AA essential car accessories

– a comprehensive range of motoring must-haves.

AA

Theory Test

The official questions and answers for car drivers and motorcyclists

AA Publishing

Produced by AA Publishing.
© Automobile Association Developments Limited 2006
First edition 1996
Reprinted 1996 (5 times)
Second edition with revised questions 1997
Reprinted 1998 (twice)
Third edition with revised questions 1998
Reprinted with amendments 1998 (twice)
Fourth edition with revised questions 1999
Reprinted 2000
Fifth edition with revised questions 2000
Sixth edition with revised questions 2001
Reprinted 2002 (twice) and June 2002 with amendments
Seventh edition with revised questions 2003
Reprinted with amendments 2005
Eighth edition with revised questions 2005
Ninth edition with revised questions 2006
Tenth edition with revised questions 2007

ISBN-10: 0-7495-5254-9
ISBN-13: 978-0-7495-5254-1

Published by AA Publishing (a trading name of Automobile Association Developments
Limited, whose registered office is Fanum House, Basing View, Basingstoke, Hampshire
RG21 4EA; registered number 1878835). A03394

Visit the AA website *www.theAA.com*

Colour separation by Keene Group, Andover
Printed in Spain by Graficas Estella

> While every effort has been made to include the
> widest possible range of questions available at the
> time of printing, the Government may from time to
> time change, add or remove questions, and the
> publisher cannot be held responsible for questions
> that may appear on a question paper which were
> not available for inclusion in this book.

Contents

Introduction

About the Theory Test

You have to pass two tests before you can apply for a full car or motorcycle licence, the Theory Test and the Practical Test. You will have to pass both the question part and the video part (Hazard Perception) to pass your Theory Test. This book contains the official theory questions from the Driving Standards Agency (DSA) that you may have to answer in your Theory Test.

During the test you will have 57 minutes to complete the questions, using a touch-screen, and all questions are multiple choice. You have to score 43 out of 50 to pass the test and the Government may, from time to time, introduce new or amended questions.

About this book

This book will help you to pass the questions section of your Theory Test.
- The questions and answers are arranged under the 14 official syllabus topics.
- Questions dealing with related aspects of a topic are grouped together.
- All the correct answers are at the back of the book.
- Each question is marked as relevant to car drivers, motorcycle riders or car and motorcycle drivers.

Questions marked with an **NI** symbol are those **not** found in Theory Test papers in Northern Ireland

Hazard Perception

The aim of the Hazard Perception test is to find out how quickly you are able to detect developing hazards coming up on the road ahead. A hazard is anything that might cause you to change speed or direction when you are driving or riding. Learners need a lot of training in how to spot hazards, because they are often so busy thinking about using the vehicle's controls and the process of driving that they forget to watch the road and traffic ahead.

First you will get a short talk explaining how the test works. You will also get a chance to practise with the computer and mouse before you start the test 'for real'. Then you will see video clips of real street scenes with traffic such as motor vehicles, pedestrians and cyclists. The scenes are shot from the point of view of a driver or rider. You have to notice hazards that are developing on the road ahead – that is, problems that could lead to an accident. As soon as you see a hazard coming up in the video clip, you click the mouse control. You score points depending on how quickly you are able to identify the developing hazard. The test lasts about 20 minutes and you currently you have to score 44 out of 75, but the pass mark may change and you should check with your instructor or the Driving Standards Agency before sitting your test.

Preparing for both tests

You are strongly recommended to prepare for the Theory Test at the same time as you develop your skills on the road for the Practical Test. Obviously, there are many similarities between the two tests – it is all about helping to make you a safer driver or rider on today's busy roads. By preparing for both tests at the same time, you will reinforce your knowledge and understanding of all aspects of driving or riding and you will improve your chances of passing both tests first time.

It is important that you should not take your Theory Test too early in your course of practical lessons. This is because you need the experience of meeting real hazards while you are learning to drive, so that you will be able to pass the Hazard Perception part of the Theory Test. However, you must pass the Theory Test before you can take the Practical Test. Agree a plan of action with your driving instructor.

Get more information

For more practical information on the Theory Test and Hazard Perception visit **www.theAA.com** and **www.dsa.gov.uk**

1 MOTORCYCLE
You want to change lanes in busy, moving traffic. Why could looking over your shoulder help?

Mark two answers

- A. Mirrors may not cover blind spots
- B. To avoid having to give a signal
- C. So traffic ahead will make room for you
- D. So your balance will not be affected
- E. Drivers behind you would be warned

2 MOTORCYCLE
You are about to turn right. What should you do just before you turn?

Mark one answer

- A. Give the correct signal
- B. Take a 'lifesaver' glance over your shoulder
- C. Select the correct gear
- D. Get in position ready for the turn

3 MOTORCYCLE
What is the 'lifesaver' when riding a motorcycle?

Mark one answer

- A. A certificate every motorcyclist must have
- B. A final rearward glance before changing direction
- C. A part of the motorcycle tool kit
- D. A mirror fitted to check blind spots

4 MOTORCYCLE
You see road signs showing a sharp bend ahead. What should you do?

Mark one answer

- A. Continue at the same speed
- B. Slow down as you go around the bend
- C. Slow down as you come out of the bend
- D. Slow down before the bend

5 MOTORCYCLE
You are riding at night and are dazzled by the headlights of an oncoming car. You should

Mark one answer

- A. slow down or stop
- B. close your eyes
- C. flash your headlight
- D. turn your head away

6 MOTORCYCLE
When riding, your shoulders obstruct the view in your mirrors. To overcome this you should

Mark one answer

- A. indicate earlier than normal
- B. fit smaller mirrors
- C. extend the mirror arms
- D. brake earlier than normal

7 MOTORCYCLE
On a motorcycle you should only use a mobile telephone when you

Mark one answer

- A. have a pillion passenger to help
- B. have parked in a safe place
- C. have a motorcycle with automatic gears
- D. are travelling on a quiet road

8 MOTORCYCLE
You are riding along a motorway. You see an accident on the other side of the road. Your lane is clear. You should

Mark one answer

- A. assist the emergency services
- B. stop and cross the road to help
- C. concentrate on what is happening ahead
- D. place a warning triangle in the road

Alertness – Section 1

9 MOTORCYCLE
You are riding at night. You have your headlight on main beam. Another vehicle is overtaking you. When should you dip your headlight?

Mark one answer
- A. When the other vehicle signals to overtake
- B. As soon as the other vehicle moves out to overtake
- C. As soon as the other vehicle passes you
- D. After the other vehicle pulls in front of you

10 MOTORCYCLE
To move off safely from a parked position you should

Mark one answer
- A. signal if other drivers will need to slow down
- B. leave your motorcycle on its stand until the road is clear
- C. give an arm signal as well as using your indicators
- D. look over your shoulder for a final check

11 MOTORCYCLE
In motorcycling, the term 'lifesaver' refers to

Mark one answer
- A. a final rearward glance
- B. an approved safety helmet
- C. a reflective jacket
- D. the two-second rule

12 MOTORCYCLE
Riding a motorcycle when you are cold could cause you to

Mark one answer
- A. be more alert
- B. be more relaxed
- C. react more quickly
- D. lose concentration

13 MOTORCYCLE
You are riding at night and are dazzled by the lights of an approaching vehicle. What should you do?

Mark one answer
- A. Switch off your headlight
- B. Switch to main beam
- C. Slow down and stop
- D. Flash your headlight

14 MOTORCYCLE
You should always check the 'blind areas' before

Mark one answer
- A. moving off
- B. slowing down
- C. changing gear
- D. giving a signal

15 MOTORCYCLE
The 'blind area' should be checked before

Mark one answer
- A. giving a signal
- B. applying the brakes
- C. changing direction
- D. giving an arm signal

16 MOTORCYCLE
It is vital to check the 'blind area' before

Mark one answer
- A. changing gear
- B. giving signals
- C. slowing down
- D. changing lanes

17 MOTORCYCLE
You are about to emerge from a junction. Your pillion passenger tells you it's clear. When should you rely on their judgement?

Mark one answer
- A. Never, you should always look for yourself
- B. When the roads are very busy
- C. When the roads are very quiet
- D. Only when they are a qualified rider

10 The Theory Test

18 MOTORCYCLE
You are about to emerge from a junction. Your pillion passenger tells you it's safe to go. What should you do?

Mark one answer

- A. Go if you are sure they can see clearly
- B. Check for yourself before pulling out
- C. Take their advice and ride on
- D. Ask them to check again before you go

19 MOTORCYCLE
What must you do before stopping normally?

Mark one answer

- A. Put both feet down
- B. Select first gear
- C. Use your mirrors
- D. Move into neutral

20 MOTORCYCLE
You have been waiting for some time to make a right turn into a side road. What should you do just before you make the turn?

Mark one answer

- A. Move close to the kerb
- B. Select a higher gear
- C. Make a 'lifesaver' check
- D. Wave to the oncoming traffic

21 MOTORCYCLE
You are turning right onto a dual carriageway. What should you do before emerging?

Mark one answer

- A. Stop, and then select a very low gear
- B. Position in the left gutter of the side road
- C. Check that the central reservation is wide enough
- D. Check there is enough room for vehicles behind you

22 MOTORCYCLE
When riding a different motorcycle you should

Mark one answer

- A. ask someone to ride with you for the first time
- B. ride as soon as possible, as all controls and switches are the same
- C. leave your gloves behind so switches can be operated more easily
- D. be sure you know where all controls and switches are

23 MOTORCYCLE
Why can it be helpful to have mirrors fitted on each side of your motorcycle?

Mark one answer

- A. To judge the gap when filtering in traffic
- B. To give protection when riding in poor weather
- C. To make your motorcycle appear larger to other drivers
- D. To give you the best view of the road behind

24 CAR & MOTORCYCLE
Before you make a U-turn in the road, you should

Mark one answer

- A. give an arm signal as well as using your indicators
- B. signal so that other drivers can slow down for you
- C. look over your shoulder for a final check
- D. select a higher gear than normal

25 CAR & MOTORCYCLE
As you approach this bridge you should

Mark three answers

- **A.** move into the middle of the road to get a better view
- **B.** slow down
- **C.** get over the bridge as quickly as possible
- **D.** consider using your horn
- **E.** find another route
- **F.** beware of pedestrians

26 CAR & MOTORCYCLE
When following a large vehicle you should keep well back because this

Mark one answer

- **A.** allows you to corner more quickly
- **B.** helps the large vehicle to stop more easily
- **C.** allows the driver to see you in the mirrors
- **D.** helps you to keep out of the wind

27 CAR & MOTORCYCLE
In which of these situations should you avoid overtaking?

Mark one answer

- **A.** Just after a bend
- **B.** In a one-way street
- **C.** On a 30mph road
- **D.** Approaching a dip in the road

28 CAR & MOTORCYCLE
This road marking warns

Mark one answer

- **A.** drivers to use the hard shoulder
- **B.** overtaking drivers there is a bend to the left
- **C.** overtaking drivers to move back to the left
- **D.** drivers that it is safe to overtake

29 CAR & MOTORCYCLE
Your mobile phone rings while you are travelling. You should

Mark one answer

- **A.** stop immediately
- **B.** answer it immediately
- **C.** pull up in a suitable place
- **D.** pull up at the nearest kerb

30 CAR & MOTORCYCLE
Why are these yellow lines painted across the road?

Mark one answer

- **A.** To help you choose the correct lane
- **B.** To help you keep the correct separation distance
- **C.** To make you aware of your speed
- **D.** To tell you the distance to the roundabout

31 CAR & MOTORCYCLE
You are approaching traffic lights that have been on green for some time. You should

Mark one answer
- A. accelerate hard
- B. maintain your speed
- C. be ready to stop
- D. brake hard

32 CAR & MOTORCYCLE
Which of the following should you do before stopping?

Mark one answer
- A. Sound the horn
- B. Use the mirrors
- C. Select a higher gear
- D. Flash your headlights

33 CAR
What does the term 'blind spot' mean for a driver?

Mark one answer
- A. An area covered by your right-hand mirror
- B. An area not covered by your headlights
- C. An area covered by your left-hand mirror
- D. An area not covered by your mirrors

34 CAR
Objects hanging from your interior mirror may

Mark two answers
- A. restrict your view
- B. improve your driving
- C. distract your attention
- D. help your concentration

35 CAR
Which of the following may cause loss of concentration on a long journey?

Mark four answers
- A. Loud music
- B. Arguing with a passenger
- C. Using a mobile phone
- D. Putting in a cassette tape
- E. Stopping regularly to rest
- F. Pulling up to tune the radio

36 CAR
On a long motorway journey boredom can cause you to feel sleepy. You should

Mark two answers
- A. leave the motorway and find a safe place to stop
- B. keep looking around at the surrounding landscape
- C. drive faster to complete your journey sooner
- D. ensure a supply of fresh air into your vehicle
- E. stop on the hard shoulder for a rest

37 CAR
You are driving at dusk. You should switch your lights on

Mark two answers
- A. even when street lights are not lit
- B. so others can see you
- C. only when others have done so
- D. only when street lights are lit

38 CAR
You are most likely to lose concentration when driving if you

Mark two answers
- A. use a mobile phone
- B. listen to very loud music
- C. switch on the heated rear window
- D. look at the door mirrors

39 CAR
Which FOUR are most likely to cause you to lose concentration while you are driving?

Mark four answers
- A. Using a mobile phone
- B. Talking into a microphone
- C. Tuning your car radio
- D. Looking at a map
- E. Checking the mirrors
- F. Using the demisters

40 CAR
Your vehicle is fitted with a hands-free phone system. Using this equipment whilst driving

Mark one answer
- A. is quite safe as long as you slow down
- B. could distract your attention from the road
- C. is recommended by *The Highway Code*
- D. could be very good for road safety

41 CAR
Using a hands-free phone is likely to

Mark one answer
- A. improve your safety
- B. increase your concentration
- C. reduce your view
- D. divert your attention

42 CAR
You should ONLY use a mobile phone when

Mark one answer
- A. receiving a call
- B. suitably parked
- C. driving at less than 30mph
- D. driving an automatic vehicle

43 CAR
Using a mobile phone while you are driving

Mark one answer
- A. is acceptable in a vehicle with power steering
- B. will reduce your field of vision
- C. could distract your attention from the road
- D. will affect your vehicle's electronic systems

44 CAR
What is the safest way to use a mobile phone in your vehicle?

Mark one answer
- A. Use hands-free equipment
- B. Find a suitable place to stop
- C. Drive slowly on a quiet road
- D. Direct your call through the operator

45 CAR
You are driving on a wet road. You have to stop your vehicle in an emergency. You should

Mark one answer
- A. apply the handbrake and footbrake together
- B. keep both hands on the wheel
- C. select reverse gear
- D. give an arm signal

46 CAR
When you are moving off from behind a parked car you should

Mark three answers
- A. look round before you move off
- B. use all the mirrors on the vehicle
- C. look round after moving off
- D. use the exterior mirrors only
- E. give a signal if necessary
- F. give a signal after moving off

47 CAR
You are travelling along this narrow country road. When passing the cyclist you should go

Mark one answer
- A. slowly, sounding the horn as you pass
- B. quickly, leaving plenty of room
- C. slowly, leaving plenty of room
- D. quickly, sounding the horn as you pass

48 CAR
Your vehicle is fitted with a hand-held telephone. To use the telephone you should

Mark one answer
- A. reduce your speed
- B. find a safe place to stop
- C. steer the vehicle with one hand
- D. be particularly careful at junctions

49 CAR
To answer a call on your mobile phone while travelling you should

Mark one answer
- A. reduce your speed wherever you are
- B. stop in a proper and convenient place
- C. keep the call time to a minimum
- D. slow down and allow others to overtake

50 CAR
Your mobile phone rings while you are on the motorway. Before answering you should

Mark one answer
- A. reduce your speed to 30mph
- B. pull up on the hard shoulder
- C. move into the left-hand lane
- D. stop in a safe place

51 CAR
You are turning right onto a dual carriageway. What should you do before emerging?

Mark one answer
- A. Stop, apply the handbrake and then select a low gear
- B. Position your vehicle well to the left of the side road
- C. Check that the central reservation is wide enough for your vehicle
- D. Make sure that you leave enough room for a vehicle behind

52 CAR
You lose your way on a busy road. What is the best action to take?

Mark one answer

- A. Stop at traffic lights and ask pedestrians
- B. Shout to other drivers to ask them the way
- C. Turn into a side road, stop and check a map
- D. Check a map, and keep going with the traffic flow

53 CAR
You are waiting to emerge from a junction. The windscreen pillar is restricting your view. What should you be particularly aware of?

Mark one answer

- A. Lorries
- B. Buses
- C. Motorcyclists
- D. Coaches

54 CAR
When emerging from junctions which is most likely to obstruct your view?

Mark one answer

- A. Windscreen pillars
- B. Steering wheel
- C. Interior mirror
- D. Windscreen wipers

55 CAR
Windscreen pillars can obstruct your view. You should take particular care when

Mark one answer

- A. driving on a motorway
- B. driving on a dual carriageway
- C. approaching a one-way street
- D. approaching bends and junctions

56 CAR
You cannot see clearly behind when reversing. What should you do?

Mark one answer

- A. Open your window to look behind
- B. Open the door and look behind
- C. Look in the nearside mirror
- D. Ask someone to guide you

57 CAR & MOTORCYCLE
When you see a hazard ahead you should use the mirrors. Why is this?

Mark one answer

- A. Because you will need to accelerate out of danger
- B. To assess how your actions will affect following traffic
- C. Because you will need to brake sharply to a stop
- D. To check what is happening on the road ahead

58 CAR & MOTORCYCLE
You are waiting to turn right at the end of a road. Your view is obstructed by parked vehicles. What should you do?

Mark one answer

- [ ] **A.** Stop and then move forward slowly and carefully for a proper view
- [ ] **B.** Move quickly to where you can see so you only block traffic from one direction
- [ ] **C.** Wait for a pedestrian to let you know when it is safe for you to emerge
- [ ] **D.** Turn your vehicle around immediately and find another junction to use

59 CAR
Your vehicle is fitted with a navigation system. How should you avoid letting this distract you while driving?

Mark one answer

- [ ] **A.** Keep going and input your destination into the system
- [ ] **B.** Keep going as the system will adjust to your route
- [ ] **C.** Stop immediately to view and use the system
- [ ] **D.** Stop in a safe place before using the system

60 CAR
Using a mobile phone when driving is illegal. The chance of you having an accident while using one is

Mark one answer

- [ ] **A.** two times higher
- [ ] **B.** four times higher
- [ ] **C.** six times higher
- [ ] **D.** ten times higher

61 CAR
You are driving on a motorway and want to use your mobile phone. What should you do?

Mark one answer

- [ ] **A.** Try to find a safe place on the hard shoulder
- [ ] **B.** Leave the motorway and stop in a safe place
- [ ] **C.** Use the next exit and pull up on the slip road
- [ ] **D.** Move to the left lane and reduce your speed

62 CAR
Using a mobile phone when driving is illegal. Your chances of having an accident increase by

Mark one answer

- [ ] **A.** two times
- [ ] **B.** four times
- [ ] **C.** eight times
- [ ] **D.** twelve times

63 MOTORCYCLE
You are riding towards a zebra crossing. Pedestrians are waiting to cross. You should

Mark one answer
- A. give way to the elderly and infirm only
- B. slow down and prepare to stop
- C. use your headlight to indicate they can cross
- D. wave at them to cross the road

64 MOTORCYCLE
You are riding a motorcycle and following a large vehicle at 40mph. You should position yourself

Mark one answer
- A. close behind to make it easier to overtake the vehicle
- B. to the left of the road to make it easier to be seen
- C. close behind the vehicle to keep out of the wind
- D. well back so that you can see past the vehicle

65 MOTORCYCLE
You are riding on a country road. Two horses with riders are in the distance. You should

Mark one answer
- A. continue at your normal speed
- B. change down the gears quickly
- C. slow down and be ready to stop
- D. flash your headlight to warn them

66 MOTORCYCLE
You are approaching a red light at a puffin crossing. Pedestrians are on the crossing. The red light will stay on until

Mark one answer
- A. you start to edge forward on to the crossing
- B. the pedestrians have reached a safe position
- C. the pedestrians are clear of the front of your motorcycle
- D. a driver from the opposite direction reaches the crossing

67 MOTORCYCLE
You are riding a slow-moving scooter on a narrow winding road. You should

Mark one answer
- A. keep well out to stop vehicles overtaking dangerously
- B. wave vehicles behind you to pass, if you think they can overtake quickly
- C. pull in safely when you can, to let vehicles behind you overtake
- D. give a left signal when it is safe for vehicles to overtake you

68 MOTORCYCLE
When riding a motorcycle your normal road position should allow

Mark two answers
- A. other vehicles to overtake on your left
- B. the driver ahead to see you in their mirrors
- C. you to prevent vehicles behind from overtaking
- D. you to be seen by traffic that is emerging from junctions ahead
- E. you to ride within half a metre (1 foot 8 inches) of the kerb

69 CAR & MOTORCYCLE
At a pelican crossing the flashing amber light means you MUST

Mark one answer
- A. stop and wait for the green light
- B. stop and wait for the red light
- C. give way to pedestrians waiting to cross
- D. give way to pedestrians already on the crossing

70 CAR & MOTORCYCLE
You should never wave people across at pedestrian crossings because

Mark one answer
- A. there may be another vehicle coming
- B. they may not be looking
- C. it is safer for you to carry on
- D. they may not be ready to cross

71 CAR & MOTORCYCLE
At a puffin crossing, which colour follows the green signal?

Mark one answer
- A. Steady red
- B. Flashing amber
- C. Steady amber
- D. Flashing green

72 CAR & MOTORCYCLE
The conditions are good and dry. You could use the 'two-second rule'

Mark one answer
- A. before restarting the engine after it has stalled
- B. to keep a safe gap from the vehicle in front
- C. before using the 'Mirror-Signal-Manoeuvre' routine
- D. when emerging on wet roads

73 CAR & MOTORCYCLE
'Tailgating' means

Mark one answer
- A. using the rear door of a hatchback car
- B. reversing into a parking space
- C. following another vehicle too closely
- D. driving with rear fog lights on

74 CAR & MOTORCYCLE
Following this vehicle too closely is unwise because

Mark one answer
- A. your brakes will overheat
- B. your view ahead is increased
- C. your engine will overheat
- D. your view ahead is reduced

75 CAR & MOTORCYCLE
You are following a vehicle on a wet road. You should leave a time gap of at least

Mark one answer
- A. one second
- B. two seconds
- C. three seconds
- D. four seconds

76 CAR & MOTORCYCLE
You are in a line of traffic. The driver behind you is following very closely. What action should you take?

Mark one answer
- A. Ignore the following driver and continue to travel within the speed limit
- B. Slow down, gradually increasing the gap between you and the vehicle in front
- C. Signal left and wave the following driver past
- D. Move over to a position just left of the centre line of the road

77 CAR & MOTORCYCLE
A long, heavily-laden lorry is taking a long time to overtake you. What should you do?

Mark one answer

- A. Speed up
- B. Slow down
- C. Hold your speed
- D. Change direction

78 CAR & MOTORCYCLE
Which of the following vehicles will use blue flashing beacons?

Mark three answers

- A. Motorway maintenance
- B. Bomb disposal
- C. Blood transfusion
- D. Police patrol
- E. Breakdown recovery

79 CAR & MOTORCYCLE
Which THREE of these emergency services might have blue flashing beacons?

Mark three answers

- A. Coastguard
- B. Bomb disposal
- C. Gritting lorries
- D. Animal ambulances
- E. Mountain rescue
- F. Doctors' cars

80 CAR & MOTORCYCLE
When being followed by an ambulance showing a flashing blue beacon you should

Mark one answer

- A. pull over as soon as safely possible to let it pass
- B. accelerate hard to get away from it
- C. maintain your speed and course
- D. brake harshly and immediately stop in the road

81 CAR & MOTORCYCLE
What type of emergency vehicle is fitted with a green flashing beacon?

Mark one answer

- A. Fire engine
- B. Road gritter
- C. Ambulance
- D. Doctor's car

82 CAR & MOTORCYCLE
A flashing green beacon on a vehicle means

Mark one answer

- A. police on non-urgent duties
- B. doctor on an emergency call
- C. road safety patrol operating
- D. gritting in progress

83 CAR & MOTORCYCLE
A vehicle has a flashing green beacon. What does this mean?

Mark one answer

- A. A doctor is answering an emergency call
- B. The vehicle is slow moving
- C. It is a motorway police patrol vehicle
- D. The vehicle is carrying hazardous chemicals

84 CAR & MOTORCYCLE
Diamond-shaped signs give instructions to

Mark one answer

- A. tram drivers
- B. bus drivers
- C. lorry drivers
- D. taxi drivers

85 CAR & MOTORCYCLE
On a road where trams operate, which of these vehicles will be most at risk from the tram rails?

Mark one answer
- A. Cars
- B. Cycles
- C. Buses
- D. Lorries

86 CAR & MOTORCYCLE
What should you use your horn for?

Mark one answer
- A. To alert others to your presence
- B. To allow you right of way
- C. To greet other road users
- D. To signal your annoyance

87 CAR & MOTORCYCLE
You are in a one-way street and want to turn right. You should position yourself

Mark one answer
- A. in the right-hand lane
- B. in the left-hand lane
- C. in either lane, depending on the traffic
- D. just left of the centre line

88 CAR & MOTORCYCLE
You wish to turn right ahead. Why should you take up the correct position in good time?

Mark one answer
- A. To allow other drivers to pull out in front of you
- B. To give a better view into the road that you're joining
- C. To help other road users know what you intend to do
- D. To allow drivers to pass you on the right

89 CAR & MOTORCYCLE
At which type of crossing are cyclists allowed to ride across with pedestrians?

Mark one answer
- A. Toucan
- B. Puffin
- C. Pelican
- D. Zebra

90 CAR & MOTORCYCLE
A bus has stopped at a bus stop ahead of you. Its right-hand indicator is flashing. You should

Mark one answer
- A. flash your headlights and slow down
- B. slow down and give way if it is safe to do so
- C. sound your horn and keep going
- D. slow down and then sound your horn

91 CAR & MOTORCYCLE
You are travelling at the legal speed limit. A vehicle comes up quickly behind, flashing its headlights. You should

Mark one answer
- A. accelerate to make a gap behind you
- B. touch the brakes sharply to show your brake lights
- C. maintain your speed to prevent the vehicle from overtaking
- D. allow the vehicle to overtake

92 CAR & MOTORCYCLE
You should ONLY flash your headlights to other road users

Mark one answer
- **A.** to show that you are giving way
- **B.** to show that you are about to turn
- **C.** to tell them that you have right of way
- **D.** to let them know that you are there

93 CAR & MOTORCYCLE
You are approaching unmarked crossroads. How should you deal with this type of junction?

Mark one answer
- **A.** Accelerate and keep to the middle
- **B.** Slow down and keep to the right
- **C.** Accelerate looking to the left
- **D.** Slow down and look both ways

94 CAR & MOTORCYCLE
You are approaching a pelican crossing. The amber light is flashing. You must

Mark one answer
- **A.** give way to pedestrians who are crossing
- **B.** encourage pedestrians to cross
- **C.** not move until the green light appears
- **D.** stop even if the crossing is clear

95 CAR
At puffin crossings, which light will not show to a driver?

Mark one answer
- **A.** Flashing amber
- **B.** Red
- **C.** Steady amber
- **D.** Green

96 CAR
You should leave at least a two-second gap between your vehicle and the one in front when conditions are

Mark one answer
- **A.** wet
- **B.** good
- **C.** damp
- **D.** foggy

97 CAR
You are driving on a clear night. There is a steady stream of oncoming traffic. The national speed limit applies. Which lights should you use?

Mark one answer
- **A.** Full beam headlights
- **B.** Sidelights
- **C.** Dipped headlights
- **D.** Fog lights

98 CAR
You are driving behind a large goods vehicle. It signals left but steers to the right. You should

Mark one answer
- **A.** slow down and let the vehicle turn
- **B.** drive on, keeping to the left
- **C.** overtake on the right of it
- **D.** hold your speed and sound your horn

99 CAR
You are driving along this road. The red van cuts in close in front of you. What should you do?

Mark one answer
- [ ] A. Accelerate to get closer to the red van
- [ ] B. Give a long blast on the horn
- [ ] C. Drop back to leave the correct separation distance
- [ ] D. Flash your headlights several times

100 CAR
You are waiting in a traffic queue at night. To avoid dazzling following drivers you should

Mark one answer
- [ ] A. apply the handbrake only
- [ ] B. apply the footbrake only
- [ ] C. switch off your headlights
- [ ] D. use both the handbrake and footbrake

101 CAR
You are driving in traffic at the speed limit for the road. The driver behind is trying to overtake. You should

Mark one answer
- [ ] A. move closer to the car ahead, so the driver behind has no room to overtake
- [ ] B. wave the driver behind to overtake when it is safe
- [ ] C. keep a steady course and allow the driver behind to overtake
- [ ] D. accelerate to get away from the driver behind

102 CAR
You are driving at night on an unlit road behind another vehicle. You should

Mark one answer
- [ ] A. flash your headlights
- [ ] B. use dipped beam headlights
- [ ] C. switch off your headlights
- [ ] D. use full beam headlights

103 CAR
A bus lane on your left shows no times of operation. This means it is

Mark one answer
- [ ] A. not in operation at all
- [ ] B. only in operation at peak times
- [ ] C. in operation 24 hours a day
- [ ] D. only in operation in daylight hours

104 CAR
You are driving along a country road. A horse and rider are approaching. What should you do?

Mark two answers
- [ ] A. Increase your speed
- [ ] B. Sound your horn
- [ ] C. Flash your headlights
- [ ] D. Drive slowly past
- [ ] E. Give plenty of room
- [ ] F. Rev your engine

105 CAR
A person herding sheep asks you to stop. You should

Mark one answer
- A. ignore them as they have no authority
- B. stop and switch off your engine
- C. continue on but drive slowly
- D. try and get past quickly

106 CAR
When overtaking a horse and rider you should

Mark one answer
- A. sound your horn as a warning
- B. go past as quickly as possible
- C. flash your headlights as a warning
- D. go past slowly and carefully

107 CAR
You are approaching a zebra crossing. Pedestrians are waiting to cross. You should

Mark one answer
- A. give way to the elderly and infirm only
- B. slow down and prepare to stop
- C. use your headlights to indicate they can cross
- D. wave at them to cross the road

108 CAR
You are driving a slow-moving vehicle on a narrow winding road. You should

Mark one answer
- A. keep well out to stop vehicles overtaking dangerously
- B. wave following vehicles past you if you think they can overtake quickly
- C. pull in safely when you can, to let following vehicles overtake
- D. give a left signal when it is safe for vehicles to overtake you

109 CAR
You have a loose filler cap on your diesel fuel tank. This will

Mark two answers
- A. waste fuel and money
- B. make roads slippery for other road users
- C. improve your vehicle's fuel consumption
- D. increase the level of exhaust emissions

110 CAR
To avoid spillage after refuelling, you should make sure that

Mark one answer
- A. your tank is only three quarters full
- B. you have used a locking filler cap
- C. you check your fuel gauge is working
- D. your filler cap is securely fastened

111 CAR
A vehicle pulls out in front of you at a junction. What should you do?

Mark one answer
- A. Swerve past it and sound your horn
- B. Flash your headlights and drive up close behind
- C. Slow down and be ready to stop
- D. Accelerate past it immediately

112 CAR
You stop for pedestrians waiting to cross at a zebra crossing. They do not start to cross. What should you do?

Mark one answer
- A. Be patient and wait
- B. Sound your horn
- C. Carry on
- D. Wave them to cross

113 CAR
You are following this lorry. You should keep well back from it to

Mark one answer

- [ ] A. give you a good view of the road ahead
- [ ] B. stop following traffic from rushing through the junction
- [ ] C. prevent traffic behind you from overtaking
- [ ] D. allow you to hurry through the traffic lights if they change

114 CAR
If your vehicle uses diesel fuel, take extra care when refuelling. Diesel fuel when spilt is

Mark one answer

- [ ] A. sticky
- [ ] B. odourless
- [ ] C. clear
- [ ] D. slippery

115 CAR
You are approaching a red light at a puffin crossing. Pedestrians are on the crossing. The red light will stay on until

Mark one answer

- [ ] A. you start to edge forward on to the crossing
- [ ] B. the pedestrians have reached a safe position
- [ ] C. the pedestrians are clear of the front of your vehicle
- [ ] D. a driver from the opposite direction reaches the crossing

116 CAR
Which instrument panel warning light would show that headlights are on full beam?

Mark one answer

- [ ] A.
- [ ] B.
- [ ] C.
- [ ] D.

117 CAR
What style of driving causes increased risk to everyone?

Mark one answer

- [ ] A. Considerate
- [ ] B. Defensive
- [ ] C. Competitive
- [ ] D. Responsible

118 MOTORCYCLE
A loose drive chain on a motorcycle could cause

Mark one answer
- A. the front wheel to wobble
- B. the ignition to cut out
- C. the brakes to fail
- D. the rear wheel to lock

119 MOTORCYCLE
What is the most important reason why you should keep your motorcycle regularly maintained?

Mark one answer
- A. To accelerate faster than other traffic
- B. So the motorcycle can carry panniers
- C. To keep the machine roadworthy
- D. So the motorcycle can carry a passenger

120 MOTORCYCLE
Your motorcycle has tubed tyres fitted as standard. When replacing a tyre you should

Mark one answer
- A. replace the tube if it is 6 months old
- B. replace the tube if it has covered 6,000 miles
- C. replace the tube only if replacing the rear tyre
- D. replace the tube with each change of tyre

121 MOTORCYCLE
How should you ride a motorcycle when NEW tyres have just been fitted?

Mark one answer
- A. Carefully, until the shiny surface is worn off
- B. By braking hard especially into bends
- C. Through normal riding with higher air pressures
- D. By riding at faster than normal speeds

122 MOTORCYCLE
Which of the following would NOT make you more visible in daylight?

Mark one answer
- A. Wearing a black helmet
- B. Wearing a white helmet
- C. Switching on your dipped headlight
- D. Wearing a fluorescent jacket

123 MOTORCYCLE
When riding and wearing brightly coloured clothing you will

Mark one answer
- A. dazzle other motorists on the road
- B. be seen more easily by other motorists
- C. create a hazard by distracting other drivers
- D. be able to ride on unlit roads at night with sidelights

124 MOTORCYCLE
You are riding a motorcycle in very hot weather. You should

Mark one answer
- A. ride with your visor fully open
- B. continue to wear protective clothing
- C. wear trainers instead of boots
- D. slacken your helmet strap

125 MOTORCYCLE
Why should you wear fluorescent clothing when riding in daylight?

Mark one answer
- A. It reduces wind resistance
- B. It prevents injury if you come off the machine
- C. It helps other road users to see you
- D. It keeps you cool in hot weather

126 MOTORCYCLE
Why should riders wear reflective clothing?

Mark one answer

- A. To protect them from the cold
- B. To protect them from direct sunlight
- C. To be seen better in daylight
- D. To be seen better at night

127 MOTORCYCLE
Which of the following fairings would give you the best weather protection?

Mark one answer

- A. Handlebar
- B. Sports
- C. Touring
- D. Windscreen

128 MOTORCYCLE
It would be illegal to ride with a helmet on when

Mark one answer

- A. the helmet is not fastened correctly
- B. the helmet is more than 4 years old
- C. you have borrowed someone else's helmet
- D. the helmet does not have chin protection

129 MOTORCYCLE
Your visor becomes badly scratched. You should

Mark one answer

- A. polish it with a fine abrasive
- B. replace it
- C. wash it in soapy water
- D. clean it with petrol

130 MOTORCYCLE
The legal minimum depth of tread for motorcycle tyres is

Mark one answer

- A. 1mm
- B. 1.6mm
- C. 2.5mm
- D. 4mm

131 MOTORCYCLE
Which of the following makes it easier for motorcyclists to be seen?

Mark three answers

- A. Using a dipped headlight
- B. Wearing a fluorescent jacket
- C. Wearing a white helmet
- D. Wearing a grey helmet
- E. Wearing black leathers
- F. Using a tinted visor

132 MOTORCYCLE
Tyre pressures should be increased on your motorcycle when

Mark one answer

- A. riding on a wet road
- B. carrying a pillion passenger
- C. travelling on an uneven surface
- D. riding on twisty roads

133 MOTORCYCLE
Your oil light comes on as you are riding. You should

Mark one answer

- A. go to a dealer for an oil change
- B. go to the nearest garage for their advice
- C. ride slowly for a few miles to see if the light goes out
- D. stop as quickly as possible and try to find the cause

134 MOTORCYCLE
When may you have to increase the tyre pressures on your motorcycle?

Mark three answers
- A. When carrying a passenger
- B. After a long journey
- C. When carrying a load
- D. When riding at high speeds
- E. When riding in hot weather

135 MOTORCYCLE
Which TWO of these items on a motorcycle MUST be kept clean?

Mark two answers
- A. Number plate
- B. Wheels
- C. Engine
- D. Fairing
- E. Headlight

136 MOTORCYCLE
Motorcycle tyres MUST

Mark two answers
- A. have the same tread pattern
- B. be correctly inflated
- C. be the same size, front and rear
- D. both be the same make
- E. have sufficient tread depth

137 MOTORCYCLE
You should use the engine cut-out switch on your motorcycle to

Mark one answer
- A. save wear and tear on the battery
- B. stop the engine for a short time
- C. stop the engine in an emergency
- D. save wear and tear on the ignition

138 MOTORCYCLE
Riding your motorcycle with a slack or worn drive chain may cause

Mark one answer
- A. an engine misfire
- B. early tyre wear
- C. increased emissions
- D. a locked wheel

139 MOTORCYCLE
You have adjusted the tension on your drive chain. You should check the

Mark one answer
- A. rear wheel alignment
- B. tyre pressures
- C. valve clearances
- D. sidelights

140 MOTORCYCLE
You forget to switch the choke off after the engine warms up. This could

Mark one answer
- A. flatten the battery
- B. reduce braking distances
- C. use less fuel
- D. cause much more engine wear

Section 3 – Safety and Your Vehicle

141 MOTORCYCLE
When riding your motorcycle a tyre bursts. What should you do?

Mark one answer
- A. Slow gently to a stop
- B. Brake firmly to a stop
- C. Change to a high gear
- D. Lower the side stand

142 MOTORCYCLE
A motorcycle engine that is properly maintained will

Mark one answer
- A. use much more fuel
- B. have lower exhaust emissions
- C. increase your insurance premiums
- D. not need to have an MOT

143 MOTORCYCLE
What should you clean visors and goggles with?

Mark one answer
- A. Petrol
- B. White spirit
- C. Antifreeze
- D. Soapy water

144 MOTORCYCLE
You are riding on a quiet road. Your visor fogs up. What should you do?

Mark one answer
- A. Continue at a reduced speed
- B. Stop as soon as possible and wipe it
- C. Build up speed to increase air flow
- D. Close the helmet air vents

145 MOTORCYCLE
You are riding in hot weather. What is the safest type of footwear?

Mark one answer
- A. Sandals
- B. Trainers
- C. Shoes
- D. Boots

146 MOTORCYCLE
A friend offers you a second-hand safety helmet for you to use. Why may this be a bad idea?

Mark one answer
- A. It may be damaged
- B. You will be breaking the law
- C. You will affect your insurance cover
- D. It may be a full-face type

147

MOTORCYCLE

Which of the following should not be used to fasten your safety helmet?

Mark one answer

- **A.** Double D ring fastening
- **B.** Velcro tab
- **C.** Quick release fastening
- **D.** Bar and buckle

148

MOTORCYCLE

After warming up the engine you leave the choke ON. What will this do?

Mark one answer

- **A.** Discharge the battery
- **B.** Use more fuel
- **C.** Improve handling
- **D.** Use less fuel

149

MOTORCYCLE

You want to ride your motorcycle in the dark. What could you wear to be seen more easily?

Mark two answers

- **A.** A black leather jacket
- **B.** Reflective clothing
- **C.** A white helmet
- **D.** A red helmet

150

MOTORCYCLE

You are riding a motorcycle of more than 50cc. Which FOUR would make a tyre illegal?

Mark four answers

- **A.** Tread less than 1.6mm deep
- **B.** Tread less than 1mm deep
- **C.** A large bulge in the wall
- **D.** A recut tread
- **E.** Exposed ply or cord
- **F.** A stone wedged in the tread

151

MOTORCYCLE

You should maintain cable-operated brakes

Mark two answers

- **A.** by regular adjustment when necessary
- **B.** at normal service times only
- **C.** yearly, before taking the motorcycle for its MOT
- **D.** by oiling cables and pivots regularly

152

MOTORCYCLE

A properly serviced motorcycle will give

Mark two answers

- **A.** lower insurance premiums
- **B.** a refund on your road tax
- **C.** better fuel economy
- **D.** cleaner exhaust emissions

153

MOTORCYCLE

Your motorcycle has a catalytic converter. Its purpose is to reduce

Mark one answer

- **A.** exhaust noise
- **B.** fuel consumption
- **C.** exhaust emissions
- **D.** engine noise

154 MOTORCYCLE
Refitting which of the following will disturb your wheel alignment?

Mark one answer
- A. front wheel
- B. front brakes
- C. rear brakes
- D. rear wheel

155 MOTORCYCLE
After refitting your rear wheel what should you check?

Mark one answer
- A. Your steering damper
- B. Your side stand
- C. Your wheel alignment
- D. Your suspension preload

156 MOTORCYCLE
You are checking your direction indicators. How often per second must they flash?

Mark one answer
- A. Between 1 and 2 times
- B. Between 3 and 4 times
- C. Between 5 and 6 times
- D. Between 7 and 8 times

157 MOTORCYCLE
After adjusting the final drive chain what should you check?

Mark one answer
- A. The rear wheel alignment
- B. The suspension adjustment
- C. The rear shock absorber
- D. The front suspension forks

158 MOTORCYCLE
Your steering feels wobbly. Which of these is a likely cause?

Mark one answer
- A. Tyre pressure is too high
- B. Incorrectly adjusted brakes
- C. Worn steering head bearings
- D. A broken clutch cable

159 MOTORCYCLE
You see oil on your front forks. Should you be concerned about this?

Mark one answer
- A. No, unless the amount of oil increases
- B. No, lubrication here is perfectly normal
- C. Yes, it is illegal to ride with an oil leak
- D. Yes, oil could drip on to your tyre

160 MOTORCYCLE
You have a faulty oil seal on a shock absorber. Why is this a serious problem?

Mark one answer
- A. It will cause excessive chain wear
- B. Dripping oil could reduce the grip of your tyre
- C. Your motorcycle will be harder to ride uphill
- D. Your motorcycle will not accelerate so quickly

161 MOTORCYCLE
Oil is leaking from your forks. Why should you NOT ride a motorcycle in this condition?

Mark one answer
- A. Your brakes could be affected by dripping oil
- B. Your steering is likely to seize up
- C. The forks will quickly begin to rust
- D. The motorcycle will become too noisy

162 MOTORCYCLE
You have adjusted your drive chain. If this is not done properly, what problem could it cause?

Mark one answer
- [ ] **A.** Inaccurate speedometer reading
- [ ] **B.** Loss of braking power
- [ ] **C.** Incorrect rear wheel alignment
- [ ] **D.** Excessive fuel consumption

163 MOTORCYCLE
You have adjusted your drive chain. Why is it also important to check rear wheel alignment?

Mark one answer
- [ ] **A.** Your tyre may be more likely to puncture
- [ ] **B.** Fuel consumption could be greatly increased
- [ ] **C.** You may not be able to reach top speed
- [ ] **D.** Your motorcycle could be unstable on bends

164 MOTORCYCLE
There is a cut in the sidewall of one of your tyres. What should you do about this?

Mark one answer
- [ ] **A.** Replace the tyre before riding the motorcycle
- [ ] **B.** Check regularly to see if it gets any worse
- [ ] **C.** Repair the puncture before riding the motorcycle
- [ ] **D.** Reduce pressure in the tyre before you ride

165 MOTORCYCLE
You need to put air into your tyres. How would you find out the correct pressure to use?

Mark one answer
- [ ] **A.** It will be shown on the tyre wall
- [ ] **B.** It will be stamped on the wheel
- [ ] **C.** By checking the vehicle owner's manual
- [ ] **D.** By checking the registration document

166 MOTORCYCLE
You can prevent a cable operated clutch from becoming stiff by keeping the cable

Mark one answer
- [ ] **A.** tight
- [ ] **B.** dry
- [ ] **C.** slack
- [ ] **D.** oiled

167 MOTORCYCLE
When adusting your chain it is important for the wheels to be aligned accurately. Incorrect wheel alignment can cause

Mark one answer
- [ ] **A.** a serious loss of power
- [ ] **B.** reduced braking performance
- [ ] **C.** increased tyre wear
- [ ] **D.** reduced ground clearance

168 MOTORCYCLE
What problem can incorrectly aligned wheels cause?

Mark one answer
- [ ] **A.** Faulty headlight adjustment
- [ ] **B.** Reduced braking performance
- [ ] **C.** Better ground clearance
- [ ] **D.** Instability when cornering

169 MOTORCYCLE
What is most likely to be affected by incorrect wheel alignment?

Mark one answer
- [ ] **A.** Braking performance
- [ ] **B.** Stability
- [ ] **C.** Acceleration
- [ ] **D.** Suspension preload

170 MOTORCYCLE
Why should you wear specialist motorcycle clothing when riding?

Mark one answer

A. Because the law requires you to do so
B. Because it looks better than ordinary clothing
C. Because it gives best protection from the weather
D. Because it will reduce your insurance

171 MOTORCYCLE
When leaving your motorcycle parked, you should always

Mark one answer

A. remove the battery lead
B. pull it on to the kerb
C. use the steering lock
D. leave the parking light on

172 MOTORCYCLE
You are parking your motorcycle. Chaining it to an immovable object will

Mark one answer

A. be against the law
B. give extra security
C. be likely to cause damage
D. leave the motorcycle unstable

173 MOTORCYCLE
You are parking your motorcycle and sidecar on a hill. What is the best way to stop it rolling away?

Mark one answer

A. Leave it in neutral
B. Put the rear wheel on the pavement
C. Leave it in a low gear
D. Park very close to another vehicle

174 MOTORCYCLE
An engine cut-out switch should be used to

Mark one answer

A. reduce speed in an emergency
B. prevent the motorcycle being stolen
C. stop the engine normally
D. stop the engine in an emergency

175 MOTORCYCLE
You enter a road where there are road humps. What should you do?

Mark one answer

A. Maintain a reduced speed throughout
B. Accelerate quickly between each one
C. Always keep to the maximum legal speed
D. Ride slowly at school times only

176 MOTORCYCLE
When should you especially check the engine oil level?

Mark one answer

A. Before a long journey
B. When the engine is hot
C. Early in the morning
D. Every 6,000 miles

177 MOTORCYCLE
You service your own motorcycle. How should you get rid of the old engine oil?

Mark one answer
- A. Take it to a local authority site
- B. Pour it down a drain
- C. Tip it into a hole in the ground
- D. Put it into your dustbin

178 MOTORCYCLE
You are leaving your motorcycle parked on a road. When may you leave the engine running?

Mark one answer
- A. If you will be parked for less than 5 minutes
- B. If the battery is flat
- C. When in a 20mph zone
- D. Not on any occasion

179 MOTORCYCLE
What safeguard could you take against fire risk to your motorcycle?

Mark one answer
- A. Keep water levels above maximum
- B. Check out any strong smell of petrol
- C. Avoid riding with a full tank of petrol
- D. Use unleaded petrol

180 CAR & MOTORCYCLE
Which of these, if allowed to get low, could cause an accident?

Mark one answer
- A. Anti-freeze level
- B. Brake fluid level
- C. Battery water level
- D. Radiator coolant level

181 CAR & MOTORCYCLE
Which TWO are badly affected if the tyres are under-inflated?

Mark two answers
- A. Braking
- B. Steering
- C. Changing gear
- D. Parking

182 CAR & MOTORCYCLE
Motor vehicles can harm the environment. This has resulted in

Mark three answers
- A. air pollution
- B. damage to buildings
- C. less risk to health
- D. improved public transport
- E. less use of electrical vehicles
- F. using up of natural resources

183 CAR & MOTORCYCLE
Excessive or uneven tyre wear can be caused by faults in which THREE of the following?

Mark three answers
- A. The gearbox
- B. The braking system
- C. The accelerator
- D. The exhaust system
- E. Wheel alignment
- F. The suspension

184 CAR & MOTORCYCLE
You must NOT sound your horn

Mark one answer
- A. between 10pm and 6am in a built-up area
- B. at any time in a built-up area
- C. between 11.30pm and 7am in a built-up area
- D. between 11.30pm and 6am on any road

185 CAR & MOTORCYCLE
The pictured vehicle is 'environmentally friendly' because it

Mark three answers
- A. reduces noise pollution
- B. uses diesel fuel
- C. uses electricity
- D. uses unleaded fuel
- E. reduces parking spaces
- F. reduces town traffic

186 CAR & MOTORCYCLE
Supertrams or Light Rapid Transit (LRT) systems are environmentally friendly because

Mark one answer
- A. they use diesel power
- B. they use quieter roads
- C. they use electric power
- D. they do not operate during rush hour

187 CAR & MOTORCYCLE
'Red routes' in major cities have been introduced to

Mark one answer
- A. raise the speed limits
- B. help the traffic flow
- C. provide better parking
- D. allow lorries to load more freely

188 CAR & MOTORCYCLE
Road humps, chicanes and narrowings are

Mark one answer
- A. always at major road works
- B. used to increase traffic speed
- C. at toll-bridge approaches only
- D. traffic calming measures

189 CAR & MOTORCYCLE
The purpose of a catalytic converter is to reduce

Mark one answer
- A. fuel consumption
- B. the risk of fire
- C. toxic exhaust gases
- D. engine wear

190 CAR & MOTORCYCLE
Catalytic converters are fitted to make the

Mark one answer
- A. engine produce more power
- B. exhaust system easier to replace
- C. engine run quietly
- D. exhaust fumes cleaner

191 CAR & MOTORCYCLE
It is essential that tyre pressures are checked regularly. When should this be done?

Mark one answer
- A. After any lengthy journey
- B. After travelling at high speed
- C. When tyres are hot
- D. When tyres are cold

192 CAR & MOTORCYCLE
When should you NOT use your horn in a built-up area?

Mark one answer
- A. Between 8pm and 8am
- B. Between 9pm and dawn
- C. Between dusk and 8am
- D. Between 11.30pm and 7am

193 CAR & MOTORCYCLE
You will use more fuel if your tyres are

Mark one answer

- A. under-inflated
- B. of different makes
- C. over-inflated
- D. new and hardly used

194 CAR & MOTORCYCLE
How should you dispose of a used battery?

Mark two answers

- A. Take it to a local authority site
- B. Put it in the dustbin
- C. Break it up into pieces
- D. Leave it on waste land
- E. Take it to a garage
- F. Burn it on a fire

195 CAR & MOTORCYCLE
What is most likely to cause high fuel consumption?

Mark one answer

- A. Poor steering control
- B. Accelerating around bends
- C. Staying in high gears
- D. Harsh braking and accelerating

196 CAR & MOTORCYCLE
The fluid level in your battery is low. What should you top it up with?

Mark one answer

- A. Battery acid
- B. Distilled water
- C. Engine oil
- D. Engine coolant

197 CAR & MOTORCYCLE
You need to top up your battery. What level should you fill to?

Mark one answer

- A. The top of the battery
- B. Half-way up the battery
- C. Just below the cell plates
- D. Just above the cell plates

198 CAR & MOTORCYCLE
You have too much oil in your engine. What could this cause?

Mark one answer

- A. Low oil pressure
- B. Engine overheating
- C. Chain wear
- D. Oil leaks

199 CAR & MOTORCYCLE
You are parking on a two-way road at night. The speed limit is 40mph. You should park on the

Mark one answer

- A. left with parking lights on
- B. left with no lights on
- C. right with parking lights on
- D. right with dipped headlights on

200 CAR & MOTORCYCLE
You are parked on the road at night. Where must you use parking lights?

Mark one answer

- A. Where there are continuous white lines in the middle of the road
- B. Where the speed limit exceeds 30mph
- C. Where you are facing oncoming traffic
- D. Where you are near a bus stop

201 CAR
Which FOUR of these must be in good working order for your car to be roadworthy?

Mark four answers

- A. The temperature gauge
- B. The speedometer
- C. The windscreen washers
- D. The windscreen wipers
- E. The oil warning light
- F. The horn

202 CAR
New petrol-engined cars must be fitted with catalytic converters. The reason for this is to

Mark one answer

- A. control exhaust noise levels
- B. prolong the life of the exhaust system
- C. allow the exhaust system to be recycled
- D. reduce harmful exhaust emissions

203 CAR
What can cause heavy steering?

Mark one answer

- A. Driving on ice
- B. Badly worn brakes
- C. Over-inflated tyres
- D. Under-inflated tyres

204 CAR
Driving with under-inflated tyres can affect

Mark two answers

- A. engine temperature
- B. fuel consumption
- C. braking
- D. oil pressure

205 CAR
Excessive or uneven tyre wear can be caused by faults in the

Mark two answers

- A. gearbox
- B. braking system
- C. suspension
- D. exhaust system

206 CAR
The main cause of brake fade is

Mark one answer

- A. the brakes overheating
- B. air in the brake fluid
- C. oil on the brakes
- D. the brakes out of adjustment

207 CAR
Your anti-lock brakes warning light stays on. You should

Mark one answer

- A. check the brake fluid level
- B. check the footbrake free play
- C. check that the handbrake is released
- D. have the brakes checked immediately

208 CAR
While driving, this warning light on your dashboard comes on. It means

Mark one answer

- A. a fault in the braking system
- B. the engine oil is low
- C. a rear light has failed
- D. your seat belt is not fastened

209 CAR
It is important to wear suitable shoes when you are driving. Why is this?

Mark one answer

- A. To prevent wear on the pedals
- B. To maintain control of the pedals
- C. To enable you to adjust your seat
- D. To enable you to walk for assistance if you break down

210 CAR

The most important reason for having a properly adjusted head restraint is to

Mark one answer

- A. make you more comfortable
- B. help you to avoid neck injury
- C. help you to relax
- D. help you to maintain your driving position

211 CAR

What will reduce the risk of neck injury resulting from a collision?

Mark one answer

- A. An air-sprung seat
- B. Anti-lock brakes
- C. A collapsible steering wheel
- D. A properly adjusted head restraint

212 CAR

You are driving the children of a friend home from school. They are both under 14 years old. Who is responsible for making sure they wear a seat belt or approved child restraint where required?

Mark one answer

- A. An adult passenger
- B. The children
- C. You, the driver
- D. Your friend

213 CAR

Car passengers MUST wear a seat belt/restraint if one is available, unless they are

Mark one answer

- A. under 14 years old
- B. under 1.5 metres (5 feet) in height
- C. sitting in the rear seat
- D. exempt for medical reasons

214 CAR

You are testing your suspension. You notice that your vehicle keeps bouncing when you press down on the front wing. What does this mean?

Mark one answer

- A. Worn tyres
- B. Tyres under-inflated
- C. Steering wheel not located centrally
- D. Worn shock absorbers

215 CAR

A roof rack fitted to your car will

Mark one answer

- A. reduce fuel consumption
- B. improve the road handling
- C. make your car go faster
- D. increase fuel consumption

216 CAR

It is illegal to drive with tyres that

Mark one answer

- A. have been bought second-hand
- B. have a large deep cut in the side wall
- C. are of different makes
- D. are of different tread patterns

217 CAR

The legal minimum depth of tread for car tyres over three quarters of the breadth is

Mark one answer

- A. 1mm
- B. 1.6mm
- C. 2.5mm
- D. 4mm

218 CAR
You are carrying two 13-year-old children and their parents in your car. Who is responsible for seeing that the children wear seat belts?

Mark one answer

- A. The children's parents
- B. You, the driver
- C. The front-seat passenger
- D. The children

219 CAR
When a roof rack is not in use it should be removed. Why is this?

Mark one answer

- A. It will affect the suspension
- B. It is illegal
- C. It will affect your braking
- D. It will waste fuel

220 CAR
How can you, as a driver, help the environment?

Mark three answers

- A. By reducing your speed
- B. By gentle acceleration
- C. By using leaded fuel
- D. By driving faster
- E. By harsh acceleration
- F. By servicing your vehicle properly

221 CAR
To help the environment, you can avoid wasting fuel by

Mark three answers

- A. having your vehicle properly serviced
- B. making sure your tyres are correctly inflated
- C. not over-revving in the lower gears
- D. driving at higher speeds where possible
- E. keeping an empty roof rack properly fitted
- F. servicing your vehicle less regularly

222 CAR
To reduce the volume of traffic on the roads you could

Mark three answers

- A. use public transport more often
- B. share a car when possible
- C. walk or cycle on short journeys
- D. travel by car at all times
- E. use a car with a smaller engine
- F. drive in a bus lane

223 CAR
Which THREE of the following are most likely to waste fuel?

Mark three answers

- A. Reducing your speed
- B. Carrying unnecessary weight
- C. Using the wrong grade of fuel
- D. Under-inflated tyres
- E. Using different brands of fuel
- F. A fitted, empty roof rack

224 CAR
Which THREE things can you, as a road user, do to help the environment?

Mark three answers

- A. Cycle when possible
- B. Drive on under-inflated tyres
- C. Use the choke for as long as possible on a cold engine
- D. Have your vehicle properly tuned and serviced
- E. Watch the traffic and plan ahead
- F. Brake as late as possible without skidding

225 CAR
As a driver you can cause more damage to the environment by

Mark two answers
- [ ] A. choosing a fuel-efficient vehicle
- [ ] B. making a lot of short journeys
- [ ] C. driving in as high a gear as possible
- [ ] D. accelerating as quickly as possible
- [ ] E. having your vehicle regularly serviced

226 CAR
To help protect the environment you should NOT

Mark one answer
- [ ] A. remove your roof rack when unloaded
- [ ] B. use your car for very short journeys
- [ ] C. walk, cycle or use public transport
- [ ] D. empty the boot of unnecessary weight

227 CAR
Which THREE does the law require you to keep in good condition?

Mark three answers
- [ ] A. Gears
- [ ] B. Transmission
- [ ] C. Headlights
- [ ] D. Windscreen
- [ ] E. Seat belts

228 CAR
Driving at 70mph uses more fuel than driving at 50mph by up to

Mark one answer
- [ ] A. 10%
- [ ] B. 30%
- [ ] C. 75%
- [ ] D. 100%

229 CAR
Your vehicle pulls to one side when braking. You should

Mark one answer
- [ ] A. change the tyres around
- [ ] B. consult your garage as soon as possible
- [ ] C. pump the pedal when braking
- [ ] D. use your handbrake at the same time

230 CAR
As a driver, you can help reduce pollution levels in town centres by

Mark one answer
- [ ] A. driving more quickly
- [ ] B. over-revving in a low gear
- [ ] C. walking or cycling
- [ ] D. driving short journeys

231 CAR
Unbalanced wheels on a car may cause

Mark one answer
- [ ] A. the steering to pull to one side
- [ ] B. the steering to vibrate
- [ ] C. the brakes to fail
- [ ] D. the tyres to deflate

232 CAR
Turning the steering wheel while your car is stationary can cause damage to the

Mark two answers
- [ ] A. gearbox
- [ ] B. engine
- [ ] C. brakes
- [ ] D. steering
- [ ] E. tyres

233 CAR
How can you reduce the chances of your car being broken into when leaving it unattended?

Mark one answer
- [ ] A. Take all valuables with you
- [ ] B. Park near a taxi rank
- [ ] C. Place any valuables on the floor
- [ ] D. Park near a fire station

234 CAR
You have to leave valuables in your car. It would be safer to

Mark one answer
- [ ] A. put them in a carrier bag
- [ ] B. park near a school entrance
- [ ] C. lock them out of sight
- [ ] D. park near a bus stop

235 CAR
How could you deter theft from your car when leaving it unattended?

Mark one answer
- [ ] **A.** Leave valuables in a carrier bag
- [ ] **B.** Lock valuables out of sight
- [ ] **C.** Put valuables on the seats
- [ ] **D.** Leave valuables on the floor

236 CAR
Which of the following may help to deter a thief from stealing your car?

Mark one answer
- [ ] **A.** Always keeping the headlights on
- [ ] **B.** Fitting reflective glass windows
- [ ] **C.** Always keeping the interior light on
- [ ] **D.** Etching the car number on the windows

237 CAR
How can you help to prevent your car radio being stolen?

Mark one answer
- [ ] **A.** Park in an unlit area
- [ ] **B.** Hide the radio with a blanket
- [ ] **C.** Park near a busy junction
- [ ] **D.** Install a security-coded radio

238 CAR
Which of the following should not be kept in your vehicle?

Mark one answer
- [ ] **A.** A first aid kit
- [ ] **B.** A road atlas
- [ ] **C.** The tax disc
- [ ] **D.** The vehicle documents

239 CAR
What should you do when leaving your vehicle?

Mark one answer
- [ ] **A.** Put valuable documents under the seats
- [ ] **B.** Remove all valuables
- [ ] **C.** Cover valuables with a blanket
- [ ] **D.** Leave the interior light on

240 CAR
You are parking your car. You have some valuables which you are unable to take with you. What should you do?

Mark one answer
- [ ] **A.** Park near a police station
- [ ] **B.** Put them under the driver's seat
- [ ] **C.** Lock them out of sight
- [ ] **D.** Park in an unlit side road

241 CAR
Which of these is most likely to deter the theft of your vehicle?

Mark one answer
- [ ] **A.** An immobiliser
- [ ] **B.** Tinted windows
- [ ] **C.** Locking wheel nuts
- [ ] **D.** A sun screen

242 CAR
Wherever possible, which one of the following should you do when parking at night?

Mark one answer
- [ ] **A.** Park in a quiet car park
- [ ] **B.** Park in a well-lit area
- [ ] **C.** Park facing against the flow of traffic
- [ ] **D.** Park next to a busy junction

243 CAR
When parking and leaving your car you should

Mark one answer
- [ ] **A.** park under a shady tree
- [ ] **B.** remove the tax disc
- [ ] **C.** park in a quiet road
- [ ] **D.** engage the steering lock

244 CAR
When leaving your vehicle parked and unattended you should

Mark one answer
- A. park near a busy junction
- B. park in a housing estate
- C. remove the key and lock it
- D. leave the left indicator on

245 CAR
How can you lessen the risk of your vehicle being broken into at night?

Mark one answer
- A. Leave it in a well-lit area
- B. Park in a quiet side road
- C. Don't engage the steering lock
- D. Park in a poorly-lit area

246 CAR
To help keep your car secure you could join a

Mark one answer
- A. vehicle breakdown organisation
- B. vehicle watch scheme
- C. advanced driver's scheme
- D. car maintenance class

247 CAR
Which TWO of the following will improve fuel consumption?

Mark two answers
- A. Reducing your road speed
- B. Planning well ahead
- C. Late and harsh braking
- D. Driving in lower gears
- E. Short journeys with a cold engine
- F. Rapid acceleration

248 CAR
You service your own vehicle. How should you get rid of the old engine oil?

Mark one answer
- A. Take it to a local authority site
- B. Pour it down a drain
- C. Tip it into a hole in the ground
- D. Put it into your dustbin

249 CAR
On a vehicle, where would you find a catalytic converter?

Mark one answer
- A. In the fuel tank
- B. In the air filter
- C. On the cooling system
- D. On the exhaust system

250 CAR
Why do MOT tests include a strict exhaust emission test?

Mark one answer
- A. To recover the cost of expensive garage equipment
- B. To help protect the environment against pollution
- C. To discover which fuel supplier is used the most
- D. To make sure diesel and petrol engines emit the same fumes

251 CAR
To reduce the damage your vehicle causes to the environment you should

Mark three answers
- A. use narrow side streets
- B. avoid harsh acceleration
- C. brake in good time
- D. anticipate well ahead
- E. use busy routes

252 CAR
Your vehicle has a catalytic converter. Its purpose is to reduce

Mark one answer
- **A.** exhaust noise
- **B.** fuel consumption
- **C.** exhaust emissions
- **D.** engine noise

253 CAR
A properly serviced vehicle will give

Mark two answers
- **A.** lower insurance premiums
- **B.** you a refund on your road tax
- **C.** better fuel economy
- **D.** cleaner exhaust emissions

254 CAR
You enter a road where there are road humps. What should you do?

Mark one answer
- **A.** Maintain a reduced speed throughout
- **B.** Accelerate quickly between each one
- **C.** Always keep to the maximum legal speed
- **D.** Drive slowly at school times only

255 CAR
When should you especially check the engine oil level?

Mark one answer
- **A.** Before a long journey
- **B.** When the engine is hot
- **C.** Early in the morning
- **D.** Every 6,000 miles

256 CAR
You are having difficulty finding a parking space in a busy town. You can see there is space on the zigzag lines of a zebra crossing. Can you park there?

Mark one answer
- **A.** No, unless you stay with your car
- **B.** Yes, in order to drop off a passenger
- **C.** Yes, if you do not block people from crossing
- **D.** No, not in any circumstances

257 CAR
When leaving your car unattended for a few minutes you should

Mark one answer
- **A.** leave the engine running
- **B.** switch the engine off but leave the key in
- **C.** lock it and remove the key
- **D.** park near a traffic warden

258 CAR
When parking and leaving your car for a few minutes you should

Mark one answer
- **A.** leave it unlocked
- **B.** lock it and remove the key
- **C.** leave the hazard warning lights on
- **D.** leave the interior light on

259 CAR
When leaving your car to help keep it secure you should

Mark one answer

- [ ] **A.** leave the hazard warning lights on
- [ ] **B.** lock it and remove the key
- [ ] **C.** park on a one-way street
- [ ] **D.** park in a residential area

260 CAR
When leaving your vehicle where should you park if possible?

Mark one answer

- [ ] **A.** Opposite a traffic island
- [ ] **B.** In a secure car park
- [ ] **C.** On a bend
- [ ] **D.** At or near a taxi rank

261 CAR
You are leaving your vehicle parked on a road. When may you leave the engine running?

Mark one answer

- [ ] **A.** If you will be parking for less than 5 minutes
- [ ] **B.** If the battery is flat
- [ ] **C.** When in a 20mph zone
- [ ] **D.** Never on any occasion

262 CAR
In which THREE places would parking your vehicle cause danger or obstruction to other road users?

Mark three answers

- [ ] **A.** In front of a property entrance
- [ ] **B.** At or near a bus stop
- [ ] **C.** On your driveway
- [ ] **D.** In a marked parking space
- [ ] **E.** On the approach to a level crossing

263 CAR
In which THREE places would parking cause an obstruction to others?

Mark three answers

- [ ] **A.** Near the brow of a hill
- [ ] **B.** In a lay-by
- [ ] **C.** Where the kerb is raised
- [ ] **D.** Where the kerb has been lowered for wheelchairs
- [ ] **E.** At or near a bus stop

264 CAR
You are away from home and have to park your vehicle overnight. Where should you leave it?

Mark one answer

- [ ] **A.** Opposite another parked vehicle
- [ ] **B.** In a quiet road
- [ ] **C.** Opposite a traffic island
- [ ] **D.** In a secure car park

265 CAR & MOTORCYCLE
Before starting a journey it is wise to plan your route. How can you do this?

Mark one answer

- [ ] **A.** Look at a map
- [ ] **B.** Contact your local garage
- [ ] **C.** Look in your vehicle handbook
- [ ] **D.** Check your vehicle registration document

266 CAR & MOTORCYCLE
It can help to plan your route before starting a journey. You can do this by contacting

NI

Mark one answer

- [ ] **A.** your local filling station
- [ ] **B.** a motoring organisation
- [ ] **C.** the Driver Vehicle Licensing Agency
- [ ] **D.** your vehicle manufacturer

267 CAR & MOTORCYCLE
How can you plan your route before starting a long journey?

Mark one answer
- [ ] **A.** Check your vehicle's workshop manual
- [ ] **B.** Ask your local garage
- [ ] **C.** Use a route planner on the internet
- [ ] **D.** Consult your travel agents

268 CAR & MOTORCYCLE
Planning your route before setting out can be helpful. How can you do this?

Mark one answer
- [ ] **A.** Look in a motoring magazine
- [ ] **B.** Only visit places you know
- [ ] **C.** Try to travel at busy times
- [ ] **D.** Print or write down the route

269 CAR & MOTORCYCLE
Why is it a good idea to plan your journey to avoid busy times?

Mark one answer
- [ ] **A.** You will have an easier journey
- [ ] **B.** You will have a more stressful journey
- [ ] **C.** Your journey time will be longer
- [ ] **D.** It will cause more traffic congestion

270 CAR & MOTORCYCLE
Planning your journey to avoid busy times has a number of advantages. One of these is

Mark one answer
- [ ] **A.** your journey will take longer
- [ ] **B.** you will have a more pleasant journey
- [ ] **C.** you will cause more pollution
- [ ] **D.** your stress level will be greater

271 CAR & MOTORCYCLE
It is a good idea to plan your journey to avoid busy times. This is because

Mark one answer
- [ ] **A.** your vehicle will use more fuel
- [ ] **B.** you will see less road works
- [ ] **C.** it will help to ease congestion
- [ ] **D.** you will travel a much shorter distance

272 CAR & MOTORCYCLE
By avoiding busy times when travelling

Mark one answer
- [ ] **A.** you are more likely to be held up
- [ ] **B.** your journey time will be longer
- [ ] **C.** you will travel a much shorter distance
- [ ] **D.** you are less likely to be delayed

273 CAR & MOTORCYCLE
It can help to plan your route before starting a journey. Why should you also plan an alternative route?

Mark one answer
- [ ] **A.** Your original route may be blocked
- [ ] **B.** Your maps may have different scales
- [ ] **C.** You may find you have to pay a congestion charge
- [ ] **D.** Because you may get held up by a tractor

274 CAR
You will find that driving smoothly can

Mark one answer
- [ ] **A.** reduce journey times by about 15%
- [ ] **B.** increase fuel consumption by about 15%
- [ ] **C.** reduce fuel consumption by about 15%
- [ ] **D.** increase journey times by about 15%

275 CAR
You can save fuel when conditions allow by

Mark one answer

- A. using lower gears as often as possible
- B. accelerating sharply in each gear
- C. using each gear in turn
- D. missing out some gears

276 CAR & MOTORCYCLE
As well as planning your route before starting a journey, you should also plan an alternative route. Why is this?

Mark one answer

- A. To let another driver overtake
- B. Your first route may be blocked
- C. To avoid a railway level crossing
- D. In case you have to avoid emergency vehicles

277 CAR & MOTORCYCLE
Who of these will not have to pay Congestion Charges in London?

Mark one answer

- A. A van driver making deliveries
- B. A rider of a two-wheeled vehicle
- C. A car driver whose vehicle is more than 1000 cc
- D. A driver who just wants to park in the area

278 CAR & MOTORCYCLE
You are making an appointment and will have to travel a long distance. You should

Mark one answer

- A. allow plenty of time for your journey
- B. plan to go at busy times
- C. avoid all national speed limit roads
- D. prevent other drivers from overtaking

279 MOTORCYCLE
A loosely adjusted drive chain could

Mark one answer

- A. lock the rear wheel
- B. make wheels wobble
- C. cause a braking fault
- D. affect your headlight beam

280 MOTORCYCLE
Your motorcycle is NOT fitted with daytime running lights. When MUST you use a dipped headlight during the day?

Mark one answer

- A. On country roads
- B. In poor visibility
- C. Along narrow streets
- D. When parking

281 CAR

You are checking your trailer tyres. What is the legal minimum tread depth over the central three quarters of its breadth?

Mark one answer

- A. 1mm
- B. 1.6mm
- C. 2mm
- D. 2.6mm

282 CAR

How can driving in an Eco-safe manner help protect the environment?

Mark one answer

- A. Through the legal enforcement of speed regulations
- B. By increasing the number of cars on the road
- C. Through increased fuel bills
- D. By reducing exhaust emissions

283 CAR

What does Eco-safe driving achieve?

Mark one answer

- A. Increased fuel consumption
- B. Improved road safety
- C. Damage to the environment
- D. Increased exhaust emissions

284 CAR

How can missing out some gear changes save fuel?

Mark one answer

- A. By reducing the amount of time you are accelerating
- B. Because there is less need to use the footbrake
- C. By controlling the amount of steering
- D. Because coasting is kept to a minimum

285 CAR

Fuel consumption is at its highest when you are

Mark one answer

- A. braking
- B. coasting
- C. accelerating
- D. steering

286 CAR

Missing out some gears saves fuel by reducing the amount of time you spend

Mark one answer

- A. braking
- B. coasting
- C. steering
- D. accelerating

287 CAR & MOTORCYCLE
Rapid acceleration and heavy braking can lead to

Mark one answer

- A. reduced pollution
- B. increased fuel consumption
- C. reduced exhaust emissions
- D. increased road safety

288 CAR & MOTORCYCLE
What percentage of all emissions does road transport account for?

Mark one answer

- A. 10%
- B. 20%
- C. 30%
- D. 40%

289 CAR
Car passengers MUST wear a seat belt if one is available, unless they are

Mark one answer

- A. in a vehicle fitted with air bags
- B. travelling within a congestion charging zone
- C. sitting in the rear seat
- D. exempt for medical reasons

290 CAR
You are carrying a 5-year-old child in the back seat of your car. They are under 1.35 metres (4 feet 5 inches). A correct child restraint is NOT available. They MUST

Mark one answer

- A. sit behind the passenger seat
- B. use an adult seat belt
- C. share a belt with an adult
- D. sit between two other children

291 CAR
You are carrying a child using a rear-facing baby seat. You want to put it on the front passenger seat. What MUST you do before setting off?

Mark one answer

- A. Deactivate all front and rear airbags
- B. Make sure any front passenger airbag is deactivated
- C. Make sure all the child safety locks are off
- D. Recline the front passenger seat

292 CAR
You are carrying an 11-year-old child in the back seat of your car. They are under 1.35 metres (4 feet 5 inches) in height. You MUST make sure that

Mark one answer

- A. they sit between two belted people
- B. they can fasten their own seat belt
- C. a suitable child restraint is available
- D. they can see clearly out of the front window

293 CAR
You are parked at the side of the road. You will be waiting for some time for a passenger. What should you do?

Mark one answer

- A. Switch off the engine
- B. Apply the steering lock
- C. Switch off the radio
- D. Use your headlights

294 CAR
You are using a rear-facing baby seat. You want to put it on the front passenger seat which is protected by a frontal airbag. What MUST you do before setting off?

Mark one answer
- **A.** Deactivate the airbag
- **B.** Turn the seat to face sideways
- **C.** Ask a passenger to hold the baby
- **D.** Put the child in an adult seat belt

295 CAR
You are carrying a 5-year-old child in the back seat of your car. They are under 1.35 metres (4 feet 5 inches) in height. They MUST use an adult seat belt ONLY if

Mark one answer
- **A.** a correct child restraint is not available
- **B.** it is a lap type belt
- **C.** they sit between two adults
- **D.** it can be shared with another adult

296 MOTORCYCLE
You have too much oil in your engine. What could this cause?

Mark one answer
- **A.** Low oil pressure
- **B.** Engine overheating
- **C.** Chain wear
- **D.** Oil leaks

297 MOTORCYCLE
Your overall stopping distance will be longer when riding

Mark one answer
- **A.** at night
- **B.** in the fog
- **C.** with a passenger
- **D.** up a hill

298 MOTORCYCLE
Only a fool breaks the two-second rule refers to

Mark one answer
- **A.** the time recommended when using the choke
- **B.** the separation distance when riding in good conditions
- **C.** restarting a stalled engine in busy traffic
- **D.** the time you should keep your foot down at a junction

299 MOTORCYCLE
On a wet road what is the safest way to stop?

Mark one answer
- **A.** Change gear without braking
- **B.** Use the back brake only
- **C.** Use the front brake only
- **D.** Use both brakes

300 MOTORCYCLE
You are riding in heavy rain when your rear wheel skids as you accelerate. To get control again you must

Mark one answer
- **A.** change down to a lower gear
- **B.** ease off the throttle
- **C.** brake to reduce speed
- **D.** put your feet down

301 MOTORCYCLE
It is snowing. Before starting your journey you should

Mark one answer
- **A.** think if you need to ride at all
- **B.** try to avoid taking a passenger
- **C.** plan a route avoiding towns
- **D.** take a hot drink before setting out

302 MOTORCYCLE
Why should you ride with a dipped headlight on in the daytime?

Mark one answer
- **A.** It helps other road users to see you
- **B.** It means that you can ride faster
- **C.** Other vehicles will get out of the way
- **D.** So that it is already on when it gets dark

303 MOTORCYCLE
Motorcyclists are only allowed to use high-intensity rear fog lights when

Mark one answer
- **A.** a pillion passenger is being carried
- **B.** they ride a large touring machine
- **C.** visibility is 100 metres (328 feet) or less
- **D.** they are riding on the road for the first time

304 MOTORCYCLE
When riding at night you should

Mark two answers
- **A.** ride with your headlight on dipped beam
- **B.** wear reflective clothing
- **C.** wear a tinted visor
- **D.** ride in the centre of the road
- **E.** give arm signals

305 MOTORCYCLE
You MUST use your headlight

Mark three answers
- A. when riding in a group
- B. at night when street lighting is poor
- C. when carrying a passenger
- D. on motorways during darkness
- E. at times of poor visibility
- F. when parked on an unlit road

306 MOTORCYCLE
You are riding in town at night. The roads are wet after rain. The reflections from wet surfaces will

Mark one answer
- A. affect your stopping distance
- B. affect your road holding
- C. make it easy to see unlit objects
- D. make it hard to see unlit objects

307 MOTORCYCLE
You are riding through a flood. Which TWO should you do?

Mark two answers
- A. Keep in a high gear and stand up on the footrests
- B. Keep the engine running fast to keep water out of the exhaust
- C. Ride slowly and test your brakes when you are out of the water
- D. Turn your headlight off to avoid any electrical damage

308 MOTORCYCLE
You have just ridden through a flood. When clear of the water you should test your

Mark one answer
- A. starter motor
- B. headlight
- C. steering
- D. brakes

309 MOTORCYCLE
When going through flood water you should ride

Mark one answer
- A. quickly in a high gear
- B. slowly in a high gear
- C. quickly in a low gear
- D. slowly in a low gear

310 MOTORCYCLE
When riding at night you should NOT

Mark one answer
- A. switch on full beam headlights
- B. overtake slower vehicles in front
- C. use dipped beam headlights
- D. use tinted glasses, lenses or visors

311 MOTORCYCLE
At a mini-roundabout it is important that a motorcyclist should avoid

Mark one answer
- A. turning right
- B. using signals
- C. taking 'lifesavers'
- D. the painted area

312 MOTORCYCLE
Which of the following should you do when riding in fog?

Mark two answers
- A. Keep close to the vehicle in front
- B. Use your dipped headlight
- C. Ride close to the centre of the road
- D. Keep your visor or goggles clear
- E. Keep the vehicle in front in view

313 MOTORCYCLE
You are riding on a motorway in a crosswind. You should take extra care when

Mark two answers
- **A.** approaching service areas
- **B.** overtaking a large vehicle
- **C.** riding in slow-moving traffic
- **D.** approaching an exit
- **E.** riding in exposed places

314 MOTORCYCLE
You are riding in heavy rain. Why should you try to avoid this marked area?

Mark one answer
- **A.** It is illegal to ride over bus stops
- **B.** The painted lines may be slippery
- **C.** Cyclists may be using the bus stop
- **D.** Only emergency vehicles may drive over bus stops

315 MOTORCYCLE
Why should you try to avoid riding over this marked area?

Mark one answer
- **A.** It is illegal to ride over bus stops
- **B.** It will alter your machine's centre of gravity
- **C.** Pedestrians may be waiting at the bus stop
- **D.** A bus may have left patches of oil

316 MOTORCYCLE
When riding at night you should

Mark one answer
- **A.** wear reflective clothing
- **B.** wear a tinted visor
- **C.** ride in the middle of the road
- **D.** always give arm signals

317 MOTORCYCLE
When riding in extremely cold conditions what can you do to keep warm?

Mark one answer
- **A.** Stay close to the vehicles in front
- **B.** Wear suitable clothing
- **C.** Lie flat on the tank
- **D.** Put one hand on the exhaust pipe

318 MOTORCYCLE
You are riding at night. To be seen more easily you should

Mark two answers
- **A.** ride with your headlight on dipped beam
- **B.** wear reflective clothing
- **C.** keep the motorcycle clean
- **D.** stay well out to the right
- **E.** wear waterproof clothing

319 MOTORCYCLE
Your overall stopping distance will be much longer when riding

Mark one answer
- **A.** in the rain
- **B.** in fog
- **C.** at night
- **D.** in strong winds

320 MOTORCYCLE

The road surface is very important to motorcyclists. Which FOUR of these are more likely to reduce the stability of your motorcycle?

Mark four answers
- A. Potholes
- B. Drain covers
- C. Concrete
- D. Oil patches
- E. Tarmac
- F. Loose gravel

321 MOTORCYCLE

You are riding in very hot weather. What are TWO effects that melting tar has on the control of your motorcycle?

Mark two answers
- A. It can make the surface slippery
- B. It can reduce tyre grip
- C. It can reduce stopping distances
- D. It can improve braking efficiency

322 MOTORCYCLE

Your overall stopping distance comprises thinking and braking distance. You are on a good, dry road surface with good brakes and tyres. What is the typical BRAKING distance at 50mph?

Mark one answer
- A. 14 metres (46 feet)
- B. 24 metres (79 feet)
- C. 38 metres (125 feet)
- D. 55 metres (180 feet)

323 MOTORCYCLE

You are riding past queuing traffic. Why should you be more cautious when approaching this road marking?

Mark one answer
- A. Lorries will be unloading here
- B. Schoolchildren will be crossing here
- C. Pedestrians will be standing in the road
- D. Traffic could be emerging and may not see you

324 MOTORCYCLE

What can cause your tyres to skid and lose their grip on the road surface?

Mark one answer
- A. Giving hand signals
- B. Riding one handed
- C. Looking over your shoulder
- D. Heavy braking

325 MOTORCYCLE

It has rained after a long dry spell. You should be very careful because the road surface will be unusually

Mark one answer
- A. loose
- B. dry
- C. sticky
- D. slippery

326 MOTORCYCLE

You are riding at speed through surface water. A thin film of water has built up between your tyres and the road surface. To keep control what should you do?

Mark one answer

- A. Turn the steering quickly
- B. Use the rear brake gently
- C. Use both brakes gently
- D. Ease off the throttle

327 MOTORCYCLE

When riding in heavy rain a film of water can build up between your tyres and the road surface. This may result in loss of control. What can you do to avoid this happening?

Mark one answer

- A. Keep your speed down
- B. Increase your tyre pressures
- C. Decrease your tyre pressures
- D. Keep trying your brakes

328 MOTORCYCLE

When riding in heavy rain a film of water can build up between your tyres and the road. This is known as aquaplaning. What should you do to keep control?

Mark one answer

- A. Use your rear brakes gently
- B. Steer to the crown of the road
- C. Ease off the throttle smoothly
- D. Change up into a higher gear

329 MOTORCYCLE

You are on a good, dry road surface and your motorcycle has good brakes and tyres. What is the typical overall stopping distance at 40mph?

Mark one answer

- A. 23 metres (75 feet)
- B. 36 metres (120 feet)
- C. 53 metres (175 feet)
- D. 96 metres (315 feet)

330 MOTORCYCLE

After riding through deep water you notice your scooter brakes do not work properly. What would be the best way to dry them out?

Mark one answer

- A. Ride slowly, braking lightly
- B. Ride quickly, braking harshly
- C. Stop and dry them with a cloth
- D. Stop and wait for a few minutes

331 MOTORCYCLE

You have to ride in foggy weather. You should

Mark two answers

- A. stay close to the centre of the road
- B. switch only your sidelights on
- C. switch on your dipped headlights
- D. be aware of others not using their headlights
- E. always ride in the gutter to see the kerb

332 CAR & MOTORCYCLE

Braking distances on ice can be

Mark one answer

- A. twice the normal distance
- B. five times the normal distance
- C. seven times the normal distance
- D. ten times the normal distance

333 CAR & MOTORCYCLE
Freezing conditions will affect the distance it takes you to come to a stop. You should expect stopping distances to increase by up to

Mark one answer
- A. two times
- B. three times
- C. five times
- D. ten times

334 CAR & MOTORCYCLE
In very hot weather the road surface can become soft. Which TWO of the following will be most affected?

Mark two answers
- A. The suspension
- B. The grip of the tyres
- C. The braking
- D. The exhaust

335 CAR & MOTORCYCLE
Where are you most likely to be affected by a side wind?

Mark one answer
- A. On a narrow country lane
- B. On an open stretch of road
- C. On a busy stretch of road
- D. On a long, straight road

336 CAR & MOTORCYCLE
In windy conditions you need to take extra care when

Mark one answer
- A. using the brakes
- B. making a hill start
- C. turning into a narrow road
- D. passing pedal cyclists

337 CAR & MOTORCYCLE
In good conditions, what is the typical stopping distance at 70mph?

Mark one answer
- A. 53 metres (175 feet)
- B. 60 metres (197 feet)
- C. 73 metres (240 feet)
- D. 96 metres (315 feet)

338 CAR & MOTORCYCLE
What is the shortest overall stopping distance on a dry road at 60mph?

Mark one answer
- A. 53 metres (175 feet)
- B. 58 metres (190 feet)
- C. 73 metres (240 feet)
- D. 96 metres (315 feet)

339 CAR & MOTORCYCLE
You are following a vehicle at a safe distance on a wet road. Another driver overtakes you and pulls into the gap you have left. What should you do?

Mark one answer
- A. Flash your headlights as a warning
- B. Try to overtake safely as soon as you can
- C. Drop back to regain a safe distance
- D. Stay close to the other vehicle until it moves on

340 CAR & MOTORCYCLE
When approaching a right-hand bend you should keep well to the left. Why is this?

Mark one answer
- A. To improve your view of the road
- B. To overcome the effect of the road's slope
- C. To let faster traffic from behind overtake
- D. To be positioned safely if you skid

341 CAR & MOTORCYCLE
You have just gone through deep water. To dry off the brakes you should

Mark one answer

- **A.** accelerate and keep to a high speed for a short time
- **B.** go slowly while gently applying the brakes
- **C.** avoid using the brakes at all for a few miles
- **D.** stop for at least an hour to allow them time to dry

342 CAR
You are on a fast, open road in good conditions. For safety, the distance between you and the vehicle in front should be

Mark one answer

- **A.** a two-second time gap
- **B.** one car length
- **C.** 2 metres (6 feet 6 inches)
- **D.** two car lengths

343 CAR
What is the most common cause of skidding?

Mark one answer

- **A.** Worn tyres
- **B.** Driver error
- **C.** Other vehicles
- **D.** Pedestrians

344 CAR
You are driving on an icy road. How can you avoid wheelspin?

Mark one answer

- **A.** Drive at a slow speed in as high a gear as possible
- **B.** Use the handbrake if the wheels start to slip
- **C.** Brake gently and repeatedly
- **D.** Drive in a low gear at all times

345 CAR
Skidding is mainly caused by

Mark one answer

- **A.** the weather
- **B.** the driver
- **C.** the vehicle
- **D.** the road

346 CAR
You are driving in freezing conditions. What should you do when approaching a sharp bend?

Mark two answers

- **A.** Slow down before you reach the bend
- **B.** Gently apply your handbrake
- **C.** Firmly use your footbrake
- **D.** Coast into the bend
- **E.** Avoid sudden steering movements

347 CAR
You are turning left on a slippery road. The back of your vehicle slides to the right. You should

Mark one answer

- **A.** brake firmly and not turn the steering wheel
- **B.** steer carefully to the left
- **C.** steer carefully to the right
- **D.** brake firmly and steer to the left

348 CAR
You are braking on a wet road. Your vehicle begins to skid. It does not have anti-lock brakes. What is the FIRST thing you should do?

Mark one answer **NI**
- A. Quickly pull up the handbrake
- B. Release the footbrake fully
- C. Push harder on the brake pedal
- D. Gently use the accelerator

349 CAR
Travelling for long distances in neutral (known as coasting)

Mark one answer
- A. improves the driver's control
- B. makes steering easier
- C. reduces the driver's control
- D. uses more fuel

350 CAR
Before starting a journey in freezing weather you should clear ice and snow from your vehicle's

Mark four answers
- A. aerial
- B. windows
- C. bumper
- D. lights
- E. mirrors
- F. number plates

351 CAR
You are trying to move off on snow. You should use

Mark one answer
- A. the lowest gear you can
- B. the highest gear you can
- C. a high engine speed
- D. the handbrake and footbrake together

352 CAR
When driving in falling snow you should

Mark one answer
- A. brake firmly and quickly
- B. be ready to steer sharply
- C. use sidelights only
- D. brake gently in plenty of time

353 CAR
The main benefit of having four-wheel drive is to improve

Mark one answer
- A. road holding
- B. fuel consumption
- C. stopping distances
- D. passenger comfort

354 CAR
You are about to go down a steep hill. To control the speed of your vehicle you should

Mark one answer
- A. select a high gear and use the brakes carefully
- B. select a high gear and use the brakes firmly
- C. select a low gear and use the brakes carefully
- D. select a low gear and avoid using the brakes

355 CAR
How can you use your vehicle's engine as a brake?

Mark one answer
- A. By changing to a lower gear
- B. By selecting reverse gear
- C. By changing to a higher gear
- D. By selecting neutral gear

356 CAR
You wish to park facing DOWNHILL. Which TWO of the following should you do?

Mark two answers

- **A.** Turn the steering wheel towards the kerb
- **B.** Park close to the bumper of another car
- **C.** Park with two wheels on the kerb
- **D.** Put the handbrake on firmly
- **E.** Turn the steering wheel away from the kerb

357 CAR
You are driving in a built-up area. You approach a speed hump. You should

Mark one answer

- **A.** move across to the left-hand side of the road
- **B.** wait for any pedestrians to cross
- **C.** slow your vehicle right down
- **D.** stop and check both pavements

358 CAR
You are on a long, downhill slope. What should you do to help control the speed of your vehicle?

Mark one answer

- **A.** Select neutral
- **B.** Select a lower gear
- **C.** Grip the handbrake firmly
- **D.** Apply the parking brake gently

359 CAR
Your vehicle is fitted with anti-lock brakes. To stop quickly in an emergency you should

Mark one answer

- **A.** brake firmly and pump the brake pedal on and off
- **B.** brake rapidly and firmly without releasing the brake pedal
- **C.** brake gently and pump the brake pedal on and off
- **D.** brake rapidly once, and immediately release the brake pedal

360 CAR
Anti-lock brakes prevent wheels from locking. This means the tyres are less likely to

Mark one answer

- **A.** aquaplane
- **B.** skid
- **C.** puncture
- **D.** wear

361 CAR
Anti-lock brakes reduce the chances of a skid occurring particularly when

Mark one answer

- **A.** driving down steep hills
- **B.** braking during normal driving
- **C.** braking in an emergency
- **D.** driving on good road surfaces

362 CAR
Anti-lock brakes are most effective when you

Mark one answer

- **A.** keep pumping the footbrake to prevent skidding
- **B.** brake normally, but grip the steering wheel tightly
- **C.** brake promptly and firmly until you have slowed down
- **D.** apply the handbrake to reduce the stopping distance

363 CAR
Your car is fitted with anti-lock brakes. You need to stop in an emergency. You should

Mark one answer
- A. brake normally and avoid turning the steering wheel
- B. press the brake pedal promptly and firmly until you have stopped
- C. keep pushing and releasing the footbrake quickly to prevent skidding
- D. apply the handbrake to reduce the stopping distance

364 CAR
Vehicles fitted with anti-lock brakes

Mark one answer
- A. are impossible to skid
- B. can be steered while you are braking
- C. accelerate much faster
- D. are not fitted with a handbrake

365 CAR
Anti-lock brakes may not work as effectively if the road surface is

Mark two answers
- A. dry
- B. loose
- C. wet
- D. good
- E. firm

366 CAR
Anti-lock brakes are of most use when you are

Mark one answer
- A. braking gently
- B. driving on worn tyres
- C. braking excessively
- D. driving normally

367 CAR
Driving a vehicle fitted with anti-lock brakes allows you to

Mark one answer
- A. brake harder because it is impossible to skid
- B. drive at higher speeds
- C. steer and brake at the same time
- D. pay less attention to the road ahead

368 CAR
Anti-lock brakes can greatly assist with

Mark one answer
- A. a higher cruising speed
- B. steering control when braking
- C. control when accelerating
- D. motorway driving

369 CAR
When would an anti-lock braking system start to work?

Mark one answer
- A. After the parking brake has been applied
- B. Whenever pressure on the brake pedal is applied
- C. Just as the wheels are about to lock
- D. When the normal braking system fails to operate

370 CAR
You are driving a vehicle fitted with anti-lock brakes. You need to stop in an emergency. You should apply the footbrake

Mark one answer
- A. slowly and gently
- B. slowly but firmly
- C. rapidly and gently
- D. rapidly and firmly

371

CAR

Your vehicle has anti-lock brakes, but they may not always prevent skidding. This is most likely to happen when driving

Mark two answers

- A. in foggy conditions
- B. on surface water
- C. on loose road surfaces
- D. on dry tarmac
- E. at night on unlit roads

372

CAR

Anti-lock brakes will take effect when

Mark one answer

- A. you do not brake quickly enough
- B. maximum brake pressure has been applied
- C. you have not seen a hazard ahead
- D. speeding on slippery road surfaces

373

CAR

When driving in fog, which of the following are correct?

Mark three answers

- A. Use dipped headlights
- B. Use headlights on full beam
- C. Allow more time for your journey
- D. Keep close to the car in front
- E. Slow down   F. Use sidelights only

374

CAR

You are driving along a country road. You see this sign. AFTER dealing safely with the hazard you should always

Ford

Mark one answer

- A. check your tyre pressures
- B. switch on your hazard warning lights
- C. accelerate briskly
- D. test your brakes

375

CAR

You are driving in heavy rain. Your steering suddenly becomes very light. You should

Mark one answer

- A. steer towards the side of the road
- B. apply gentle acceleration
- C. brake firmly to reduce speed
- D. ease off the accelerator

376

CAR

How can you tell when you are driving over black ice?

Mark one answer

- A. It is easier to brake
- B. The noise from your tyres sounds louder
- C. You will see tyre tracks on the road
- D. Your steering feels light

377

CAR

The roads are icy. You should drive slowly

Mark one answer

- A. in the highest gear possible
- B. in the lowest gear possible
- C. with the handbrake partly on
- D. with your left foot on the brake

378

CAR

You are driving along a wet road. How can you tell if your vehicle is aquaplaning?

Mark one answer

- A. The engine will stall
- B. The engine noise will increase
- C. The steering will feel very heavy
- D. The steering will feel very light

379 CAR
How can you tell if you are driving on ice?

Mark two answers
- [ ] **A.** The tyres make a rumbling noise
- [ ] **B.** The tyres make hardly any noise
- [ ] **C.** The steering becomes heavier
- [ ] **D.** The steering becomes lighter

380 CAR
You are driving along a wet road. How can you tell if your vehicle's tyres are losing their grip on the surface?

Mark one answer
- [ ] **A.** The engine will stall
- [ ] **B.** The steering will feel very heavy
- [ ] **C.** The engine noise will increase
- [ ] **D.** The steering will feel very light

381 CAR
You are travelling at 50mph on a good, dry road. What is your shortest overall stopping distance?

Mark one answer
- [ ] **A.** 36 metres (120 feet)
- [ ] **B.** 53 metres (175 feet)
- [ ] **C.** 75 metres (245 feet)
- [ ] **D.** 96 metres (315 feet)

382 CAR
Your overall stopping distance will be much longer when driving

Mark one answer
- [ ] **A.** in the rain
- [ ] **B.** in fog
- [ ] **C.** at night
- [ ] **D.** in strong winds

383 CAR
You have driven through a flood. What is the first thing you should do?

Mark one answer
- [ ] **A.** Stop and check the tyres
- [ ] **B.** Stop and dry the brakes
- [ ] **C.** Check your exhaust
- [ ] **D.** Test your brakes

384 CAR
You are on a good, dry road surface. Your vehicle has good brakes and tyres. What is the BRAKING distance at 50mph?

Mark one answer
- [ ] **A.** 38 metres (125 feet)
- [ ] **B.** 14 metres (46 feet)
- [ ] **C.** 24 metres (79 feet)
- [ ] **D.** 55 metres (180 feet)

385 CAR
You are on a good, dry road surface and your vehicle has good brakes and tyres. What is the typical overall STOPPING distance at 40mph?

Mark one answer
- [ ] **A.** 23 metres (75 feet)
- [ ] **B.** 36 metres (120 feet)
- [ ] **C.** 53 metres (175 feet)
- [ ] **D.** 96 metres (315 feet)

386 CAR
You are on a wet motorway with surface spray. You should use

Mark one answer
- [ ] **A.** hazard flashers
- [ ] **B.** dipped headlights
- [ ] **C.** rear fog lights
- [ ] **D.** sidelights

387 MOTORCYCLE
You get cold and wet when riding. Which TWO are likely to happen?

Mark two answers
- A. You may lose concentration
- B. You may slide off the seat
- C. Your visor may freeze up
- D. Your reaction times may be slower
- E. Your helmet may loosen

388 MOTORCYCLE
You are riding up to a zebra crossing. You intend to stop for waiting pedestrians. How could you let them know you are stopping?

Mark one answer
- A. By signalling with your left arm
- B. By waving them across
- C. By flashing your headlight
- D. By signalling with your right arm

389 MOTORCYCLE
You are about to ride home. You cannot find the glasses you need to wear. You should

Mark one answer
- A. ride home slowly, keeping to quiet roads
- B. borrow a friend's glasses and use those
- C. ride home at night, so that the lights will help you
- D. find a way of getting home without riding

390 MOTORCYCLE
Which THREE of these are likely effects of drinking alcohol?

Mark three answers
- A. Reduced co-ordination
- B. Increased confidence
- C. Poor judgement
- D. Increased concentration
- E. Faster reactions
- F. Colour blindness

391 MOTORCYCLE
You find that you need glasses to read vehicle number plates at the required distance. When MUST you wear them?

Mark one answer
- A. Only in bad weather conditions
- B. At all times when riding
- C. Only when you think it necessary
- D. Only in bad light or at night time

392 MOTORCYCLE
Drinking any amount of alcohol is likely to

Mark three answers
- A. slow down your reactions to hazards
- B. increase the speed of your reactions
- C. worsen your judgement of speed
- D. improve your awareness of danger
- E. give a false sense of confidence

393 MOTORCYCLE
Which of the following types of glasses should NOT be worn when riding at night?

Mark one answer
- A. Half-moon
- B. Round
- C. Bi-focal
- D. Tinted

394 MOTORCYCLE
You are not sure if your cough medicine will affect you. What TWO things should you do?

Mark two answers
- A. Ask your doctor
- B. Check the medicine label
- C. Ride if you feel alright
- D. Ask a friend or relative for advice

395 MOTORCYCLE
For which of these may you use hazard warning lights?

Mark one answer
- A. When riding on a motorway to warn traffic behind of a hazard ahead
- B. When you are double parked on a two-way road
- C. When your direction indicators are not working
- D. When warning oncoming traffic that you intend to stop

396 MOTORCYCLE
When should you use hazard warning lights?

Mark one answer
- A. When you are double parked on a two-way road
- B. When your direction indicators are not working
- C. When warning oncoming traffic that you intend to stop
- D. When your motorcycle has broken down and is causing an obstruction

397 MOTORCYCLE
Why should you check over your shoulder before turning right into a side road?

Mark one answer
- A. To make sure the side road is clear
- B. To check for emerging traffic
- C. To check for overtaking vehicles
- D. To confirm your intention to turn

398 MOTORCYCLE
When riding how can you help to reduce the risk of hearing damage?

Mark one answer
- A. Wearing goggles
- B. Using ear plugs
- C. Wearing a scarf
- D. Keeping the visor up

399 MOTORCYCLE
It is a very hot day. What would you expect to find?

Mark one answer
- A. Mud on the road
- B. A soft road surface
- C. Road works ahead
- D. Banks of fog

400 MOTORCYCLE
You see this road marking in between queuing traffic. What should you look out for?

Mark one answer
- A. Overhanging trees
- B. Road works
- C. Traffic wardens
- D. Traffic emerging

KEEP CLEAR

401 MOTORCYCLE
When riding long distances at speed, noise can cause fatigue. What can you do to help reduce this?

Mark one answer
- A. Vary your speed
- B. Wear ear plugs
- C. Use an open-face helmet
- D. Ride in an upright position

402 MOTORCYCLE
Why should you wear ear plugs when riding a motorcycle?

Mark one answer
- A. To help to prevent ear damage
- B. To make you less aware of traffic
- C. To help to keep you warm
- D. To make your helmet fit better

403 MOTORCYCLE
You are going out to a social event and alcohol will be available. You will be riding your motorcycle shortly afterwards. What is the safest thing to do?

Mark one answer
- A. Stay just below the legal limit
- B. Have soft drinks and alcohol in turn
- C. Don't go beyond the legal limit
- D. Stick to non-alcoholic drinks

404 MOTORCYCLE
You are convicted of riding after drinking too much alcohol. How could this affect your insurance?

Mark one answer
- A. Your insurance may become invalid
- B. The amount of excess you pay will be reduced
- C. You will only be able to get third party cover
- D. Cover will only be given for riding smaller motorcycles

405 CAR & MOTORCYCLE
You see this sign on the rear of a slow-moving lorry that you want to pass. It is travelling in the middle lane of a three-lane motorway. You should

Mark one answer
- A. cautiously approach the lorry then pass on either side
- B. follow the lorry until you can leave the motorway
- C. wait on the hard shoulder until the lorry has stopped
- D. approach with care and keep to the left of the lorry

406 CAR & MOTORCYCLE
To avoid an accident when entering a contraflow system, you should

Mark three answers
- A. reduce speed in good time
- B. switch lanes any time to make progress
- C. choose an appropriate lane early
- D. keep the correct separation distance
- E. increase speed to pass through quickly
- F. follow other motorists closely to avoid long queues

407 CAR & MOTORCYCLE
Where would you expect to see these markers?

Mark two answers

- A. On a motorway sign
- B. At the entrance to a narrow bridge
- C. On a large goods vehicle
- D. On a builder's skip placed on the road

408 CAR & MOTORCYCLE
What does this signal from a police officer mean to oncoming traffic?

Mark one answer

- A. Go ahead
- B. Stop
- C. Turn left
- D. Turn right

409 CAR & MOTORCYCLE
What is the main hazard shown in this picture?

Mark one answer

- A. Vehicles turning right
- B. Vehicles doing U-turns
- C. The cyclist crossing the road
- D. Parked cars around the corner

410 CAR & MOTORCYCLE
Which road user has caused a hazard?

Mark one answer

- A. The parked car (arrowed A)
- B. The pedestrian waiting to cross (arrowed B)
- C. The moving car (arrowed C)
- D. The car turning (arrowed D)

411 CAR & MOTORCYCLE
What should the driver of the car approaching the crossing do?

Mark one answer
- **A.** Continue at the same speed
- **B.** Sound the horn
- **C.** Drive through quickly
- **D.** Slow down and get ready to stop

412 CAR & MOTORCYCLE
What THREE things should the driver of the grey car (arrowed) be especially aware of?

Mark three answers
- **A.** Pedestrians stepping out between cars
- **B.** Other cars behind the grey car
- **C.** Doors opening on parked cars
- **D.** The bumpy road surface
- **E.** Cars leaving parking spaces
- **F.** Empty parking spaces

413 CAR & MOTORCYCLE
You think the driver of the vehicle in front has forgotten to cancel their right indicator. You should

Mark one answer
- **A.** flash your lights to alert the driver
- **B.** sound your horn before overtaking
- **C.** overtake on the left if there is room
- **D.** stay behind and not overtake

414 CAR & MOTORCYCLE
What is the main hazard the driver of the red car (arrowed) should be aware of?

Mark one answer
- **A.** Glare from the sun may affect the driver's vision
- **B.** The black car may stop suddenly
- **C.** The bus may move out into the road
- **D.** Oncoming vehicles will assume the driver is turning right

415 CAR & MOTORCYCLE

In heavy motorway traffic you are being followed closely by the vehicle behind. How can you lower the risk of an accident?

Mark one answer

- **A.** Increase your distance from the vehicle in front
- **B.** Tap your foot on the brake pedal sharply
- **C.** Switch on your hazard lights
- **D.** Move on to the hard shoulder and stop

416 CAR & MOTORCYCLE

You see this sign ahead. You should expect the road to

Mark one answer

- **A.** go steeply uphill
- **B.** go steeply downhill
- **C.** bend sharply to the left
- **D.** bend sharply to the right

417 CAR & MOTORCYCLE

You are approaching this cyclist. You should

Mark one answer

- **A.** overtake before the cyclist gets to the junction
- **B.** flash your headlights at the cyclist
- **C.** slow down and allow the cyclist to turn
- **D.** overtake the cyclist on the left-hand side

418 CAR & MOTORCYCLE

Why must you take extra care when turning right at this junction?

Mark one answer

- **A.** Road surface is poor
- **B.** Footpaths are narrow
- **C.** Road markings are faint
- **D.** There is reduced visibility

419 CAR & MOTORCYCLE
This yellow sign on a vehicle indicates this is

Mark one answer
- [ ] **A.** a broken-down vehicle
- [ ] **B.** a school bus
- [ ] **C.** an ice-cream van
- [ ] **D.** a private ambulance

420 CAR & MOTORCYCLE
When approaching this bridge you should give way to

Mark one answer
- [ ] **A.** bicycles
- [ ] **B.** buses
- [ ] **C.** motorcycles
- [ ] **D.** cars

421 CAR & MOTORCYCLE
What type of vehicle could you expect to meet in the middle of the road?

Mark one answer
- [ ] **A.** Lorry
- [ ] **B.** Bicycle
- [ ] **C.** Car
- [ ] **D.** Motorcycle

422 CAR & MOTORCYCLE
At this blind junction you must stop

Mark one answer
- [ ] **A.** behind the line, then edge forward to see clearly
- [ ] **B.** beyond the line at a point where you can see clearly
- [ ] **C.** only if there is traffic on the main road
- [ ] **D.** only if you are turning to the right

423 CAR & MOTORCYCLE
A driver pulls out of a side road in front of you. You have to brake hard. You should

Mark one answer
- [ ] **A.** ignore the error and stay calm
- [ ] **B.** flash your lights to show your annoyance
- [ ] **C.** sound your horn to show your annoyance
- [ ] **D.** overtake as soon as possible

424 CAR & MOTORCYCLE
An elderly person's driving ability could be affected because they may be unable to

Mark one answer
- [ ] **A.** obtain car insurance
- [ ] **B.** understand road signs
- [ ] **C.** react very quickly
- [ ] **D.** give signals correctly

425 CAR & MOTORCYCLE
You have just passed these warning lights. What hazard would you expect to see next?

Mark one answer
- **A.** A level crossing with no barrier
- **B.** An ambulance station
- **C.** A school crossing patrol
- **D.** An opening bridge

426 CAR & MOTORCYCLE
Why should you be especially cautious when going past this stationary bus?

Mark two answers
- **A.** There is traffic approaching in the distance
- **B.** The driver may open the door
- **C.** It may suddenly move off
- **D.** People may cross the road in front of it
- **E.** There are bicycles parked on the pavement

427 CAR & MOTORCYCLE
In areas where there are 'traffic calming' measures you should

Mark one answer
- **A.** travel at a reduced speed
- **B.** always travel at the speed limit
- **C.** position in the centre of the road
- **D.** only slow down if pedestrians are near

428 CAR & MOTORCYCLE
You are planning a long journey. Do you need to plan rest stops?

Mark one answer
- **A.** Yes, you should plan to stop every half an hour
- **B.** Yes, regular stops help concentration
- **C.** No, you will be less tired if you get there as soon as possible
- **D.** No, only fuel stops will be needed

429 CAR & MOTORCYCLE
A driver does something that upsets you. You should

Mark one answer
- **A.** try not to react
- **B.** let them know how you feel
- **C.** flash your headlights several times
- **D.** sound your horn

430 CAR & MOTORCYCLE
Some two-way roads are divided into three lanes. Why are these particularly dangerous?

Mark one answer
- **A.** Traffic in both directions can use the middle lane to overtake
- **B.** Traffic can travel faster in poor weather conditions
- **C.** Traffic can overtake on the left
- **D.** Traffic uses the middle lane for emergencies only

431 CAR & MOTORCYCLE
The red lights are flashing. What should you do when approaching this level crossing?

Mark one answer

- [ ] **A.** Go through quickly
- [ ] **B.** Go through carefully
- [ ] **C.** Stop before the barrier
- [ ] **D.** Switch on hazard warning lights

432 CAR & MOTORCYCLE
What TWO main hazards should you be aware of when going along this street?

Mark two answers

- [ ] **A.** Glare from the sun
- [ ] **B.** Car doors opening suddenly
- [ ] **C.** Lack of road markings
- [ ] **D.** The headlights on parked cars being switched on
- [ ] **E.** Large goods vehicles
- [ ] **F.** Children running out from between vehicles

433 CAR & MOTORCYCLE
What is the main hazard you should be aware of when following this cyclist?

Mark one answer

- [ ] **A.** The cyclist may move to the left and dismount
- [ ] **B.** The cyclist may swerve out into the road
- [ ] **C.** The contents of the cyclist's carrier may fall on to the road
- [ ] **D.** The cyclist may wish to turn right at the end of the road

434 CAR & MOTORCYCLE
When approaching this hazard why should you slow down?

Mark two answers

- [ ] **A.** Because of the bend
- [ ] **B.** Because it's hard to see to the right
- [ ] **C.** Because of approaching traffic
- [ ] **D.** Because of animals crossing
- [ ] **E.** Because of the level crossing

435 CAR & MOTORCYCLE
A driver's behaviour has upset you. It may help if you

Mark one answer

- **A.** stop and take a break
- **B.** shout abusive language
- **C.** gesture to them with your hand
- **D.** follow their car, flashing your headlights

436 CAR & MOTORCYCLE
You are on a dual carriageway. Ahead you see a vehicle with an amber flashing light. What will this be?

Mark one answer

- **A.** An ambulance
- **B.** A fire engine
- **C.** A doctor on call
- **D.** A disabled person's vehicle

437 CAR & MOTORCYCLE
You are approaching crossroads. The traffic lights have failed. What should you do?

Mark one answer

- **A.** Brake and stop only for large vehicles
- **B.** Brake sharply to a stop before looking
- **C.** Be prepared to brake sharply to a stop
- **D.** Be prepared to stop for any traffic

438 CAR & MOTORCYCLE
Why are place names painted on the road surface?

Mark one answer

- **A.** To restrict the flow of traffic
- **B.** To warn you of oncoming traffic
- **C.** To enable you to change lanes early
- **D.** To prevent you changing lanes

439 CAR & MOTORCYCLE
What should the driver of the red car (arrowed) do?

Mark one answer

- **A.** Wave the pedestrians who are waiting to cross
- **B.** Wait for the pedestrian in the road to cross
- **C.** Quickly drive behind the pedestrian in the road
- **D.** Tell the pedestrian in the road she should not have crossed

440 CAR & MOTORCYCLE
You are following a slower-moving vehicle on a narrow country road. There is a junction just ahead on the right. What should you do?

Mark one answer

- **A.** Overtake after checking your mirrors and signalling
- **B.** Stay behind until you are past the junction
- **C.** Accelerate quickly to pass before the junction
- **D.** Slow down and prepare to overtake on the left

441 CAR & MOTORCYCLE
What should you do as you approach this overhead bridge?

Mark one answer

- **A.** Move out to the centre of the road before going through
- **B.** Find another route, this is only for high vehicles
- **C.** Be prepared to give way to large vehicles in the middle of the road
- **D.** Move across to the right-hand side before going through

442 CAR & MOTORCYCLE
Why are mirrors often slightly curved (convex)?

Mark one answer

- **A.** They give a wider field of vision
- **B.** They totally cover blind spots
- **C.** They make it easier to judge the speed of following traffic
- **D.** They make following traffic look bigger

443 CAR
What does the solid white line at the side of the road indicate?

Mark one answer

- **A.** Traffic lights ahead
- **B.** Edge of the carriageway
- **C.** Footpath on the left
- **D.** Cycle path

444 CAR
You are driving towards this level crossing. What would be the first warning of an approaching train?

Mark one answer

- **A.** Both half barriers down
- **B.** A steady amber light
- **C.** One half barrier down
- **D.** Twin flashing red lights

445 CAR
You are driving along this motorway. It is raining. When following this lorry you should

Mark two answers

- **A.** allow at least a two-second gap
- **B.** move left and drive on the hard shoulder
- **C.** allow at least a four-second gap
- **D.** be aware of spray reducing your vision
- **E.** move right and stay in the right-hand lane

446 CAR
You are behind this cyclist. When the traffic lights change, what should you do?

Mark one answer
- **A.** Try to move off before the cyclist
- **B.** Allow the cyclist time and room
- **C.** Turn right but give the cyclist room
- **D.** Tap your horn and drive through first

447 CAR
You are driving towards this left-hand bend. What dangers should you be aware of?

Mark one answer
- **A.** A vehicle overtaking you
- **B.** No white lines in the centre of the road
- **C.** No sign to warn you of the bend
- **D.** Pedestrians walking towards you

448 CAR
While driving, you see this sign ahead. You should

Mark one answer
- **A.** stop at the sign
- **B.** slow, but continue around the bend
- **C.** slow to a crawl and continue
- **D.** stop and look for open farm gates

449 CAR
Why should the junction on the left be kept clear?

Mark one answer
- **A.** To allow vehicles to enter and emerge
- **B.** To allow the bus to reverse
- **C.** To allow vehicles to make a U-turn
- **D.** To allow vehicles to park

450 CAR
When the traffic lights change to green the white car should

Mark one answer

- **A.** wait for the cyclist to pull away
- **B.** move off quickly and turn in front of the cyclist
- **C.** move close up to the cyclist to beat the lights
- **D.** sound the horn to warn the cyclist

451 CAR
You intend to turn left at the traffic lights. Just before turning you should

Mark one answer

- **A.** check your right mirror
- **B.** move close up to the white car
- **C.** straddle the lanes
- **D.** check for bicycles on your left

452 CAR
You should reduce your speed when driving along this road because

Mark one answer

- **A.** there is a staggered junction ahead
- **B.** there is a low bridge ahead
- **C.** there is a change in the road surface
- **D.** the road ahead narrows

453 CAR
You are driving at 60mph. As you approach this hazard you should

Mark one answer

- **A.** maintain your speed
- **B.** reduce your speed
- **C.** take the next right turn
- **D.** take the next left turn

454 CAR
The traffic ahead of you in the left-hand lane is slowing. You should

Mark two answers

- A. be wary of cars on your right cutting in
- B. accelerate past the vehicles in the left-hand lane
- C. pull up on the left-hand verge
- D. move across and continue in the right-hand lane
- E. slow down, keeping a safe separation distance

455 CAR
What might you expect to happen in this situation?

Mark one answer

- A. Traffic will move into the right-hand lane
- B. Traffic speed will increase
- C. Traffic will move into the left-hand lane
- D. Traffic will not need to change position

456 CAR
You are driving on a road with several lanes. You see these signs above the lanes. What do they mean?

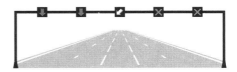

Mark one answer

- A. The two right lanes are open
- B. The two left lanes are open
- C. Traffic in the left lanes should stop
- D. Traffic in the right lanes should stop

457 CAR
As a provisional licence holder, you must not drive a motor car

Mark two answers

- A. at more than 40mph
- B. on your own
- C. on the motorway
- D. under the age of 18 years at night
- E. with passengers in the rear seats

458 CAR
After passing your driving test, you suffer from ill health. This affects your driving. You MUST

Mark one answer

- A. inform your local police station
- B. avoid using motorways
- C. always drive accompanied
- D. inform the licensing authority

459
CAR

You are invited to a pub lunch. You know that you will have to drive in the evening. What is your best course of action?

Mark one answer
- [ ] **A.** Avoid mixing your alcoholic drinks
- [ ] **B.** Not drink any alcohol at all
- [ ] **C.** Have some milk before drinking alcohol
- [ ] **D.** Eat a hot meal with your alcoholic drinks

460
CAR

You have been convicted of driving whilst unfit through drink or drugs. You will find this is likely to cause the cost of one of the following to rise considerably. Which one?

Mark one answer
- [ ] **A.** Road fund licence
- [ ] **B.** Insurance premiums
- [ ] **C.** Vehicle test certificate
- [ ] **D.** Driving licence

461
CAR

What advice should you give to a driver who has had a few alcoholic drinks at a party?

Mark one answer
- [ ] **A.** Have a strong cup of coffee and then drive home
- [ ] **B.** Drive home carefully and slowly
- [ ] **C.** Go home by public transport
- [ ] **D.** Wait a short while and then drive home

462
CAR

You have been taking medicine for a few days which made you feel drowsy. Today you feel better but still need to take the medicine. You should only drive

Mark one answer
- [ ] **A.** if your journey is necessary
- [ ] **B.** at night on quiet roads
- [ ] **C.** if someone goes with you
- [ ] **D.** after checking with your doctor

463
CAR

You are about to return home from holiday when you become ill. A doctor prescribes drugs which are likely to affect your driving. You should

Mark one answer
- [ ] **A.** drive only if someone is with you
- [ ] **B.** avoid driving on motorways
- [ ] **C.** not drive yourself
- [ ] **D.** never drive at more than 30mph

464
CAR

During periods of illness your ability to drive may be impaired. You MUST

Mark two answers
- [ ] **A.** see your doctor each time before you drive
- [ ] **B.** only take smaller doses of any medicines
- [ ] **C.** be medically fit to drive
- [ ] **D.** not drive after taking certain medicines
- [ ] **E.** take all your medicines with you when you drive

465 CAR
You feel drowsy when driving. You should

Mark two answers
- A. stop and rest as soon as possible
- B. turn the heater up to keep you warm and comfortable
- C. make sure you have a good supply of fresh air
- D. continue with your journey but drive more slowly
- E. close the car windows to help you concentrate

466 CAR
You are driving along a motorway and become tired. You should

Mark two answers
- A. stop at the next service area and rest
- B. leave the motorway at the next exit and rest
- C. increase your speed and turn up the radio volume
- D. close all your windows and set heating to warm
- E. pull up on the hard shoulder and change drivers

467 CAR
You are taking drugs that are likely to affect your driving. What should you do?

Mark one answer
- A. Seek medical advice before driving
- B. Limit your driving to essential journeys
- C. Only drive if accompanied by a full licence-holder
- D. Drive only for short distances

468 CAR
You are about to drive home. You feel very tired and have a severe headache. You should

Mark one answer
- A. wait until you are fit and well before driving
- B. drive home, but take a tablet for headaches
- C. drive home if you can stay awake for the journey
- D. wait for a short time, then drive home slowly

469 CAR
If you are feeling tired it is best to stop as soon as you can. Until then you should

Mark one answer
- A. increase your speed to find a stopping place quickly
- B. ensure a supply of fresh air
- C. gently tap the steering wheel
- D. keep changing speed to improve concentration

470 CAR
If your motorway journey seems boring and you feel drowsy while driving, you should

Mark one answer
- A. open a window and drive to the next service area
- B. stop on the hard shoulder for a sleep
- C. speed up to arrive at your destination sooner
- D. slow down and let other drivers overtake

471 CAR
Driving long distances can be tiring. You can prevent this by

Mark three answers

- [ ] **A.** stopping every so often for a walk
- [ ] **B.** opening a window for some fresh air
- [ ] **C.** ensuring plenty of refreshment breaks
- [ ] **D.** completing the journey without stopping
- [ ] **E.** eating a large meal before driving

472 CAR
You go to a social event and need to drive a short time after. What precaution should you take?

Mark one answer

- [ ] **A.** Avoid drinking alcohol on an empty stomach
- [ ] **B.** Drink plenty of coffee after drinking alcohol
- [ ] **C.** Avoid drinking alcohol completely
- [ ] **D.** Drink plenty of milk before drinking alcohol

473 CAR
You take some cough medicine given to you by a friend. What should you do before driving?

Mark one answer

- [ ] **A.** Ask your friend if taking the medicine affected their driving
- [ ] **B.** Drink some strong coffee one hour before driving
- [ ] **C.** Check the label to see if the medicine will affect your driving
- [ ] **D.** Drive a short distance to see if the medicine is affecting your driving

474 CAR
You take the wrong route and find you are on a one-way street. You should

Mark one answer

- [ ] **A.** reverse out of the road
- [ ] **B.** turn round in a side road
- [ ] **C.** continue to the end of the road
- [ ] **D.** reverse into a driveway

475 CAR
Which THREE are likely to make you lose concentration while driving?

Mark three answers

- [ ] **A.** Looking at road maps
- [ ] **B.** Listening to loud music
- [ ] **C.** Using your windscreen washers
- [ ] **D.** Looking in your wing mirror
- [ ] **E.** Using a mobile phone

476 CAR
You are driving along this road. The driver on the left is reversing from a driveway. You should

Mark one answer

- [ ] **A.** move to the opposite side of the road
- [ ] **B.** drive through as you have priority
- [ ] **C.** sound your horn and be prepared to stop
- [ ] **D.** speed up and drive through quickly

477 CAR
You have been involved in an argument before starting your journey. This has made you feel angry. You should

Mark one answer
- A. start to drive, but open a window
- B. drive slower than normal and turn your radio on
- C. have an alcoholic drink to help you relax before driving
- D. calm down before you start to drive

478 CAR
You start to feel tired while driving. What should you do?

Mark one answer
- A. Increase your speed slightly
- B. Decrease your speed slightly
- C. Find a less busy route
- D. Pull over at a safe place to rest

479 CAR
You are driving on this dual carriageway. Why may you need to slow down?

Mark one answer
- A. There is a broken white line in the centre
- B. There are solid white lines either side
- C. There are road works ahead of you
- D. There are no footpaths

480 CAR
You have just been overtaken by this motorcyclist who is cutting in sharply. You should

Mark one answer
- A. sound the horn
- B. brake firmly
- C. keep a safe gap
- D. flash your lights

481 CAR
You are about to drive home. You cannot find the glasses you need to wear. You should

Mark one answer
- A. drive home slowly, keeping to quiet roads
- B. borrow a friend's glasses and use those
- C. drive home at night, so that the lights will help you
- D. find a way of getting home without driving

482 CAR
Which THREE result from drinking alcohol?

Mark three answers
- A. Less control
- B. A false sense of confidence
- C. Faster reactions
- D. Poor judgement of speed
- E. Greater awareness of danger

483 CAR
Which THREE of these are likely effects of drinking alcohol?

Mark three answers
- [ ] **A.** Reduced co-ordination
- [ ] **B.** Increased confidence
- [ ] **C.** Poor judgement
- [ ] **D.** Increased concentration
- [ ] **E.** Faster reactions
- [ ] **F.** Colour blindness

484 CAR
How does alcohol affect you?

Mark one answer
- [ ] **A.** It speeds up your reactions
- [ ] **B.** It increases your awareness
- [ ] **C.** It improves your co-ordination
- [ ] **D.** It reduces your concentration

485 CAR
Your doctor has given you a course of medicine. Why should you ask how it will affect you?

Mark one answer
- [ ] **A.** Drugs make you a better driver by quickening your reactions
- [ ] **B.** You will have to let your insurance company know about the medicine
- [ ] **C.** Some types of medicine can cause your reactions to slow down
- [ ] **D.** The medicine you take may affect your hearing

486 CAR
You are not sure if your cough medicine will affect you. What TWO things should you do?

Mark two answers
- [ ] **A.** Ask your doctor
- [ ] **B.** Check the medicine label
- [ ] **C.** Drive if you feel alright
- [ ] **D.** Ask a friend or relative for advice

487 CAR
You are on a motorway. You feel tired. You should

Mark one answer
- [ ] **A.** carry on but go slowly
- [ ] **B.** leave the motorway at the next exit
- [ ] **C.** complete your journey as quickly as possible
- [ ] **D.** stop on the hard shoulder

488 CAR
You find that you need glasses to read vehicle number plates at the required distance. When MUST you wear them?

Mark one answer
- [ ] **A.** Only in bad weather conditions
- [ ] **B.** At all times when driving
- [ ] **C.** Only when you think it necessary
- [ ] **D.** Only in bad light or at night time

489 CAR
Which TWO things would help to keep you alert during a long journey?

Mark two answers
- [ ] **A.** Finishing your journey as fast as you can
- [ ] **B.** Keeping off the motorways and using country roads
- [ ] **C.** Making sure that you get plenty of fresh air
- [ ] **D.** Making regular stops for refreshments

490 CAR
Which of the following types of glasses should NOT be worn when driving at night?

Mark one answer
- [ ] **A.** Half-moon
- [ ] **B.** Round
- [ ] **C.** Bi-focal
- [ ] **D.** Tinted

491 CAR
Drinking any amount of alcohol is likely to

Mark three answers

- **A.** slow down your reactions to hazards
- **B.** increase the speed of your reactions
- **C.** worsen your judgement of speed
- **D.** improve your awareness of danger
- **E.** give a false sense of confidence

492 CAR
What else can seriously affect your concentration, other than alcoholic drinks?

Mark three answers

- **A.** Drugs
- **B.** Tiredness
- **C.** Tinted windows
- **D.** Contact lenses
- **E.** Loud music

493 CAR
As a driver you find that your eyesight has become very poor. Your optician says they cannot help you. The law says that you should tell

Mark one answer

- **A.** the licensing authority
- **B.** your own doctor
- **C.** the local police station
- **D.** another optician

494 CAR
For which of these may you use hazard warning lights?

Mark one answer

- **A.** When driving on a motorway to warn traffic behind of a hazard ahead
- **B.** When you are double parked on a two-way road
- **C.** When your direction indicators are not working
- **D.** When warning oncoming traffic that you intend to stop

495 CAR
When should you use hazard warning lights?

Mark one answer

- **A.** When you are double parked on a two-way road
- **B.** When your direction indicators are not working
- **C.** When warning oncoming traffic that you intend to stop
- **D.** When your vehicle has broken down and is causing an obstruction

496 CAR
You want to turn left at this junction. The view of the main road is restricted. What should you do?

Mark one answer

- **A.** Stay well back and wait to see if something comes
- **B.** Build up your speed so that you can emerge quickly
- **C.** Stop and apply the handbrake even if the road is clear
- **D.** Approach slowly and edge out until you can see more clearly

497 CAR
You are driving on a motorway. The traffic ahead is braking sharply because of an accident. How could you warn traffic behind you?

Mark one answer
- [ ] **A.** Briefly use the hazard warning lights
- [ ] **B.** Switch on the hazard warning lights continuously
- [ ] **C.** Briefly use the rear fog lights
- [ ] **D.** Switch on the headlights continuously

498 CAR
When may you use hazard warning lights?

Mark one answer
- [ ] **A.** To park alongside another car
- [ ] **B.** To park on double yellow lines
- [ ] **C.** When you are being towed
- [ ] **D.** When you have broken down

499 CAR
Hazard warning lights should be used when vehicles are

Mark one answer
- [ ] **A.** broken down and causing an obstruction
- [ ] **B.** faulty and moving slowly
- [ ] **C.** being towed along a road
- [ ] **D.** reversing into a side road

500 CAR
When driving a car fitted with automatic transmission what would you use 'kick down' for?

Mark one answer
- [ ] **A.** Cruise control
- [ ] **B.** Quick acceleration
- [ ] **C.** Slow braking
- [ ] **D.** Fuel economy

501 CAR
You are waiting to emerge at a junction. Your view is restricted by parked vehicles. What can help you to see traffic on the road you are joining?

Mark one answer
- [ ] **A.** Looking for traffic behind you
- [ ] **B.** Reflections of traffic in shop windows
- [ ] **C.** Making eye contact with other road users
- [ ] **D.** Checking for traffic in your interior mirror

502 CAR & MOTORCYCLE
Overtaking is a major cause of collisions. In which THREE of these situations should you NOT overtake?

Mark three answers
- [ ] **A.** If you are turning left shortly afterwards
- [ ] **B.** When you are in a one-way street
- [ ] **C.** When you are approaching a junction
- [ ] **D.** If you are travelling up a long hill
- [ ] **E.** When your view ahead is blocked

503 CAR & MOTORCYCLE
It is an offence to drive under the influence of illegal drugs. Many of the effects are unpredictable. The direct effects of some drugs can last for up to

Mark one answer
- [ ] **A.** 24 hours
- [ ] **B.** 48 hours
- [ ] **C.** 72 hours
- [ ] **D.** 96 hours

504 MOTORCYCLE
You should not ride too closely behind a lorry because

Mark one answer

- A. you will breathe in the lorry's exhaust fumes
- B. wind from the lorry will slow you down
- C. drivers behind you may not be able to see you
- D. it will reduce your view ahead

505 MOTORCYCLE
You are riding along a main road with many side roads. Why should you be particularly careful?

Mark one answer

- A. Gusts of wind from the side roads may push you off course
- B. Drivers coming out from side roads may not see you
- C. The road will be more slippery where cars have been turning
- D. Drivers will be travelling slowly when they approach a junction

506 MOTORCYCLE
You are riding on a country lane. You see cattle on the road. You should

Mark three answers

- A. slow down
- B. stop if necessary
- C. give plenty of room
- D. rev your engine
- E. sound your horn
- F. ride up close behind them

507 MOTORCYCLE
A learner driver has begun to emerge into your path from a side road on the left. You should

Mark one answer

- A. be ready to slow down and stop
- B. let them emerge then ride close behind
- C. turn into the side road
- D. brake hard, then wave them out

508 MOTORCYCLE
The vehicle ahead is being driven by a learner. You should

Mark one answer

- A. keep calm and be patient
- B. ride up close behind
- C. put your headlight on full beam
- D. sound your horn and overtake

509 MOTORCYCLE
Why is it vital for a rider to make a 'lifesaver' check before turning right?

Mark one answer

- A. To check for any overtaking traffic
- B. To confirm that they are about to turn
- C. To make sure the side road is clear
- D. To check that the rear indicator is flashing

510 MOTORCYCLE
You are riding in fast-flowing traffic. The vehicle behind is following too closely. You should

Mark one answer

- A. slow down gradually to increase the gap in front of you
- B. slow down as quickly as possible by braking
- C. accelerate to get away from the vehicle behind you
- D. apply the brakes sharply to warn the driver behind

511 MOTORCYCLE
You are riding towards a zebra crossing. Waiting to cross is a person in a wheelchair. You should

Mark one answer

- A. continue on your way
- B. wave to the person to cross
- C. wave to the person to wait
- D. be prepared to stop

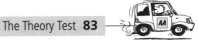

512 MOTORCYCLE
Why should you allow extra room when overtaking another motorcyclist on a windy day?

Mark one answer

A. The rider may turn off suddenly to get out of the wind

B. The rider may be blown across in front of you

C. The rider may stop suddenly

D. The rider may be travelling faster than normal

513 MOTORCYCLE
You have stopped at a pelican crossing. A disabled person is crossing slowly in front of you. The lights have now changed to green. You should

Mark two answers

A. allow the person to cross

B. ride in front of the person

C. ride behind the person

D. sound your horn

E. be patient

F. edge forward slowly

514 MOTORCYCLE
Where should you take particular care to look out for other motorcyclists and cyclists?

Mark one answer

A. On dual carriageways

B. At junctions

C. At zebra crossings

D. On one-way streets

515 MOTORCYCLE
What is a main cause of accidents among young and new motorcyclists?

Mark one answer

A. Using borrowed equipment

B. Lack of experience and judgement

C. Riding in bad weather conditions

D. Riding on country roads

516 MOTORCYCLE
Young motorcyclists can often be the cause of accidents due to

Mark one answer

A. being too cautious at junctions

B. riding in the middle of their lane

C. showing off and being competitive

D. riding when the weather is poor

517 MOTORCYCLE
Which of the following is applicable to young motorcyclists?

Mark one answer

A. They are normally better than experienced riders

B. They are usually less likely to have accidents

C. They are often over-confident of their own ability

D. They are more likely to get cheaper insurance

518 MOTORCYCLE
You are about to overtake horse riders. Which TWO of the following could scare the horses?

Mark two answers

A. Sounding your horn

B. Giving arm signals

C. Riding slowly

D. Revving your engine

519 MOTORCYCLE
The road outside this school is marked with yellow zigzag lines. What do these lines mean?

Mark one answer

- A. You may park on the lines when dropping off schoolchildren
- B. You may park on the lines when picking up schoolchildren
- C. You must not wait or park your motorcycle here
- D. You must stay with your motorcycle if you park here

520 CAR & MOTORCYCLE
Which sign means that there may be people walking along the road?

Mark one answer

- A.
- B.
- C.
- D.

521 CAR & MOTORCYCLE
You are turning left at a junction. Pedestrians have started to cross the road. You should

Mark one answer

- A. go on, giving them plenty of room
- B. stop and wave at them to cross
- C. blow your horn and proceed
- D. give way to them

522 CAR & MOTORCYCLE
You are turning left from a main road into a side road. People are already crossing the road into which you are turning. You should

Mark one answer

- A. continue, as it is your right of way
- B. signal to them to continue crossing
- C. wait and allow them to cross
- D. sound your horn to warn them of your presence

523 CAR & MOTORCYCLE
You are at a road junction, turning into a minor road. There are pedestrians crossing the minor road. You should

Mark one answer
- [ ] **A.** stop and wave the pedestrians across
- [ ] **B.** sound your horn to let the pedestrians know that you are there
- [ ] **C.** give way to the pedestrians who are already crossing
- [ ] **D.** carry on; the pedestrians should give way to you

524 CAR & MOTORCYCLE
You are turning left into a side road. What hazards should you be especially aware of?

Mark one answer
- [ ] **A.** One-way street
- [ ] **B.** Pedestrians
- [ ] **C.** Traffic congestion
- [ ] **D.** Parked vehicles

525 CAR & MOTORCYCLE
You intend to turn right into a side road. Just before turning you should check for motorcyclists who might be

Mark one answer
- [ ] **A.** overtaking on your left
- [ ] **B.** following you closely
- [ ] **C.** emerging from the side road
- [ ] **D.** overtaking on your right

526 CAR & MOTORCYCLE
A toucan crossing is different from other crossings because

Mark one answer
- [ ] **A.** moped riders can use it
- [ ] **B.** it is controlled by a traffic warden
- [ ] **C.** it is controlled by two flashing lights
- [ ] **D.** cyclists can use it

527 CAR & MOTORCYCLE
At toucan crossings

Mark one answer
- [ ] **A.** you only stop if someone is waiting to cross
- [ ] **B.** cyclists are not permitted
- [ ] **C.** there is a continuously flashing amber beacon
- [ ] **D.** pedestrians and cyclists may cross

528 CAR & MOTORCYCLE
What does this sign tell you?

Mark one answer
- [ ] **A.** No cycling
- [ ] **B.** Cycle route ahead
- [ ] **C.** Cycle parking only
- [ ] **D.** End of cycle route

529 CAR & MOTORCYCLE
How will a school crossing patrol signal you to stop?

Mark one answer
- [ ] **A.** By pointing to children on the opposite pavement
- [ ] **B.** By displaying a red light
- [ ] **C.** By displaying a stop sign
- [ ] **D.** By giving you an arm signal

530 CAR & MOTORCYCLE
Where would you see this sign?

Mark one answer

- **A.** In the window of a car taking children to school
- **B.** At the side of the road
- **C.** At playground areas
- **D.** On the rear of a school bus or coach

531 CAR & MOTORCYCLE
Which sign tells you that pedestrians may be walking in the road as there is no pavement?

Mark one answer

- **A.**
- **B.**
- **C.**
- **D.**

532 CAR & MOTORCYCLE
What does this sign mean?

Mark one answer

- **A.** No route for pedestrians and cyclists
- **B.** A route for pedestrians only
- **C.** A route for cyclists only
- **D.** A route for pedestrians and cyclists

533 CAR & MOTORCYCLE
You see a pedestrian with a white stick and red band. This means that the person is

Mark one answer

- **A.** physically disabled
- **B.** deaf only
- **C.** blind only
- **D.** deaf and blind

534 CAR & MOTORCYCLE
What action would you take when elderly people are crossing the road?

Mark one answer

- **A.** Wave them across so they know that you have seen them
- **B.** Be patient and allow them to cross in their own time
- **C.** Rev the engine to let them know that you are waiting
- **D.** Tap the horn in case they are hard of hearing

535 CAR & MOTORCYCLE
You see two elderly pedestrians about to cross the road ahead. You should

Mark one answer

- **A.** expect them to wait for you to pass
- **B.** speed up to get past them quickly
- **C.** stop and wave them across the road
- **D.** be careful, they may misjudge your speed

536 CAR & MOTORCYCLE
What does this sign mean?

Mark one answer
- **A.** Contraflow pedal cycle lane
- **B.** With-flow pedal cycle lane
- **C.** Pedal cycles and buses only
- **D.** No pedal cycles or buses

537 CAR & MOTORCYCLE
You are coming up to a roundabout. A cyclist is signalling to turn right. What should you do?

Mark one answer
- **A.** Overtake on the right
- **B.** Give a horn warning
- **C.** Signal the cyclist to move across
- **D.** Give the cyclist plenty of room

538 CAR & MOTORCYCLE
You are approaching this roundabout and see the cyclist signal right. Why is the cyclist keeping to the left?

Mark one answer
- **A.** It is a quicker route for the cyclist
- **B.** The cyclist is going to turn left instead
- **C.** The cyclist thinks *The Highway Code* does not apply to bicycles
- **D.** The cyclist is slower and more vulnerable

539 CAR & MOTORCYCLE
When you are overtaking a cyclist you should leave as much room as you would give to a car. What is the main reason for this?

Mark one answer
- **A.** The cyclist might change lanes
- **B.** The cyclist might get off the bike
- **C.** The cyclist might swerve
- **D.** The cyclist might have to make a right turn

540 CAR & MOTORCYCLE
Which TWO should you allow extra room when overtaking?

Mark two answers
- **A.** Motorcycles
- **B.** Tractors
- **C.** Bicycles
- **D.** Road-sweeping vehicles

541 CAR & MOTORCYCLE
Why should you look particularly for motorcyclists and cyclists at junctions?

Mark one answer
- **A.** They may want to turn into the side road
- **B.** They may slow down to let you turn
- **C.** They are harder to see
- **D.** They might not see you turn

542 CAR & MOTORCYCLE
You are waiting to come out of a side road. Why should you watch carefully for motorcycles?

Mark one answer
- **A.** Motorcycles are usually faster than cars
- **B.** Police patrols often use motorcycles
- **C.** Motorcycles are small and hard to see
- **D.** Motorcycles have right of way

543 CAR & MOTORCYCLE
In daylight, an approaching motorcyclist is using a dipped headlight. Why?

Mark one answer

- A. So that the rider can be seen more easily
- B. To stop the battery overcharging
- C. To improve the rider's vision
- D. The rider is inviting you to proceed

544 CAR & MOTORCYCLE
Motorcyclists should wear bright clothing mainly because

Mark one answer

- A. they must do so by law
- B. it helps keep them cool in summer
- C. the colours are popular
- D. drivers often do not see them

545 CAR & MOTORCYCLE
There is a slow-moving motorcyclist ahead of you. You are unsure what the rider is going to do. You should

Mark one answer

- A. pass on the left
- B. pass on the right
- C. stay behind
- D. move closer

546 CAR & MOTORCYCLE
Motorcyclists will often look round over their right shoulder just before turning right. This is because

Mark one answer

- A. they need to listen for following traffic
- B. motorcycles do not have mirrors
- C. looking around helps them balance as they turn
- D. they need to check for traffic in their blind area

547 CAR & MOTORCYCLE
At road junctions which of the following are most vulnerable?

Mark three answers

- A. Cyclists
- B. Motorcyclists
- C. Pedestrians
- D. Car drivers
- E. Lorry drivers

548 CAR & MOTORCYCLE
Motorcyclists are particularly vulnerable

Mark one answer

- A. when moving off
- B. on dual carriageways
- C. when approaching junctions
- D. on motorways

549 CAR & MOTORCYCLE
An injured motorcyclist is lying unconscious in the road. You should

Mark one answer

- A. remove the safety helmet
- B. seek medical assistance
- C. move the person off the road
- D. remove the leather jacket

550 CAR & MOTORCYCLE
You notice horse riders in front. What should you do FIRST?

Mark one answer

- A. Pull out to the middle of the road
- B. Slow down and be ready to stop
- C. Accelerate around them
- D. Signal right

551 CAR & MOTORCYCLE
You are approaching a roundabout. There are horses just ahead of you. You should

Mark two answers

- [ ] A. be prepared to stop
- [ ] B. treat them like any other vehicle
- [ ] C. give them plenty of room
- [ ] D. accelerate past as quickly as possible
- [ ] E. sound your horn as a warning

552 CAR & MOTORCYCLE
Which THREE should you do when passing sheep on a road?

Mark three answers

- [ ] A. Allow plenty of room
- [ ] B. Go very slowly
- [ ] C. Pass quickly but quietly
- [ ] D. Be ready to stop
- [ ] E. Briefly sound your horn

553 CAR & MOTORCYCLE
At night you see a pedestrian wearing reflective clothing and carrying a bright red light. What does this mean?

Mark one answer

- [ ] A. You are approaching road works
- [ ] B. You are approaching an organised walk
- [ ] C. You are approaching a slow-moving vehicle
- [ ] D. You are approaching an accident black spot

554 CAR & MOTORCYCLE
As you approach a pelican crossing the lights change to green. Elderly people are half-way across. You should

Mark one answer

- [ ] A. wave them to cross as quickly as they can
- [ ] B. rev your engine to make them hurry
- [ ] C. flash your lights in case they have not heard you
- [ ] D. wait because they will take longer to cross

555 CAR & MOTORCYCLE
There are flashing amber lights under a school warning sign. What action should you take?

Mark one answer

- [ ] A. Reduce speed until you are clear of the area
- [ ] B. Keep up your speed and sound the horn
- [ ] C. Increase your speed to clear the area quickly
- [ ] D. Wait at the lights until they change to green

556 CAR & MOTORCYCLE
You are approaching this crossing. You should

Mark one answer

- [ ] A. prepare to slow down and stop
- [ ] B. stop and wave the pedestrians across
- [ ] C. speed up and pass by quickly
- [ ] D. continue unless the pedestrians step out

557 CAR & MOTORCYCLE
You see a pedestrian with a dog. The dog has a yellow or burgundy coat. This especially warns you that the pedestrian is

Mark one answer

A. elderly	B. dog training
C. colour blind	D. deaf

558 CAR & MOTORCYCLE
These road markings must be kept clear to allow

Mark one answer

A. schoolchildren to be dropped off
B. for teachers to park
C. schoolchildren to be picked up
D. a clear view of the crossing area

559 CAR & MOTORCYCLE
You must not stop on these road markings because you may obstruct

Mark one answer

A. children's view of the crossing area
B. teachers' access to the school
C. delivery vehicles' access to the school
D. emergency vehicles' access to the school

560 CAR & MOTORCYCLE
The left-hand pavement is closed due to street repairs. What should you do?

Mark one answer

A. Watch out for pedestrians walking in the road
B. Use your right-hand mirror more often
C. Speed up to get past the road works quicker
D. Position close to the left-hand kerb

561 CAR & MOTORCYCLE
Where would you see this sign?

Mark one answer

A. Near a school crossing
B. At a playground entrance
C. On a school bus
D. At a 'pedestrians only' area

562 CAR & MOTORCYCLE
You are following a motorcyclist on an uneven road. You should

Mark one answer

A. allow less room so you can be seen in their mirrors
B. overtake immediately
C. allow extra room in case they swerve to avoid potholes
D. allow the same room as normal because road surfaces do not affect motorcyclists

563 CAR & MOTORCYCLE
You are following two cyclists. They approach a roundabout in the left-hand lane. In which direction should you expect the cyclists to go?

Mark one answer
- [ ] A. Left
- [ ] B. Right
- [ ] C. Any direction
- [ ] D. Straight ahead

564 CAR & MOTORCYCLE
You are travelling behind a moped. You want to turn left just ahead. You should

Mark one answer
- [ ] A. overtake the moped before the junction
- [ ] B. pull alongside the moped and stay level until just before the junction
- [ ] C. sound your horn as a warning and pull in front of the moped
- [ ] D. stay behind until the moped has passed the junction

565 CAR & MOTORCYCLE
Which THREE of the following are hazards motorcyclists present in queues of traffic?

Mark three answers
- [ ] A. Cutting in just in front of you
- [ ] B. Riding in single file
- [ ] C. Passing very close to you
- [ ] D. Riding with their headlight on dipped beam
- [ ] E. Filtering between the lanes

566 CAR & MOTORCYCLE
You see a horse rider as you approach a roundabout. They are signalling right but keeping well to the left. You should

Mark one answer
- [ ] A. proceed as normal
- [ ] B. keep close to them
- [ ] C. cut in front of them
- [ ] D. stay well back

567 CAR & MOTORCYCLE
How would you react to drivers who appear to be inexperienced?

Mark one answer
- [ ] A. Sound your horn to warn them of your presence
- [ ] B. Be patient and prepare for them to react more slowly
- [ ] C. Flash your headlights to indicate that it is safe for them to proceed
- [ ] D. Overtake them as soon as possible

568 CAR & MOTORCYCLE
You are following a learner driver who stalls at a junction. You should

Mark one answer
- [ ] A. be patient as you expect them to make mistakes
- [ ] B. stay very close behind and flash your headlights
- [ ] C. start to rev your engine if they take too long to restart
- [ ] D. immediately steer around them and drive on

569 CAR & MOTORCYCLE
You are on a country road. What should you expect to see coming towards you on YOUR side of the road?

Mark one answer

- A. Motorcycles
- B. Bicycles
- C. Pedestrians
- D. Horse riders

570 CAR & MOTORCYCLE
You are turning left into a side road. Pedestrians are crossing the road near the junction. You must

Mark one answer

- A. wave them on
- B. sound your horn
- C. switch on your hazard lights
- D. wait for them to cross

571 CAR & MOTORCYCLE
You are following a car driven by an elderly driver. You should

Mark one answer

- A. expect the driver to drive badly
- B. flash your lights and overtake
- C. be aware that the driver's reactions may not be as fast as yours
- D. stay very close behind but be careful

572 CAR & MOTORCYCLE
You are following a cyclist. You wish to turn left just ahead. You should

Mark one answer

- A. overtake the cyclist before the junction
- B. pull alongside the cyclist and stay level until after the junction
- C. hold back until the cyclist has passed the junction
- D. go around the cyclist on the junction

573 CAR & MOTORCYCLE
A horse rider is in the left-hand lane approaching a roundabout. You should expect the rider to

Mark one answer

- A. go in any direction
- B. turn right
- C. turn left
- D. go ahead

574 CAR & MOTORCYCLE
You have just passed your test. How can you decrease your risk of accidents on the motorway?

Mark one answer

- A. By keeping up with the car in front
- B. By never going over 40mph
- C. By staying only in the left-hand lane
- D. By taking further training

575 CAR & MOTORCYCLE
Powered vehicles used by disabled people are small and hard to see. How do they give early warning when on a dual carriageway?

Mark one answer

- [ ] **A.** They will have a flashing red light
- [ ] **B.** They will have a flashing green light
- [ ] **C.** They will have a flashing blue light
- [ ] **D.** They will have a flashing amber light

576 CAR & MOTORCYCLE
You should never attempt to overtake a cyclist

Mark one answer

- [ ] **A.** just before you turn left
- [ ] **B.** on a left-hand bend
- [ ] **C.** on a one-way street
- [ ] **D.** on a dual carriageway

577 CAR & MOTORCYCLE
Ahead of you there is a moving vehicle with a flashing amber beacon. This means it is

Mark one answer

- [ ] **A.** slow moving
- [ ] **B.** broken down
- [ ] **C.** a doctor's car
- [ ] **D.** a school crossing patrol

578 CAR
You want to reverse into a side road. You are not sure that the area behind your car is clear. What should you do?

Mark one answer

- [ ] **A.** Look through the rear window only
- [ ] **B.** Get out and check
- [ ] **C.** Check the mirrors only
- [ ] **D.** Carry on, assuming it is clear

579 CAR
You are about to reverse into a side road. A pedestrian wishes to cross behind you. You should

Mark one answer

- [ ] **A.** wave to the pedestrian to stop
- [ ] **B.** give way to the pedestrian
- [ ] **C.** wave to the pedestrian to cross
- [ ] **D.** reverse before the pedestrian starts to cross

580 CAR
Who is especially in danger of not being seen as you reverse your car?

Mark one answer

- [ ] **A.** Motorcyclists
- [ ] **B.** Car drivers
- [ ] **C.** Cyclists
- [ ] **D.** Children

581 CAR
You are reversing around a corner when you notice a pedestrian walking behind you. What should you do?

Mark one answer

- [ ] **A.** Slow down and wave the pedestrian across
- [ ] **B.** Continue reversing and steer round the pedestrian
- [ ] **C.** Stop and give way
- [ ] **D.** Continue reversing and sound your horn

582 CAR
You want to turn right from a junction but your view is restricted by parked vehicles. What should you do?

Mark one answer

- [ ] **A.** Move out quickly, but be prepared to stop
- [ ] **B.** Sound your horn and pull out if there is no reply
- [ ] **C.** Stop, then move slowly forward until you have a clear view
- [ ] **D.** Stop, get out and look along the main road to check

583 CAR

You are at the front of a queue of traffic waiting to turn right into a side road. Why is it important to check your right mirror just before turning?

Mark one answer

- A. To look for pedestrians about to cross
- B. To check for overtaking vehicles
- C. To make sure the side road is clear
- D. To check for emerging traffic

584 CAR

What must a driver do at a pelican crossing when the amber light is flashing?

Mark one answer

- A. Signal the pedestrian to cross
- B. Always wait for the green light before proceeding
- C. Give way to any pedestrians on the crossing
- D. Wait for the red-and-amber light before proceeding

585 CAR

You have stopped at a pelican crossing. A disabled person is crossing slowly in front of you. The lights have now changed to green. You should

Mark two answers

- A. allow the person to cross
- B. drive in front of the person
- C. drive behind the person
- D. sound your horn
- E. be patient
- F. edge forward slowly

586 CAR

You are driving past parked cars. You notice a bicycle wheel sticking out between them. What should you do?

Mark one answer

- A. Accelerate past quickly and sound your horn
- B. Slow down and wave the cyclist across
- C. Brake sharply and flash your headlights
- D. Slow down and be prepared to stop for a cyclist

587 CAR

You are driving past a line of parked cars. You notice a ball bouncing out into the road ahead. What should you do?

Mark one answer

- A. Continue driving at the same speed and sound your horn
- B. Continue driving at the same speed and flash your headlights
- C. Slow down and be prepared to stop for children
- D. Stop and wave the children across to fetch their ball

588 CAR

You want to turn right from a main road into a side road. Just before turning you should

Mark one answer

- A. cancel your right-turn signal
- B. select first gear
- C. check for traffic overtaking on your right
- D. stop and set the handbrake

589 CAR
You are driving in slow-moving queues of traffic. Just before changing lane you should

Mark one answer
- [ ] **A.** sound the horn
- [ ] **B.** look for motorcyclists filtering through the traffic
- [ ] **C.** give a 'slowing down' arm signal
- [ ] **D.** change down to first gear

590 CAR
You are driving in town. There is a bus at the bus stop on the other side of the road. Why should you be careful?

Mark one answer
- [ ] **A.** The bus may have broken down
- [ ] **B.** Pedestrians may come from behind the bus
- [ ] **C.** The bus may move off suddenly
- [ ] **D.** The bus may remain stationary

591 CAR
How should you overtake horse riders?

Mark one answer
- [ ] **A.** Drive up close and overtake as soon as possible
- [ ] **B.** Speed is not important but allow plenty of room
- [ ] **C.** Use your horn just once to warn them
- [ ] **D.** Drive slowly and leave plenty of room

592 CAR
A friend wants to help you to learn to drive. They must be

Mark one answer
- [ ] **A.** over 21 and have held a full licence for at least two years
- [ ] **B.** over 18 and hold an advanced driver's certificate
- [ ] **C.** over 18 and have fully comprehensive insurance
- [ ] **D.** over 21 and have held a full licence for at least three years

593 CAR
You are dazzled at night by a vehicle behind you. You should

Mark one answer
- [ ] **A.** set your mirror to anti-dazzle
- [ ] **B.** set your mirror to dazzle the other driver
- [ ] **C.** brake sharply to a stop
- [ ] **D.** switch your rear lights on and off

594 CAR
You have a collision whilst your car is moving. What is the first thing you must do?

Mark one answer
- [ ] **A.** Stop only if there are injured people
- [ ] **B.** Call the emergency services
- [ ] **C.** Stop at the scene of the accident
- [ ] **D.** Call your insurance company

595 CAR
Yellow zigzag lines on the road outside schools mean

Mark one answer
- A. sound your horn to alert other road users
- B. stop to allow children to cross
- C. you must not wait or park on these lines
- D. you must not drive over these lines

596 CAR
What do these road markings outside a school mean?

Mark one answer
- A. You may park here if you are a teacher
- B. Sound your horn before parking
- C. When parking, use your hazard warning lights
- D. You must not wait or park your vehicle here

597 CAR
You are driving on a main road. You intend to turn right into a side road. Just before turning you should

Mark one answer
- A. adjust your interior mirror
- B. flash your headlamps
- C. steer over to the left
- D. check for traffic overtaking on your right

598 CAR
Why should you allow extra room when overtaking a motorcyclist on a windy day?

Mark one answer
- A. The rider may turn off suddenly to get out of the wind
- B. The rider may be blown across in front of you
- C. The rider may stop suddenly
- D. The rider may be travelling faster than normal

599 CAR
Which age group of drivers is most likely to be involved in a road accident?

Mark one answer
- A. 17–25-year-olds
- B. 36–45-year-olds
- C. 46–55-year-olds
- D. over 55-year-olds

600 CAR
You are driving towards a zebra crossing. A person in a wheelchair is waiting to cross. What should you do?

Mark one answer
- A. Continue on your way
- B. Wave to the person to cross
- C. Wave to the person to wait
- D. Be prepared to stop

601 CAR
Where in particular should you look out for motorcyclists?

Mark one answer
- A. In a filling station
- B. At a road junction
- C. Near a service area
- D. When entering a car park

602 CAR
Where should you take particular care to look out for motorcyclists and cyclists?

Mark one answer
- A. On dual carriageways
- B. At junctions
- C. At zebra crossings
- D. On one-way streets

603 CAR
The road outside this school is marked with yellow zigzag lines. What do these lines mean?

Mark one answer
- A. You may park on the lines when dropping off schoolchildren
- B. You may park on the lines when picking schoolchildren up
- C. You must not wait or park your vehicle here at all
- D. You must stay with your vehicle if you park here

604 CAR & MOTORCYCLE
Some junctions controlled by traffic lights have a marked area between two stop lines. What is this for?

Mark one answer
- A. To allow taxis to position in front of other traffic
- B. To allow people with disabilities to cross the road
- C. To allow cyclists and pedestrians to cross the road together
- D. To allow cyclists to position in front of other traffic

605 CAR & MOTORCYCLE
At some traffic lights there are advance stop lines and a marked area. What are these for?

Mark one answer
- A. To allow cyclists to position in front of other traffic
- B. To let pedestrians cross when the lights change
- C. To prevent traffic from jumping the lights
- D. To let passengers get off a bus which is queuing

606 MOTORCYCLE

You are riding behind a long vehicle. There is a mini-roundabout ahead. The vehicle is signalling left, but positioned to the right. You should

Mark one answer

- A. sound your horn
- B. overtake on the left
- C. keep well back
- D. flash your headlights

607 MOTORCYCLE

Why should you be careful when riding on roads where electric trams operate?

Mark two answers

- A. They cannot steer to avoid you
- B. They move quickly and quietly
- C. They are noisy and slow
- D. They can steer to avoid you
- E. They give off harmful exhaust fumes

608 CAR & MOTORCYCLE

You are about to overtake a slow-moving motorcyclist. Which one of these signs would make you take special care?

Mark one answer

- A.
- B.
- C.
- D.

609 CAR & MOTORCYCLE

You are waiting to emerge left from a minor road. A large vehicle is approaching from the right. You have time to turn, but you should wait. Why?

Mark one answer

- A. The large vehicle can easily hide an overtaking vehicle
- B. The large vehicle can turn suddenly
- C. The large vehicle is difficult to steer in a straight line
- D. The large vehicle can easily hide vehicles from the left

610 CAR & MOTORCYCLE

You are following a long vehicle. It approaches a crossroads and signals left, but moves out to the right. You should

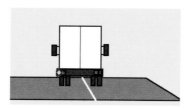

Mark one answer

- A. get closer in order to pass it quickly
- B. stay well back and give it room
- C. assume the signal is wrong and it is really turning right
- D. overtake as it starts to slow down

611 CAR & MOTORCYCLE

You are following a long vehicle approaching a crossroads. The driver signals right but moves close to the left-hand kerb. What should you do?

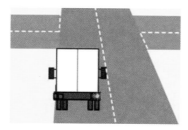

Mark one answer

- A. Warn the driver of the wrong signal
- B. Wait behind the long vehicle
- C. Report the driver to the police
- D. Overtake on the right-hand side

612 CAR & MOTORCYCLE

You are approaching a mini-roundabout. The long vehicle in front is signalling left but positioned over to the right. You should

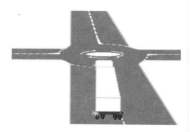

Mark one answer

- A. sound your horn
- B. overtake on the left
- C. follow the same course as the lorry
- D. keep well back

613 CAR & MOTORCYCLE

Before overtaking a large vehicle you should keep well back. Why is this?

Mark one answer

- A. To give acceleration space to overtake quickly on blind bends
- B. To get the best view of the road ahead
- C. To leave a gap in case the vehicle stops and rolls back
- D. To offer other drivers a safe gap if they want to overtake you

614 CAR & MOTORCYCLE

Why is passing a lorry more risky than passing a car?

Mark one answer

- A. Lorries are longer than cars
- B. Lorries may suddenly pull up
- C. The brakes of lorries are not as good
- D. Lorries climb hills more slowly

615 CAR & MOTORCYCLE
You are travelling behind a bus that pulls up at a bus stop. What should you do?

Mark two answers

- **A.** Accelerate past the bus sounding your horn
- **B.** Watch carefully for pedestrians
- **C.** Be ready to give way to the bus
- **D.** Pull in closely behind the bus

616 CAR & MOTORCYCLE
When you approach a bus signalling to move off from a bus stop you should

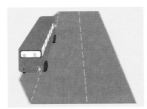

Mark one answer

- **A.** get past before it moves
- **B.** allow it to pull away, if it is safe to do so
- **C.** flash your headlights as you approach
- **D.** signal left and wave the bus on

617 CAR & MOTORCYCLE
Which of these is LEAST likely to be affected by crosswinds?

Mark one answer

- **A.** Cyclists
- **B.** Motorcyclists
- **C.** High-sided vehicles
- **D.** Cars

618 CAR & MOTORCYCLE
You are following a large lorry on a wet road. Spray makes it difficult to see. You should

Mark one answer

- **A.** drop back until you can see better
- **B.** put your headlights on full beam
- **C.** keep close to the lorry, away from the spray
- **D.** speed up and overtake quickly

619 CAR & MOTORCYCLE
What should you do as you approach this lorry?

Mark one answer

- **A.** Slow down and be prepared to wait
- **B.** Make the lorry wait for you
- **C.** Flash your lights at the lorry
- **D.** Move to the right-hand side of the road

620 CAR & MOTORCYCLE

You are following a large articulated vehicle. It is going to turn left into a narrow road. What action should you take?

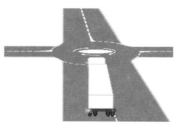

Mark one answer

- **A.** Move out and overtake on the right
- **B.** Pass on the left as the vehicle moves out
- **C.** Be prepared to stop behind
- **D.** Overtake quickly before the lorry moves out

621 CAR & MOTORCYCLE

You keep well back while waiting to overtake a large vehicle. A car fills the gap. You should

Mark one answer

- **A.** sound your horn
- **B.** drop back further
- **C.** flash your headlights
- **D.** start to overtake

622 CAR & MOTORCYCLE

You are following a large vehicle approaching crossroads. The driver signals to turn left. What should you do?

Mark one answer

- **A.** Overtake if you can leave plenty of room
- **B.** Overtake only if there are no oncoming vehicles
- **C.** Do not overtake until the vehicle begins to turn
- **D.** Do not overtake when at or approaching a junction

623 CAR & MOTORCYCLE

You are following a long lorry. The driver signals to turn left into a narrow road. What should you do?

Mark one answer

- **A.** Overtake on the left before the lorry reaches the junction
- **B.** Overtake on the right as soon as the lorry slows down
- **C.** Do not overtake unless you can see there is no oncoming traffic
- **D.** Do not overtake, stay well back and be prepared to stop

624 CAR & MOTORCYCLE

You wish to overtake a long, slow-moving vehicle on a busy road. You should

Mark one answer

- **A.** follow it closely and keep moving out to see the road ahead
- **B.** flash your headlights for the oncoming traffic to give way
- **C.** stay behind until the driver waves you past
- **D.** keep well back until you can see that it is clear

625 CAR

It is very windy. You are behind a motorcyclist who is overtaking a high-sided vehicle. What should you do?

Mark one answer

- **A.** Overtake the motorcyclist immediately
- **B.** Keep well back
- **C.** Stay level with the motorcyclist
- **D.** Keep close to the motorcyclist

626 CAR
It is very windy. You are about to overtake a motorcyclist. You should

Mark one answer

- A. overtake slowly
- B. allow extra room
- C. sound your horn
- D. keep close as you pass

627 CAR
You are towing a caravan. Which is the safest type of rear-view mirror to use?

Mark one answer

- A. Interior wide-angle mirror
- B. Extended-arm side mirrors
- C. Ordinary door mirrors
- D. Ordinary interior mirror

628 CAR
You are driving in town. Ahead of you a bus is at a bus stop. Which TWO of the following should you do?

Mark two answers

- A. Be prepared to give way if the bus suddenly moves off
- B. Continue at the same speed but sound your horn as a warning
- C. Watch carefully for the sudden appearance of pedestrians
- D. Pass the bus as quickly as you possibly can

629 CAR
You are driving in heavy traffic on a wet road. Spray makes it difficult to be seen. You should use your

Mark two answers

- A. full beam headlights
- B. rear fog lights if visibility is less than 100 metres (328 feet)
- C. rear fog lights if visibility is more than 100 metres (328 feet)
- D. dipped headlights
- E. sidelights only

630 CAR
You are driving along this road. What should you be prepared to do?

Mark one answer

- A. Sound your horn and continue
- B. Slow down and give way
- C. Report the driver to the police
- D. Squeeze through the gap

631 CAR
As a driver why should you be more careful where trams operate?

Mark one answer

- A. Because they do not have a horn
- B. Because they do not stop for cars
- C. Because they do not have lights
- D. Because they cannot steer to avoid you

632 CAR
It is a very windy day and you are about to overtake a cyclist. What should you do?

Mark one answer

- A. Overtake very closely
- B. Keep close as you pass
- C. Sound your horn repeatedly
- D. Allow extra room

633 CAR & MOTORCYCLE
Powered vehicles, such as wheelchairs or scooters, used by disabled people have a maximum speed of

Mark one answer

- A. 8mph
- B. 12mph
- C. 16mph
- D. 20mph

634 CAR & MOTORCYCLE
In front of you is a powered vehicle (powered wheelchair) driven by a disabled person. These vehicles have a maximum speed of

Mark one answer

- A. 8mph
- B. 18mph
- C. 28mph
- D. 38mph

635 MOTORCYCLE
You are sitting on a stationary motorcycle and checking your riding position. You should be able to

Mark one answer

- **A.** just touch the ground with your toes
- **B.** place both feet on the ground
- **C.** operate the centre stand
- **D.** adjust your mirrors by stretching

636 MOTORCYCLE
As a safety measure before starting your engine, you should

Mark two answers

- **A.** push the motorcycle forward to check the rear wheel turns freely
- **B.** engage first gear and apply the rear brake
- **C.** engage first gear and apply the front brake
- **D.** glance at the neutral light on your instrument panel

637 MOTORCYCLE
Your motorcycle does NOT have linked brakes. What should you do when braking to a normal stop?

Mark one answer

- **A.** only apply the front brake
- **B.** rely just on the rear brake
- **C.** apply both brakes smoothly
- **D.** apply either of the brakes gently

638 MOTORCYCLE
You are going ahead and will have to cross tram lines. Why should you be especially careful?

Mark one answer

- **A.** Tram lines are always 'live'
- **B.** Trams will be stopping here
- **C.** Pedestrians will be crossing here
- **D.** The steel rails can be slippery

639 MOTORCYCLE
You are approaching this junction. As the motorcyclist you should

Mark two answers

- **A.** prepare to slow down
- **B.** sound your horn
- **C.** keep near the left kerb
- **D.** speed up to clear the junction
- **E.** stop, as the car has right of way

640 MOTORCYCLE
What can you do to improve your safety on the road as a motorcyclist?

Mark one answer

- **A.** Anticipate the actions of others
- **B.** Stay just above the speed limits
- **C.** Keep positioned close to the kerbs
- **D.** Remain well below speed limits

641 MOTORCYCLE
Which THREE of these can cause skidding?

Mark three answers

- **A.** Braking too gently
- **B.** Leaning too far over when cornering
- **C.** Staying upright when cornering
- **D.** Braking too hard
- **E.** Changing direction suddenly

642 MOTORCYCLE
It is very cold and the road looks wet. You cannot hear any road noise. You should

Mark two answers
- A. continue riding at the same speed
- B. ride slower in as high a gear as possible
- C. ride in as low a gear as possible
- D. keep revving your engine
- E. slow down as there may be black ice

643 MOTORCYCLE
When riding a motorcycle you should wear full protective clothing

Mark one answer
- A. at all times
- B. only on faster, open roads
- C. just on long journeys
- D. only during bad weather

644 MOTORCYCLE
You have to make a journey in fog. What are the TWO most important things you should do before you set out?

Mark two answers
- A. Fill up with fuel
- B. Make sure that you have a warm drink with you
- C. Check that your lights are working
- D. Check the battery
- E. Make sure that your visor is clean

645 MOTORCYCLE
The best place to park your motorcycle is

Mark one answer
- A. on soft tarmac
- B. on bumpy ground
- C. on grass
- D. on firm, level ground

646 MOTORCYCLE
When riding in windy conditions, you should

Mark one answer
- A. stay close to large vehicles
- B. keep your speed up
- C. keep your speed down
- D. stay close to the gutter

647 MOTORCYCLE
In normal riding your position on the road should be

Mark one answer
- A. about a foot from the kerb
- B. about central in your lane
- C. on the right of your lane
- D. near the centre of the road

648 MOTORCYCLE
Your motorcycle is parked on a two-way road. You should get on from the

Mark one answer
- A. right and apply the rear brake
- B. left and leave the brakes alone
- C. left and apply the front brake
- D. right and leave the brakes alone

649 MOTORCYCLE
To gain basic skills in how to ride a motorcycle you should

Mark one answer
- A. practise off-road with an approved training body
- B. ride on the road on the first dry day
- C. practise off-road in a public park or in a quiet cul-de-sac
- D. ride on the road as soon as possible

650 MOTORCYCLE
You should not ride with your clutch lever pulled in for longer than necessary because it

Mark one answer
- A. increases wear on the gearbox
- B. increases petrol consumption
- C. reduces your control of the motorcycle
- D. reduces the grip of the tyres

651 MOTORCYCLE
You are approaching a road with a surface of loose chippings. What should you do?

Mark one answer
- A. Ride normally
- B. Speed up
- C. Slow down
- D. Stop suddenly

652 MOTORCYCLE
It rains after a long dry, hot spell. This may cause the road surface to

Mark one answer
- A. be unusually slippery
- B. give better grip
- C. become covered in grit
- D. melt and break up

653 MOTORCYCLE
The main causes of a motorcycle skidding are

Mark three answers
- A. heavy and sharp braking
- B. excessive acceleration
- C. leaning too far when cornering
- D. riding in wet weather
- E. riding in the winter

654 MOTORCYCLE
To stop your motorcycle quickly in an emergency you should apply

Mark one answer
- A. the rear brake only
- B. the front brake only
- C. the front brake just before the rear
- D. the rear brake just before the front

655 MOTORCYCLE
Riding with the side stand down could cause an accident. This is most likely to happen when

Mark one answer
- A. going uphill
- B. accelerating
- C. braking
- D. cornering

656 MOTORCYCLE
You leave the choke on for too long. This causes the engine to run too fast. When is this likely to make your motorcycle most difficult to control?

Mark one answer
- A. Accelerating
- B. Going uphill
- C. Slowing down
- D. On motorways

657 MOTORCYCLE
You should NOT look down at the front wheel when riding because it can

Mark one answer

- A. make your steering lighter
- B. improve your balance
- C. use less fuel
- D. upset your balance

658 MOTORCYCLE
You are entering a bend. Your side stand is not fully raised. This could

Mark one answer

- A. cause an accident
- B. improve your balance
- C. alter the motorcycle's centre of gravity
- D. make the motorcycle more stable

659 MOTORCYCLE
In normal riding conditions you should brake

Mark one answer

- A. by using the rear brake first and then the front
- B. when the motorcycle is being turned or ridden through a bend
- C. by pulling in the clutch before using the front brake
- D. when the motorcycle is upright and moving in a straight line

660 MOTORCYCLE
You have to brake sharply and your motorcycle starts to skid. You should

Mark one answer

- A. continue braking and select a low gear
- B. apply the brakes harder for better grip
- C. select neutral and use the front brake only
- D. release the brakes and reapply

661 MOTORCYCLE
Which THREE of the following will affect your stopping distance?

Mark three answers

- A. How fast you are going
- B. The tyres on your motorcycle
- C. The time of day
- D. The weather
- E. The street lighting

662 MOTORCYCLE
You are on a motorway at night. You MUST have your headlights switched on unless

Mark one answer

- A. there are vehicles close in front of you
- B. you are travelling below 50mph
- C. the motorway is lit
- D. your motorcycle is broken down on the hard shoulder

663 MOTORCYCLE
You have to park on the road in fog. You should

Mark one answer

- A. leave parking lights on
- B. leave no lights on
- C. leave dipped headlights on
- D. leave main beam headlights on

664 MOTORCYCLE
You ride over broken glass and get a sudden puncture. What should you do?

Mark one answer

- A. Close the throttle and roll to a stop
- B. Brake to a stop as quickly as possible
- C. Release your grip on the handlebars
- D. Steer from side to side to keep your balance

665 MOTORCYCLE
You see a rainbow-coloured pattern across the road. What will this warn you of?

Mark one answer
- A. A soft uneven road surface
- B. A polished road surface
- C. Fuel spilt on the road
- D. Water on the road

666 MOTORCYCLE
You are riding in wet weather. You see diesel fuel on the road. What should you do?

Mark one answer
- A. Swerve to avoid the area
- B. Accelerate through quickly
- C. Brake sharply to a stop
- D. Slow down in good time

667 MOTORCYCLE
Spilt fuel on the road can be very dangerous for you as a motorcyclist. How can this hazard be seen?

Mark one answer
- A. By a rainbow pattern on the surface
- B. By a series of skid marks
- C. By a pitted road surface
- D. By a highly polished surface

668 MOTORCYCLE
Traction Control Systems (TCS) are fitted to some motorcycles. What does this help to prevent?

Mark one answer
- A. Wheelspin when accelerating
- B. Skidding when braking too hard
- C. Uneven front tyre wear
- D. Uneven rear tyre wear

669 MOTORCYCLE
Braking too hard has caused both wheels to skid. What should you do?

Mark one answer
- A. Release both brakes together
- B. Release the front then the rear brake
- C. Release the front brake only
- D. Release the rear brake only

670 MOTORCYCLE
You leave the choke on for too long. This could make the engine run faster than normal. This will make your motorcycle

Mark one answer
- A. handle much better
- B. corner much safer
- C. stop much more quickly
- D. more difficult to control

671 MOTORCYCLE
Which FOUR types of road surface increase the risk of skidding for motorcyclists?

Mark four answers
- A. White lines
- B. Dry tarmac
- C. Tar banding
- D. Yellow grid lines
- E. Loose chippings

672 MOTORCYCLE
You are riding on a wet road. When braking you should

Mark one answer

- [ ] **A.** apply the rear brake well before the front
- [ ] **B.** apply the front brake just before the rear
- [ ] **C.** avoid using the front brake at all
- [ ] **D.** avoid using the rear brake at all

673 MOTORCYCLE
The road is wet. You are passing a line of queuing traffic and riding on the painted road markings. You should take extra care, particularly when

Mark one answer

- [ ] **A.** signalling
- [ ] **B.** braking
- [ ] **C.** carrying a passenger
- [ ] **D.** checking your mirrors

674 CAR & MOTORCYCLE
In which THREE of these situations may you overtake another vehicle on the left?

Mark three answers

- [ ] **A.** When you are in a one-way street
- [ ] **B.** When approaching a motorway slip road where you will be turning off
- [ ] **C.** When the vehicle in front is signalling to turn right
- [ ] **D.** When a slower vehicle is travelling in the right-hand lane of a dual carriageway
- [ ] **E.** In slow-moving traffic queues when traffic in the right-hand lane is moving more slowly

675 CAR & MOTORCYCLE
You are travelling in very heavy rain. Your overall stopping distance is likely to be

Mark one answer

- [ ] **A.** doubled
- [ ] **B.** halved
- [ ] **C.** up to ten times greater
- [ ] **D.** no different

676 CAR & MOTORCYCLE
Which TWO of the following are correct? When overtaking at night you should

Mark two answers

- [ ] **A.** wait until a bend so that you can see the oncoming headlights
- [ ] **B.** sound your horn twice before moving out
- [ ] **C.** be careful because you can see less
- [ ] **D.** beware of bends in the road ahead
- [ ] **E.** put headlights on full beam

677 CAR & MOTORCYCLE
When may you wait in a box junction?

Mark one answer

- [ ] **A.** When you are stationary in a queue of traffic
- [ ] **B.** When approaching a pelican crossing
- [ ] **C.** When approaching a zebra crossing
- [ ] **D.** When oncoming traffic prevents you turning right

678 CAR & MOTORCYCLE
Which of these plates normally appear with this road sign?

Mark one answer

A.
> Humps for
> ½ mile

B.
> Hump Bridge

C.
> Low Bridge

D.
> Soft Verge

679 CAR & MOTORCYCLE
Areas reserved for trams may have

Mark three answers

A. metal studs around them
B. white line markings
C. zigzag markings
D. a different coloured surface
E. yellow hatch markings
F. a different surface texture

680 CAR & MOTORCYCLE
Traffic calming measures are used to

Mark one answer

A. stop road rage
B. help overtaking
C. slow traffic down
D. help parking

681 CAR & MOTORCYCLE
Why should you always reduce your speed when travelling in fog?

Mark one answer

A. The brakes do not work as well
B. You will be dazzled by other headlights
C. The engine will take longer to warm up
D. It is more difficult to see events ahead

682 CAR & MOTORCYCLE
You are on a motorway in fog. The left-hand edge of the motorway can be identified by reflective studs. What colour are they?

Mark one answer

A. Green
B. Amber
C. Red
D. White

683 CAR & MOTORCYCLE
A rumble device is designed to

Mark two answers

A. give directions
B. prevent cattle escaping
C. alert you to low tyre pressure
D. alert you to a hazard
E. encourage you to reduce speed

684 CAR & MOTORCYCLE
You are on a narrow road at night. A slower-moving vehicle ahead has been signalling right for some time. What should you do?

Mark one answer

- **A.** Overtake on the left
- **B.** Flash your headlights before overtaking
- **C.** Signal right and sound your horn
- **D.** Wait for the signal to be cancelled before overtaking

685 CAR & MOTORCYCLE
After this hazard you should test your brakes. Why is this?

Mark one answer

- **A.** You will be on a slippery road
- **B.** Your brakes will be soaking wet
- **C.** You will have going down a long hill
- **D.** You will have just crossed a long bridge

686 CAR & MOTORCYCLE
You have to make a journey in foggy conditions. You should

Mark one answer

- **A.** follow other vehicles' tail-lights closely
- **B.** avoid using dipped headlights
- **C.** leave plenty of time for your journey
- **D.** keep two seconds behind other vehicles

687 CAR & MOTORCYCLE
You see a vehicle coming towards you on a single-track road. You should

Mark one answer

- **A.** go back to the main road
- **B.** do an emergency stop
- **C.** stop at a passing place
- **D.** put on your hazard warning lights

688 CAR & MOTORCYCLE
You are overtaking a car at night. You must be sure that

Mark one answer

- **A.** you flash your headlights before overtaking
- **B.** you select a higher gear
- **C.** you have switched your lights to full beam before overtaking
- **D.** you do not dazzle other road users

689 CAR & MOTORCYCLE
You are on a road which has speed humps. A driver in front is travelling slower than you. You should

Mark one answer

- **A.** sound your horn
- **B.** overtake as soon as you can
- **C.** flash your headlights
- **D.** slow down and stay behind

690 CAR & MOTORCYCLE
You are following other vehicles in fog with your lights on. How else can you reduce the chances of being involved in an accident?

Mark one answer

- **A.** Keep close to the vehicle in front
- **B.** Use your main beam instead of dipped headlights
- **C.** Keep together with the faster vehicles
- **D.** Reduce your speed and increase the gap

691

CAR & MOTORCYCLE

You see these markings on the road. Why are they there?

Mark one answer

- **A.** To show a safe distance between vehicles
- **B.** To keep the area clear of traffic
- **C.** To make you aware of your speed
- **D.** To warn you to change direction

692

CAR

When MUST you use dipped headlights during the day?

Mark one answer

- **A.** All the time
- **B.** Along narrow streets
- **C.** In poor visibility
- **D.** When parking

693

CAR

What are TWO main reasons why coasting downhill is wrong?

Mark two answers

- **A.** Fuel consumption will be higher
- **B.** The vehicle will get faster
- **C.** It puts more wear and tear on the tyres
- **D.** You have less braking and steering control
- **E.** It damages the engine

694

CAR

Hills can affect the performance of your vehicle. Which TWO apply when driving up steep hills?

Mark two answers

- **A.** Higher gears will pull better
- **B.** You will slow down sooner
- **C.** Overtaking will be easier
- **D.** The engine will work harder
- **E.** The steering will feel heavier

695

CAR

Why is travelling in neutral for long distances (known as coasting) wrong?

Mark one answer

- **A.** It will cause the car to skid
- **B.** It will make the engine stall
- **C.** The engine will run faster
- **D.** There is no engine braking

696

CAR

You are driving on the motorway in windy conditions. When passing high-sided vehicles you should

Mark one answer

- **A.** increase your speed
- **B.** be wary of a sudden gust
- **C.** drive alongside very closely
- **D.** expect normal conditions

697

CAR

To correct a rear-wheel skid you should

Mark one answer

- **A.** not steer at all
- **B.** steer away from it
- **C.** steer into it
- **D.** apply your handbrake

698 CAR
You have to make a journey in fog. What are the TWO most important things you should do before you set out?

Mark two answers

- A. Top up the radiator with antifreeze
- B. Make sure that you have a warning triangle in the vehicle
- C. Check that your lights are working
- D. Check the battery
- E. Make sure that the windows are clean

699 CAR
You are driving in fog. Why should you keep well back from the vehicle in front?

Mark one answer

- A. In case it changes direction suddenly
- B. In case its fog lights dazzle you
- C. In case it stops suddenly
- D. In case its brake lights dazzle you

700 CAR
You should switch your rear fog lights on when visibility drops below

Mark one answer

- A. your overall stopping distance
- B. ten car lengths
- C. 200 metres (656 feet)
- D. 100 metres (328 feet)

701 CAR
Whilst driving, the fog clears and you can see more clearly. You must remember to

Mark one answer

- A. switch off the fog lights
- B. reduce your speed
- C. switch off the demister
- D. close any open windows

702 CAR
You have to park on the road in fog. You should

Mark one answer

- A. leave sidelights on
- B. leave dipped headlights and fog lights on
- C. leave dipped headlights on
- D. leave main beam headlights on

703 CAR
On a foggy day you unavoidably have to park your car on the road. You should

Mark one answer

- A. leave your headlights on
- B. leave your fog lights on
- C. leave your sidelights on
- D. leave your hazard lights on

704 CAR
You are travelling at night. You are dazzled by headlights coming towards you. You should

Mark one answer

- A. pull down your sun visor
- B. slow down or stop
- C. switch on your main beam headlights
- D. put your hand over your eyes

705 CAR
Which FOUR of the following may apply when dealing with this hazard?

Mark four answers
- A. It could be more difficult in winter
- B. Use a low gear and drive slowly
- C. Use a high gear to prevent wheelspin
- D. Test your brakes afterwards
- E. Always switch on fog lamps
- F. There may be a depth gauge

706 CAR
Front fog lights may be used ONLY if

Mark one answer
- A. visibility is seriously reduced
- B. they are fitted above the bumper
- C. they are not as bright as the headlights
- D. an audible warning device is used

707 CAR
Front fog lights may be used ONLY if

Mark one answer
- A. your headlights are not working
- B. they are operated with rear fog lights
- C. they were fitted by the vehicle manufacturer
- D. visibility is seriously reduced

708 CAR
You are driving with your front fog lights switched on. Earlier fog has now cleared. What should you do?

Mark one answer
- A. Leave them on if other drivers have their lights on
- B. Switch them off as long as visibility remains good
- C. Flash them to warn oncoming traffic that it is foggy
- D. Drive with them on instead of your headlights

709 CAR
Front fog lights should be used ONLY when

Mark one answer
- A. travelling in very light rain
- B. visibility is seriously reduced
- C. daylight is fading
- D. driving after midnight

710 CAR
Why is it dangerous to leave rear fog lights on when they are not needed?

Mark two answers
- A. Brake lights are less clear
- B. Following drivers can be dazzled
- C. Electrical systems could be overloaded
- D. Direction indicators may not work properly
- E. The battery could fail

711 CAR
You are driving on a clear dry night with your rear fog lights switched on. This may

Mark two answers
- A. reduce glare from the road surface
- B. make other drivers think you are braking
- C. give a better view of the road ahead
- D. dazzle following drivers
- E. help your indicators to be seen more clearly

712 CAR
You have just driven out of fog. Visibility is now good. You MUST

Mark one answer
- A. switch off all your fog lights
- B. keep your rear fog lights on
- C. keep your front fog lights on
- D. leave fog lights on in case fog returns

713 CAR
You forget to switch off your rear fog lights when the fog has cleared. This may

Mark three answers
- A. dazzle other road users
- B. reduce battery life
- C. cause brake lights to be less clear
- D. be breaking the law
- E. seriously affect engine power

714 CAR
You have been driving in thick fog which has now cleared. You must switch OFF your rear fog lights because

Mark one answer
- A. they use a lot of power from the battery
- B. they make your brake lights less clear
- C. they will cause dazzle in your rear-view mirrors
- D. they may not be properly adjusted

715 CAR
Front fog lights should be used

Mark one answer
- A. when visibility is reduced to 100 metres (328 feet)
- B. as a warning to oncoming traffic
- C. when driving during the hours of darkness
- D. in any conditions and at any time

716 CAR
Using rear fog lights in clear daylight will

Mark one answer
- A. be useful when towing a trailer
- B. give extra protection
- C. dazzle other drivers
- D. make following drivers keep back

717 CAR
Using front fog lights in clear daylight will

Mark one answer
- A. flatten the battery
- B. dazzle other drivers
- C. improve your visibility
- D. increase your awareness

718 CAR

You may use front fog lights with headlights ONLY when visibility is reduced to less than

Mark one answer
- A. 100 metres (328 feet)
- B. 200 metres (656 feet)
- C. 300 metres (984 feet)
- D. 400 metres (1,312 feet)

719 CAR

You may drive with front fog lights switched on

Mark one answer
- A. when visibility is less than 100 metres (328 feet)
- B. at any time to be noticed
- C. instead of headlights on high-speed roads
- D. when dazzled by the lights of oncoming vehicles

720 CAR

Chains can be fitted to your wheels to help prevent

Mark one answer
- A. damage to the road surface
- B. wear to the tyres
- C. skidding in deep snow
- D. the brakes locking

721 CAR

Holding the clutch pedal down or rolling in neutral for too long while driving will

Mark one answer
- A. use more fuel
- B. cause the engine to overheat
- C. reduce your control
- D. improve tyre wear

722 CAR

How can you use the engine of your vehicle to control your speed?

Mark one answer
- A. By changing to a lower gear
- B. By selecting reverse gear
- C. By changing to a higher gear
- D. By selecting neutral

723 CAR

You are driving down a steep hill. Why could keeping the clutch down or rolling in neutral for too long be dangerous?

Mark one answer
- A. Fuel consumption will be higher
- B. Your vehicle will pick up speed
- C. It will damage the engine
- D. It will wear tyres out more quickly

724 CAR
Why could keeping the clutch down or selecting neutral for long periods of time be dangerous?

Mark one answer

- A. Fuel spillage will occur
- B. Engine damage may be caused
- C. You will have less steering and braking control
- D. It will wear tyres out more quickly

725 CAR
You are driving on an icy road. What distance should you drive from the car in front?

Mark one answer

- A. four times the normal distance
- B. six times the normal distance
- C. eight times the normal distance
- D. ten times the normal distance

726 CAR
You are on a well-lit motorway at night. You must

Mark one answer

- A. use only your sidelights
- B. always use your headlights
- C. always use rear fog lights
- D. use headlights only in bad weather

727 CAR
You are on a motorway at night with other vehicles just ahead of you. Which lights should you have on?

Mark one answer

- A. Front fog lights
- B. Main beam headlights
- C. Sidelights only
- D. Dipped headlights

728 CAR
Which THREE of the following will affect your stopping distance?

Mark three answers

- A. How fast you are going
- B. The tyres on your vehicle
- C. The time of day
- D. The weather
- E. The street lighting

729 CAR
You are on a motorway at night. You MUST have your headlights switched on unless

Mark one answer

- A. there are vehicles close in front of you
- B. you are travelling below 50mph
- C. the motorway is lit
- D. your vehicle is broken down on the hard shoulder

730 CAR
You will feel the effects of engine braking when you

Mark one answer

- A. only use the handbrake
- B. only use neutral
- C. change to a lower gear
- D. change to a higher gear

731 CAR
Daytime visibility is poor but not seriously reduced. You should switch on

Mark one answer

- A. headlights and fog lights
- B. front fog lights
- C. dipped headlights
- D. rear fog lights

732 CAR
Why are vehicles fitted with rear fog lights?

Mark one answer
- A. To be seen when driving at high speed
- B. To use if broken down in a dangerous position
- C. To make them more visible in thick fog
- D. To warn drivers following closely to drop back

733 CAR
While you are driving in fog, it becomes necessary to use front fog lights. You should

Mark one answer
- A. only turn them on in heavy traffic conditions
- B. remember not to use them on motorways
- C. only use them on dual carriageways
- D. remember to switch them off as visibility improves

734 CAR
When snow is falling heavily you should

Mark one answer
- A. only drive with your hazard lights on
- B. not drive unless you have a mobile phone
- C. only drive when your journey is short
- D. not drive unless it is essential

735 CAR
You are driving down a long steep hill. You suddenly notice your brakes are not working as well as normal. What is the usual cause of this?

Mark one answer
- A. The brakes overheating
- B. Air in the brake fluid
- C. Oil on the brakes
- D. Badly adjusted brakes

736 CAR & MOTORCYCLE
The road is wet. Why might a motorcyclist steer round drain covers on a bend?

Mark one answer
- A. To avoid puncturing the tyres on the edge of the drain covers
- B. To prevent the motorcycle sliding on the metal drain covers
- C. To help judge the bend using the drain covers as marker points
- D. To avoid splashing pedestrians on the pavement

737 MOTORCYCLE
A motorcycle is not allowed on a motorway if it has an engine size smaller than

Mark one answer

- [ ] **A.** 50cc
- [ ] **B.** 125cc
- [ ] **C.** 150cc
- [ ] **D.** 250cc

738 MOTORCYCLE
You are riding on a motorway. Unless signs show otherwise you must NOT exceed

Mark one answer

NI

- [ ] **A.** 50mph
- [ ] **B.** 60mph
- [ ] **C.** 70mph
- [ ] **D.** 80mph

739 MOTORCYCLE
To ride on a motorway your motorcycle must be

Mark one answer

- [ ] **A.** 50cc or more
- [ ] **B.** 100cc or more
- [ ] **C.** 125cc or more
- [ ] **D.** 250cc or more

740 MOTORCYCLE
On a three-lane motorway why should you normally ride in the left-hand lane?

Mark one answer

- [ ] **A.** The left-hand lane is only for lorries and motorcycles
- [ ] **B.** The left-hand lane should only be used by smaller vehicles
- [ ] **C.** The lanes on the right are for overtaking
- [ ] **D.** Motorcycles are not allowed in the far right-hand lane

741 MOTORCYCLE
You are riding at 70mph on a three-lane motorway. There is no traffic ahead. Which lane should you use?

Mark one answer

- [ ] **A.** Any lane
- [ ] **B.** Middle lane
- [ ] **C.** Right-hand lane
- [ ] **D.** Left-hand lane

742 MOTORCYCLE
Why is it particularly important to carry out a check of your motorcycle before making a long motorway journey?

Mark one answer

- [ ] **A.** You will have to do more harsh braking on motorways
- [ ] **B.** Motorway service stations do not deal with breakdowns
- [ ] **C.** The road surface will wear down the tyres faster
- [ ] **D.** Continuous high speeds may increase the risk of your motorcycle breaking down

743 MOTORCYCLE
On a motorway you may ONLY stop on the hard shoulder

Mark one answer

- [ ] **A.** in an emergency
- [ ] **B.** if you feel tired and need to rest
- [ ] **C.** if you go past the exit that you wanted to take
- [ ] **D.** to pick up a hitchhiker

744 MOTORCYCLE

You are intending to leave the motorway at the next exit. Before you reach the exit you should normally position your motorcycle

Mark one answer

- **A.** in the middle lane
- **B.** in the left-hand lane
- **C.** on the hard shoulder
- **D.** in any lane

745 MOTORCYCLE

You are joining a motorway from a slip road. You should

Mark one answer

- **A.** adjust your speed to the speed of the traffic on the motorway
- **B.** accelerate as quickly as you can and ride straight out
- **C.** ride on to the hard shoulder until a gap appears
- **D.** expect drivers on the motorway to give way to you

746 CAR & MOTORCYCLE

Which FOUR of these must NOT use motorways?

Mark four answers

- **A.** Learner car drivers
- **B.** Motorcycles over 50cc
- **C.** Double-deck buses
- **D.** Farm tractors
- **E.** Horse riders
- **F.** Cyclists

747 CAR & MOTORCYCLE

Which FOUR of these must NOT use motorways?

Mark four answers

- **A.** Learner car drivers
- **B.** Motorcycles over 50cc
- **C.** Double-deck buses
- **D.** Farm tractors
- **E.** Learner motorcyclists
- **F.** Cyclists

748 CAR & MOTORCYCLE

Immediately after joining a motorway you should normally

Mark one answer

- **A.** try to overtake
- **B.** re-adjust your mirrors
- **C.** position your vehicle in the centre lane
- **D.** keep in the left-hand lane

749 CAR & MOTORCYCLE

When joining a motorway you must always

Mark one answer

- **A.** use the hard shoulder
- **B.** stop at the end of the acceleration lane
- **C.** come to a stop before joining the motorway
- **D.** give way to traffic already on the motorway

750 CAR & MOTORCYCLE

What is the national speed limit for cars and motorcycles in the centre lane of a three-lane motorway?

Mark one answer

- **A.** 40mph
- **B.** 50mph
- **C.** 60mph
- **D.** 70mph

751 CAR & MOTORCYCLE
What is the national speed limit on motorways for cars and motorcycles?

Mark one answer

- A. 30mph
- B. 50mph
- C. 60mph
- D. 70mph

752 CAR & MOTORCYCLE
The left-hand lane on a three-lane motorway is for use by

Mark one answer

- A. any vehicle
- B. large vehicles only
- C. emergency vehicles only
- D. slow vehicles only

753 CAR & MOTORCYCLE
What is the right-hand lane used for on a three-lane motorway?

Mark one answer

- A. Emergency vehicles only
- B. Overtaking
- C. Vehicles towing trailers
- D. Coaches only

754 CAR & MOTORCYCLE
Which of these IS NOT allowed to travel in the right-hand lane of a three-lane motorway?

Mark one answer

- A. A small delivery van
- B. A motorcycle
- C. A vehicle towing a trailer
- D. A motorcycle and sidecar

755 CAR & MOTORCYCLE
You are travelling on a motorway. You decide you need a rest. You should

Mark two answers

- A. stop on the hard shoulder
- B. go to a service area
- C. park on the slip road
- D. park on the central reservation
- E. leave at the next exit

756 CAR & MOTORCYCLE
You break down on a motorway. You need to call for help. Why may it be better to use an emergency roadside telephone rather than a mobile phone?

Mark one answer

- A. It connects you to a local garage
- B. Using a mobile phone will distract other drivers
- C. It allows easy location by the emergency services
- D. Mobile phones do not work on motorways

757 CAR & MOTORCYCLE
What should you use the hard shoulder of a motorway for?

Mark one answer

- A. Stopping in an emergency
- B. Leaving the motorway
- C. Stopping when you are tired
- D. Joining the motorway

758 CAR & MOTORCYCLE
After a breakdown you need to rejoin the main carriageway of a motorway from the hard shoulder. You should

Mark one answer
- A. move out onto the carriageway then build up your speed
- B. move out onto the carriageway using your hazard lights
- C. gain speed on the hard shoulder before moving out onto the carriageway
- D. wait on the hard shoulder until someone flashes their headlights at you

759 CAR & MOTORCYCLE
A crawler lane on a motorway is found

Mark one answer
- A. on a steep gradient
- B. before a service area
- C. before a junction
- D. along the hard shoulder

760 CAR & MOTORCYCLE
You are on a motorway. There are red flashing lights above every lane. You must

Mark one answer
- A. pull on to the hard shoulder
- B. slow down and watch for further signals
- C. leave at the next exit
- D. stop and wait

761 CAR & MOTORCYCLE
You are in the right-hand lane on a motorway. You see these overhead signs. This means

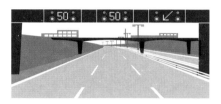

Mark one answer
- A. move to the left and reduce your speed to 50mph
- B. there are road works 50 metres (55 yards) ahead
- C. use the hard shoulder until you have passed the hazard
- D. leave the motorway at the next exit

762 CAR & MOTORCYCLE
What do these motorway signs show?

Mark one answer
- A. They are countdown markers to a bridge
- B. They are distance markers to the next telephone
- C. They are countdown markers to the next exit
- D. They warn of a police control ahead

763 CAR & MOTORCYCLE
On a motorway the amber reflective studs can be found between

Mark one answer
- A. the hard shoulder and the carriageway
- B. the acceleration lane and the carriageway
- C. the central reservation and the carriageway
- D. each pair of the lanes

764 CAR & MOTORCYCLE
What colour are the reflective studs between the lanes on a motorway?

Mark one answer
- A. Green
- B. Amber
- C. White
- D. Red

765 CAR & MOTORCYCLE
What colour are the reflective studs between a motorway and its slip road?

Mark one answer
- A. Amber
- B. White
- C. Green
- D. Red

766 CAR & MOTORCYCLE
You are allowed to stop on a motorway when you

Mark one answer
- A. need to walk and get fresh air
- B. wish to pick up hitchhikers
- C. are told to do so by flashing red lights
- D. need to use a mobile telephone

767 CAR & MOTORCYCLE
You have broken down on a motorway. To find the nearest emergency telephone you should always walk

Mark one answer
- A. with the traffic flow
- B. facing oncoming traffic
- C. in the direction shown on the marker posts
- D. in the direction of the nearest exit

768 CAR & MOTORCYCLE
You are travelling along the left-hand lane of a three-lane motorway. Traffic is joining from a slip road. You should

Mark one answer
- A. race the other vehicles
- B. move to another lane
- C. maintain a steady speed
- D. switch on your hazard flashers

769 CAR & MOTORCYCLE
You are joining a motorway. Why is it important to make full use of the slip road?

Mark one answer
- A. Because there is space available to turn round if you need to
- B. To allow you direct access to the overtaking lanes
- C. To build up a speed similar to traffic on the motorway
- D. Because you can continue on the hard shoulder

770 CAR & MOTORCYCLE
How should you use the emergency telephone on a motorway?

Mark one answer
- A. Stay close to the carriageway
- B. Face the oncoming traffic
- C. Keep your back to the traffic
- D. Stand on the hard shoulder

771 CAR & MOTORCYCLE
You are on a motorway. What colour are the reflective studs on the left of the carriageway?

Mark one answer

- A. Green
- B. Red
- C. White
- D. Amber

772 CAR & MOTORCYCLE
On a three-lane motorway which lane should you normally use?

Mark one answer

- A. Left
- B. Right
- C. Centre
- D. Either the right or centre

773 CAR & MOTORCYCLE
A basic rule when on motorways is

Mark one answer

- A. use the lane that has least traffic
- B. keep to the left-hand lane unless overtaking
- C. overtake on the side that is clearest
- D. try to keep above 50mph to prevent congestion

774 CAR & MOTORCYCLE
When going through a contraflow system on a motorway you should

Mark one answer

- A. ensure that you do not exceed 30mph
- B. keep a good distance from the vehicle ahead
- C. switch lanes to keep the traffic flowing
- D. stay close to the vehicle ahead to reduce queues

775 CAR & MOTORCYCLE
You are on a three-lane motorway. There are red reflective studs on your left and white ones to your right. Where are you?

Mark one answer

- A. In the right-hand lane
- B. In the middle lane
- C. On the hard shoulder
- D. In the left-hand lane

776 CAR & MOTORCYCLE
When should you stop on a motorway?

Mark three answers

- A. If you have to read a map
- B. When you are tired and need a rest
- C. If red lights show above every lane
- D. When told to by the police
- E. If your mobile phone rings
- F. When signalled by a Highways Agency Traffic Officer

777 CAR & MOTORCYCLE
You are approaching road works on a motorway. What should you do?

Mark one answer

- A. Speed up to clear the area quickly
- B. Always use the hard shoulder
- C. Obey all speed limits
- D. Stay very close to the vehicle in front

778 CAR & MOTORCYCLE
On motorways you should never overtake on the left unless

Mark one answer

- **A.** you can see well ahead that the hard shoulder is clear
- **B.** the traffic in the right-hand lane is signalling right
- **C.** you warn drivers behind by signalling left
- **D.** there is a queue of slow-moving traffic to your right that is moving more slowly than you are

779 CAR
You are towing a trailer on a motorway. What is your maximum speed limit?

Mark one answer

- **A.** 40mph
- **B.** 50mph
- **C.** 60mph
- **D.** 70mph

780 CAR
The left-hand lane of a motorway should be used for

Mark one answer

- **A.** breakdowns and emergencies only
- **B.** overtaking slower traffic in the other lanes
- **C.** slow vehicles only
- **D.** normal driving

781 CAR
You are driving on a motorway. You have to slow down quickly due to a hazard. You should

Mark one answer

- **A.** switch on your hazard lights
- **B.** switch on your headlights
- **C.** sound your horn
- **D.** flash your headlights

782 CAR
You get a puncture on the motorway. You manage to get your vehicle on to the hard shoulder. You should

Mark one answer

- **A.** change the wheel yourself immediately
- **B.** use the emergency telephone and call for assistance
- **C.** try to wave down another vehicle for help
- **D.** only change the wheel if you have a passenger to help you

783 CAR
You are driving on a motorway. By mistake, you go past the exit that you wanted to take. You should

Mark one answer

- **A.** carefully reverse on the hard shoulder
- **B.** carry on to the next exit
- **C.** carefully reverse in the left-hand lane
- **D.** make a U-turn at the next gap in the central reservation

784 CAR

Your vehicle breaks down on the hard shoulder of a motorway. You decide to use your mobile phone to call for help. You should

Mark one answer

- A. stand at the rear of the vehicle while making the call
- B. try to repair the vehicle yourself
- C. get out of the vehicle by the right-hand door
- D. check your location from the marker posts on the left

785 CAR & MOTORCYCLE

You are travelling on a motorway. Unless signs show a lower speed limit you must NOT exceed

Mark one answer **NI**

- A. 50mph
- B. 60mph
- C. 70mph
- D. 80mph

786 CAR

You are on a three-lane motorway towing a trailer. You may use the right-hand lane when

Mark one answer **NI**

- A. there are lane closures
- B. there is slow-moving traffic
- C. you can maintain a high speed
- D. large vehicles are in the left and centre lanes

787 CAR

You are on a motorway. There is a contraflow system ahead. What would you expect to find?

Mark one answer

- A. Temporary traffic lights
- B. Lower speed limits
- C. Wider lanes than normal
- D. Speed humps

788 CAR

You are driving at 70mph on a three-lane motorway. There is no traffic ahead. Which lane should you use?

Mark one answer

- A. Any lane
- B. Middle lane
- C. Right lane
- D. Left lane

789 CAR

Your vehicle has broken down on a motorway. You are not able to stop on the hard shoulder. What should you do?

Mark one answer

- A. Switch on your hazard warning lights
- B. Stop following traffic and ask for help
- C. Attempt to repair your vehicle quickly
- D. Stand behind your vehicle to warn others

790 CAR

Why is it particularly important to carry out a check on your vehicle before making a long motorway journey?

Mark one answer

- A. You will have to do more harsh braking on motorways
- B. Motorway service stations do not deal with breakdowns
- C. The road surface will wear down the tyres faster
- D. Continuous high speeds may increase the risk of your vehicle breaking down

791 CAR & MOTORCYCLE
For what reason may you use the right-hand lane of a motorway?

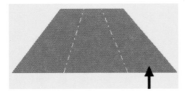

Mark one answer

- A. For keeping out of the way of lorries
- B. For travelling at more than 70mph
- C. For turning right
- D. For overtaking other vehicles

792 CAR
On a motorway you may ONLY stop on the hard shoulder

Mark one answer

- A. in an emergency
- B. if you feel tired and need to rest
- C. if you accidentally go past the exit that you wanted to take
- D. to pick up a hitchhiker

793 CAR
You are driving on a motorway. The car ahead shows its hazard lights for a short time. This tells you that

Mark one answer

- A. the driver wants you to overtake
- B. the other car is going to change lanes
- C. traffic ahead is slowing or stopping suddenly
- D. there is a police speed check ahead

794 CAR & MOTORCYCLE
Motorway emergency telephones are usually linked to the police. In some areas they are now linked to

Mark one answer

- A. the local ambulance service
- B. an Highways Agency control centre
- C. the local fire brigade
- D. a breakdown service control centre

795 CAR
You are intending to leave the motorway at the next exit. Before you reach the exit you should normally position your vehicle

Mark one answer

- A. in the middle lane
- B. in the left-hand lane
- C. on the hard shoulder
- D. in any lane

796 CAR
As a provisional licence holder you should not drive a car

Mark one answer

- A. over 30mph
- B. at night
- C. on the motorway
- D. with passengers in rear seats

797 CAR & MOTORCYCLE
Motorway emergency telephones are usually linked to the police. In some areas they are now linked to

Mark one answer **NI**
- **A.** the Highways Agency Control Centre
- **B.** the Driver Vehicle Licensing Agency
- **C.** the Driving Standards Agency
- **D.** the local Vehicle Registration Office

798 CAR & MOTORCYCLE
An Emergency Refuge Area is an area

Mark one answer
- **A.** on a motorway for use in cases of emergency or breakdown
- **B.** for use if you think you will be involved in a road rage incident
- **C.** on a motorway for a police patrol to park and watch traffic
- **D.** for construction and road workers to store emergency equipment

799 CAR & MOTORCYCLE
What is an Emergency Refuge Area on a motorway for?

Mark one answer
- **A.** An area to park in when you want to use a mobile phone
- **B.** To use in cases of emergency or breakdown
- **C.** For an emergency recovery vehicle to park in a contraflow system
- **D.** To drive in when there is queuing traffic ahead

800 CAR & MOTORCYCLE
Highways Agency Traffic Officers

Mark one answer **NI**
- **A.** will not be able to assist at a breakdown or emergency
- **B.** are not able to stop and direct anyone on a motorway
- **C.** will tow a broken down vehicle and its passengers home
- **D.** are able to stop and direct anyone on a motorway

801 CAR & MOTORCYCLE
You are on a motorway. A red cross is displayed above the hard shoulder. What does this mean?

NI

Mark one answer
- **A.** Pull up in this lane to answer your mobile phone
- **B.** Use this lane as a running lane
- **C.** This lane can be used if you need a rest
- **D.** You should not travel in this lane

802 CAR & MOTORCYCLE

You are on a motorway in an Active Traffic Management (ATM) area. A mandatory speed limit is displayed above the hard shoulder. What does this mean?

Mark one answer **NI**

- A. You should not travel in this lane
- B. The hard shoulder can be used as a running lane
- C. You can park on the hard shoulder if you feel tired
- D. You can pull up in this lane to answer a mobile phone

803 CAR & MOTORCYCLE

The aim of an Active Traffic Management scheme on a motorway is to

Mark one answer **NI**

- A. prevent overtaking
- B. reduce rest stops
- C. prevent tailgating
- D. reduce congestion

804 CAR & MOTORCYCLE

You are in an Active Traffic Management area on a motorway. When the Actively Managed mode is operating

Mark one answer **NI**

- A. speed limits are only advisory
- B. the national speed limit will apply
- C. the speed limit is always 30mph
- D. all speed limit signals are set

805 CAR & MOTORCYCLE

You are on a three-lane motorway. A red cross is shown above the hard shoulder and mandatory speed limits above all other lanes. This means

Mark one answer **NI**

- A. the hard shoulder can be used as a rest area if you feel tired
- B. the hard shoulder is for emergency or breakdown use only
- C. the hard shoulder can be used as a normal running lane
- D. the hard shoulder has a speed limit of 50mph

806 CAR & MOTORCYCLE
You are travelling on a motorway. A red cross is shown above the hard shoulder. What does this mean?

Mark one answer **NI**

- [ ] **A.** Use this lane as a rest area
- [ ] **B.** Use this as a normal running lane
- [ ] **C.** Do not use this lane to travel in
- [ ] **D.** National speed limit applies in this lane

807 CAR & MOTORCYCLE
You are on a three-lane motorway and see this sign. It means you can use

Mark one answer **NI**

- [ ] **A.** any lane except the hard shoulder
- [ ] **B.** the hard shoulder only
- [ ] **C.** the three right hand lanes only
- [ ] **D.** all the lanes including the hard shoulder

808 CAR & MOTORCYCLE
Why can it be an advantage for traffic speed to stay constant over a longer distance?

Mark one answer

- [ ] **A.** You will do more stop-start driving
- [ ] **B.** You will use far more fuel
- [ ] **C.** You will be able to use more direct routes
- [ ] **D.** Your overall journey time will normally improve

809 CAR & MOTORCYCLE
You should not normally travel on the hard shoulder of a motorway. When can you use it?

Mark one answer **NI**

- [ ] **A.** When taking the next exit
- [ ] **B.** When traffic is stopped
- [ ] **C.** When signs direct you to
- [ ] **D.** When traffic is slow moving

810 CAR & MOTORCYCLE
On a motorway what is used to reduce traffic bunching?

Mark one answer

- [ ] **A.** Variable speed limits
- [ ] **B.** Contraflow systems
- [ ] **C.** National speed limits
- [ ] **D.** Lane closures

811 CAR & MOTORCYCLE
When may you stop on a motorway?

Mark one answer

- [ ] **A.** If you have to read a map
- [ ] **B.** When you are tired and need a rest
- [ ] **C.** If your mobile phone rings
- [ ] **D.** In an emergency or breakdown

812 MOTORCYCLE
You are riding slowly in a town centre. Before turning left you should glance over your left shoulder to

Mark one answer
- [ ] A. check for cyclists
- [ ] B. help keep your balance
- [ ] C. look for traffic signs
- [ ] D. check for potholes

813 MOTORCYCLE
As a motorcycle rider which TWO lanes must you NOT use?

Mark two answers
- [ ] A. Crawler lane
- [ ] B. Overtaking lane
- [ ] C. Acceleration lane
- [ ] D. Cycle lane
- [ ] E. Tram lane

814 MOTORCYCLE
You are turning right at a large roundabout. Just before you leave the roundabout you should

Mark one answer
- [ ] A. take a 'lifesaver' glance over your left shoulder
- [ ] B. take a 'lifesaver' glance over your right shoulder
- [ ] C. put on your right indicator
- [ ] D. cancel the left indicator

815 MOTORCYCLE
When filtering through slow-moving or stationary traffic you should

Mark three answers
- [ ] A. watch for hidden vehicles emerging from side roads
- [ ] B. continually use your horn as a warning
- [ ] C. look for vehicles changing course suddenly
- [ ] D. always ride with your hazard lights on
- [ ] E. stand up on the footrests for a good view ahead
- [ ] F. look for pedestrians walking between vehicles

816 MOTORCYCLE
You want to tow a trailer with your motorcycle. Your engine must be more than

Mark one answer
- [ ] A. 50cc
- [ ] B. 125cc
- [ ] C. 525cc
- [ ] D. 1,000cc

817 MOTORCYCLE
What is the national speed limit on a single carriageway?

Mark one answer
- [ ] A. 40mph
- [ ] B. 50mph
- [ ] C. 60mph
- [ ] D. 70mph

818 MOTORCYCLE
What does this sign mean?

Mark one answer
- [ ] A. No parking for solo motorcycles
- [ ] B. Parking for solo motorcycles
- [ ] C. Passing place for motorcycles
- [ ] D. Police motorcycles only

819 MOTORCYCLE

You are riding towards road works. The temporary traffic lights are at red. The road ahead is clear. What should you do?

Mark one answer
- **A.** Ride on with extreme caution
- **B.** Ride on at normal speed
- **C.** Carry on if approaching cars have stopped
- **D.** Wait for the green light

820 MOTORCYCLE

You are riding on a busy dual carriageway. When changing lanes you should

Mark one answer
- **A.** rely totally on mirrors
- **B.** always increase your speed
- **C.** signal so others will give way
- **D.** use mirrors and shoulder checks

821 MOTORCYCLE

You are looking for somewhere to park your motorcycle. The area is full EXCEPT for spaces marked 'disabled use'. You can

Mark one answer
- **A.** use these spaces when elsewhere is full
- **B.** park if you stay with your motorcycle
- **C.** use these spaces, disabled or not
- **D.** not park there unless permitted

822 MOTORCYCLE

On which THREE occasions MUST you stop your motorcycle?

Mark three answers
- **A.** When involved in an accident
- **B.** At a red traffic light
- **C.** When signalled to do so by a police officer
- **D.** At a junction with double broken white lines
- **E.** At a pelican crossing when the amber light is flashing and no pedestrians are crossing

823 MOTORCYCLE

You are on a road with passing places. It is only wide enough for one vehicle. There is a car coming towards you. What should you do?

Mark one answer
- **A.** Pull into a passing place on your right
- **B.** Force the other driver to reverse
- **C.** Turn round and ride back to the main road
- **D.** Pull into a passing place on your left

824 MOTORCYCLE

You intend to go abroad and will be riding on the right-hand side of the road. What should you fit to your motorcycle?

Mark one answer
- **A.** Twin headlights
- **B.** Headlight deflectors
- **C.** Tinted yellow brake lights
- **D.** Tinted red indicator lenses

825 MOTORCYCLE

You are both turning right at this crossroads. It is safer to keep the car to your right so you can

Mark one answer
- **A.** see approaching traffic
- **B.** keep close to the kerb
- **C.** keep clear of following traffic
- **D.** make oncoming vehicles stop

826 CAR & MOTORCYCLE
What is the meaning of this sign?

Mark one answer
- **A.** Local speed limit applies
- **B.** No waiting on the carriageway
- **C.** National speed limit applies
- **D.** No entry to vehicular traffic

827 CAR & MOTORCYCLE
What is the national speed limit on a single carriageway road for cars and motorcycles?

Mark one answer
- **A.** 30mph
- **B.** 50mph
- **C.** 60mph
- **D.** 70mph

828 CAR & MOTORCYCLE
What is the national speed limit for cars and motorcycles on a dual carriageway?

Mark one answer
- **A.** 30mph
- **B.** 50mph
- **C.** 60mph
- **D.** 70mph

829 CAR & MOTORCYCLE
There are no speed limit signs on the road. How is a 30mph limit indicated?

Mark one answer
- **A.** By hazard warning lines
- **B.** By street lighting
- **C.** By pedestrian islands
- **D.** By double or single yellow lines

830 CAR & MOTORCYCLE
Where you see street lights but no speed limit signs the limit is usually

Mark one answer
- **A.** 30mph
- **B.** 40mph
- **C.** 50mph
- **D.** 60mph

831 CAR & MOTORCYCLE
What does this sign mean?

Mark one answer
- **A.** Minimum speed 30mph
- **B.** End of maximum speed
- **C.** End of minimum speed
- **D.** Maximum speed 30mph

832 CAR & MOTORCYCLE
There is a tractor ahead of you. You wish to overtake but you are NOT sure if it is safe to do so. You should

Mark one answer
- **A.** follow another overtaking vehicle through
- **B.** sound your horn to the slow vehicle to pull over
- **C.** speed through but flash your lights to oncoming traffic
- **D.** not overtake if you are in doubt

833 CAR & MOTORCYCLE
Which three of the following are most likely to take an unusual course at roundabouts?

Mark three answers
- A. Horse riders
- B. Milk floats
- C. Delivery vans
- D. Long vehicles
- E. Estate cars
- F. Cyclists

834 CAR & MOTORCYCLE
In which TWO places should you NOT park?

Mark two answers
- A. Near a school entrance
- B. Near a police station
- C. In a side road
- D. At a bus stop
- E. In a one-way street

835 CAR & MOTORCYCLE
On a clearway you must not stop

Mark one answer
- A. at any time
- B. when it is busy
- C. in the rush hour
- D. during daylight hours

836 CAR & MOTORCYCLE
What is the meaning of this sign?

Mark one answer
- A. No entry
- B. Waiting restrictions
- C. National speed limit
- D. School crossing patrol

837 CAR & MOTORCYCLE
You can park on the right-hand side of a road at night

Mark one answer
- A. in a one-way street
- B. with your sidelights on
- C. more than 10 metres (32 feet) from a junction
- D. under a lamppost

838 CAR & MOTORCYCLE
On a three-lane dual carriageway the right-hand lane can be used for

Mark one answer
- A. overtaking only, never turning right
- B. overtaking or turning right
- C. fast-moving traffic only
- D. turning right only, never overtaking

839 CAR & MOTORCYCLE
You are approaching a busy junction. There are several lanes with road markings. At the last moment you realise that you are in the wrong lane. You should

Mark one answer
- A. continue in that lane
- B. force your way across
- C. stop until the area has cleared
- D. use clear arm signals to cut across

840 CAR & MOTORCYCLE
Where may you overtake on a one-way street?

Mark one answer
- A. Only on the left-hand side
- B. Overtaking is not allowed
- C. Only on the right-hand side
- D. Either on the right or the left

841 CAR & MOTORCYCLE
When going straight ahead at a roundabout you should

Mark one answer
- A. indicate left before leaving the roundabout
- B. not indicate at any time
- C. indicate right when approaching the roundabout
- D. indicate left when approaching the roundabout

842 CAR & MOTORCYCLE
Which vehicle might have to use a different course to normal at roundabouts?

Mark one answer
- A. Sports car
- B. Van
- C. Estate car
- D. Long vehicle

843 CAR & MOTORCYCLE
You are going straight ahead at a roundabout. How should you signal?

Mark one answer
- A. Signal right on the approach and then left to leave the roundabout
- B. Signal left as you leave the roundabout
- C. Signal left on the approach to the roundabout and keep the signal on until you leave
- D. Signal left just after you pass the exit before the one you will take

844 CAR & MOTORCYCLE
You may only enter a box junction when

Mark one answer
- A. there are less than two vehicles in front of you
- B. the traffic lights show green
- C. your exit road is clear
- D. you need to turn left

845 CAR & MOTORCYCLE
You may wait in a yellow box junction when

Mark one answer
- A. oncoming traffic is preventing you from turning right
- B. you are in a queue of traffic turning left
- C. you are in a queue of traffic to go ahead
- D. you are on a roundabout

846
CAR & MOTORCYCLE
You MUST stop when signalled to do so by which THREE of these?

Mark three answers
- A. A police officer
- B. A pedestrian
- C. A school crossing patrol
- D. A bus driver
- E. A red traffic light

847
CAR & MOTORCYCLE
You will see these red and white markers when approaching

Mark one answer
- A. the end of a motorway
- B. a concealed level crossing
- C. a concealed speed limit sign
- D. the end of a dual carriageway

848
CAR & MOTORCYCLE
Someone is waiting to cross at a zebra crossing. They are standing on the pavement. You should normally

Mark one answer
- A. go on quickly before they step on to the crossing
- B. stop before you reach the zigzag lines and let them cross
- C. stop, let them cross, wait patiently
- D. ignore them as they are still on the pavement

849
CAR & MOTORCYCLE
At toucan crossings, apart from pedestrians you should be aware of

Mark one answer
- A. emergency vehicles emerging
- B. buses pulling out
- C. trams crossing in front
- D. cyclists riding across

850
CAR & MOTORCYCLE
Who can use a toucan crossing?

Mark two answers
- A. Trains
- B. Cyclists
- C. Buses
- D. Pedestrians
- E. Trams

851
CAR & MOTORCYCLE
At a pelican crossing, what does a flashing amber light mean?

Mark one answer
- A. You must not move off until the lights stop flashing
- B. You must give way to pedestrians still on the crossing
- C. You can move off, even if pedestrians are still on the crossing
- D. You must stop because the lights are about to change to red

852
CAR & MOTORCYCLE
You are waiting at a pelican crossing. The red light changes to flashing amber. This means you must

Mark one answer
- A. wait for pedestrians on the crossing to clear
- B. move off immediately without any hesitation
- C. wait for the green light before moving off
- D. get ready and go when the continuous amber light shows

853 CAR & MOTORCYCLE
You are travelling on a well-lit road at night in a built-up area. By using dipped headlights you will be able to

Mark one answer
- A. see further along the road
- B. go at a much faster speed
- C. switch to main beam quickly
- D. be easily seen by others

854 CAR & MOTORCYCLE
When can you park on the left opposite these road markings?

Mark one answer
- A. If the line nearest to you is broken
- B. When there are no yellow lines
- C. To pick up or set down passengers
- D. During daylight hours only

855 CAR & MOTORCYCLE
You are intending to turn right at a crossroads. An oncoming driver is also turning right. It will normally be safer to

Mark one answer
- A. keep the other vehicle to your RIGHT and turn behind it (offside to offside)
- B. keep the other vehicle to your LEFT and turn in front of it (nearside to nearside)
- C. carry on and turn at the next junction instead
- D. hold back and wait for the other driver to turn first

856 CAR & MOTORCYCLE
You are on a road that has no traffic signs. There are street lights. What is the speed limit?

Mark one answer
- A. 20mph
- B. 30mph
- C. 40mph
- D. 60mph

857 CAR & MOTORCYCLE
You are going along a street with parked vehicles on the left-hand side. For which THREE reasons should you keep your speed down?

Mark three answers
- A. So that oncoming traffic can see you more clearly
- B. You may set off car alarms
- C. Vehicles may be pulling out
- D. Drivers' doors may open
- E. Children may run out from between the vehicles

858 CAR & MOTORCYCLE
You meet an obstruction on your side of the road. You should

Mark one answer
- A. carry on, you have priority
- B. give way to oncoming traffic
- C. wave oncoming vehicles through
- D. accelerate to get past first

859 CAR & MOTORCYCLE
You are on a two-lane dual carriageway. For which TWO of the following would you use the right-hand lane?

Mark two answers
- A. Turning right
- B. Normal progress
- C. Staying at the minimum allowed speed
- D. Constant high speed
- E. Overtaking slower traffic
- F. Mending punctures

860 CAR & MOTORCYCLE
Who has priority at an unmarked crossroads?

Mark one answer
- [ ] **A.** The larger vehicle
- [ ] **B.** No one has priority
- [ ] **C.** The faster vehicle
- [ ] **D.** The smaller vehicle

861 CAR & MOTORCYCLE
What is the nearest you may park to a junction?

Mark one answer **NI**
- [ ] **A.** 10 metres (32 feet)
- [ ] **B.** 12 metres (39 feet)
- [ ] **C.** 15 metres (49 feet)
- [ ] **D.** 20 metres (66 feet)

862 CAR & MOTORCYCLE
In which THREE places must you NOT park?

Mark three answers **NI**
- [ ] **A.** Near the brow of a hill
- [ ] **B.** At or near a bus stop
- [ ] **C.** Where there is no pavement
- [ ] **D.** Within 10 metres (32 feet) of a junction
- [ ] **E.** On a 40mph road

863 CAR & MOTORCYCLE
You are waiting at a level crossing. A train has passed but the lights keep flashing. You must

Mark one answer
- [ ] **A.** carry on waiting
- [ ] **B.** phone the signal operator
- [ ] **C.** edge over the stop line and !ook for trains
- [ ] **D.** park and investigate

864 CAR & MOTORCYCLE
You park at night on a road with a 40mph speed limit. You should park

Mark one answer
- [ ] **A.** facing the traffic
- [ ] **B.** with parking lights on
- [ ] **C.** with dipped headlights on
- [ ] **D.** near a street light

865 CAR & MOTORCYCLE
The dual carriageway you are turning right on to has a very narrow central reservation. What should you do?

Mark one answer
- [ ] **A.** Proceed to the central reservation and wait
- [ ] **B.** Wait until the road is clear in both directions
- [ ] **C.** Stop in the first lane so that other vehicles give way
- [ ] **D.** Emerge slightly to show your intentions

866 CAR & MOTORCYCLE
At a crossroads there are no signs or road markings. Two vehicles approach. Which has priority?

Mark one answer
- [ ] **A.** Neither of the vehicles
- [ ] **B.** The vehicle travelling the fastest
- [ ] **C.** Oncoming vehicles turning right
- [ ] **D.** Vehicles approaching from the right

867 CAR & MOTORCYCLE
What does this sign tell you?

Mark one answer
- **A.** That it is a no-through road
- **B.** End of traffic calming zone
- **C.** Free parking zone ends
- **D.** No waiting zone ends

868 CAR & MOTORCYCLE
You are entering an area of road works. There is a temporary speed limit displayed. You should

Mark one answer
- **A.** not exceed the speed limit
- **B.** obey the limit only during rush hour
- **C.** ignore the displayed limit
- **D.** obey the limit except at night

869 CAR
You may drive over a footpath

Mark one answer
- **A.** to overtake slow-moving traffic
- **B.** when the pavement is very wide
- **C.** if no pedestrians are near
- **D.** to get into a property

870 CAR
A single-carriageway road has this sign. What is the maximum permitted speed for a car towing a trailer?

Mark one answer
- **A.** 30mph
- **B.** 40mph
- **C.** 50mph
- **D.** 60mph

871 CAR
You are towing a small caravan on a dual carriageway. You must not exceed

Mark one answer
- **A.** 50mph
- **B.** 40mph
- **C.** 70mph
- **D.** 60mph

872 CAR
You want to park and you see this sign. On the days and times shown you should

Meter
ZONE

Mon - Fri
8.30 am - 6.30 pm
Saturday
8.30 am - 1.30 pm

Mark one answer
- **A.** park in a bay and not pay
- **B.** park on yellow lines and pay
- **C.** park on yellow lines and not pay
- **D.** park in a bay and pay

873 CAR
As a car driver which THREE lanes are you NOT normally allowed to use?

Mark three answers
- **A.** Crawler lane
- **B.** Bus lane
- **C.** Overtaking lane
- **D.** Acceleration lane
- **E.** Cycle lane
- **F.** Tram lane

874 CAR
You are driving along a road that has a cycle lane. The lane is marked by a solid white line. This means that during its period of operation

Mark one answer
- **A.** the lane may be used for parking your car
- **B.** you may drive in that lane at any time
- **C.** the lane may be used when necessary
- **D.** you must not drive in that lane

875 CAR
A cycle lane is marked by a solid white line. You must not drive or park in it

Mark one answer
- **A.** at any time
- **B.** during the rush hour
- **C.** if a cyclist is using it
- **D.** during its period of operation

876 CAR
While driving, you intend to turn left into a minor road. On the approach you should

Mark one answer
- **A.** keep just left of the middle of the road
- **B.** keep in the middle of the road
- **C.** swing out wide just before turning
- **D.** keep well to the left of the road

877 CAR
You are waiting at a level crossing. The red warning lights continue to flash after a train has passed by. What should you do?

Mark one answer
- **A.** Get out and investigate
- **B.** Telephone the signal operator
- **C.** Continue to wait
- **D.** Drive across carefully

878 CAR
You are driving over a level crossing. The warning lights come on and a bell rings. What should you do?

Mark one answer
- **A.** Get everyone out of the vehicle immediately
- **B.** Stop and reverse back to clear the crossing
- **C.** Keep going and clear the crossing
- **D.** Stop immediately and use your hazard warning lights

879 CAR
You are on a busy main road and find that you are travelling in the wrong direction. What should you do?

Mark one answer
- A. Turn into a side road on the right and reverse into the main road
- B. Make a U-turn in the main road
- C. Make a 'three-point' turn in the main road
- D. Turn round in a side road

880 CAR
You may remove your seat belt when carrying out a manoeuvre that involves

Mark one answer
- A. reversing
- B. a hill start
- C. an emergency stop
- D. driving slowly

881 CAR
You must not reverse

Mark one answer
- A. for longer than necessary
- B. for more than a car's length
- C. into a side road
- D. in a built-up area

882 CAR
You are parked in a busy high street. What is the safest way to turn your vehicle around so you can go the opposite way?

Mark one answer
- A. Find a quiet side road to turn round in
- B. Drive into a side road and reverse into the main road
- C. Get someone to stop the traffic
- D. Do a U-turn

883 CAR
When you are NOT sure that it is safe to reverse your vehicle you should

Mark one answer
- A. use your horn
- B. rev your engine
- C. get out and check
- D. reverse slowly

884 CAR
When may you reverse from a side road into a main road?

Mark one answer
- A. Only if both roads are clear of traffic
- B. Not at any time
- C. At any time
- D. Only if the main road is clear of traffic

885 CAR
You want to turn right at a box junction. There is oncoming traffic. You should

Mark one answer
- A. wait in the box junction if your exit is clear
- B. wait before the junction until it is clear of all traffic
- C. drive on, you cannot turn right at a box junction
- D. drive slowly into the box junction when signalled by oncoming traffic

886 CAR
You are reversing your vehicle into a side road. When would the greatest hazard to passing traffic occur?

Mark one answer
- A. After you've completed the manoeuvre
- B. Just before you actually begin to manoeuvre
- C. After you've entered the side road
- D. When the front of your vehicle swings out

887 CAR

You are driving on a road that has a cycle lane. The lane is marked by a broken white line. This means that

Mark two answers
- A. you should not drive in the lane unless it is unavoidable
- B. you should not park in the lane unless it is unavoidable
- C. cyclists can travel in both directions in that lane
- D. the lane must be used by motorcyclists in heavy traffic

888 CAR

Where is the safest place to park your vehicle at night?

Mark one answer
- A. In a garage
- B. On a busy road
- C. In a quiet car park
- D. Near a red route

889 CAR

To help keep your vehicle secure at night where should you park?

Mark one answer
- A. Near a police station
- B. In a quiet road
- C. On a red route
- D. In a well-lit area

890 CAR

You are in the right-hand lane of a dual carriageway. You see signs showing that the right-hand lane is closed 800 yards ahead. You should

GET IN LANE

↑ ↑ ⊤

800 yards

Mark one answer
- A. keep in that lane until you reach the queue
- B. move to the left immediately
- C. wait and see which lane is moving faster
- D. move to the left in good time

891 CAR

You are driving on an urban clearway. You may stop only to

Mark one answer
- A. set down and pick up passengers
- B. use a mobile telephone
- C. ask for directions
- D. load or unload goods

892 CAR

You are looking for somewhere to park your vehicle. The area is full EXCEPT for spaces marked 'disabled use'. You can

Mark one answer
- A. use these spaces when elsewhere is full
- B. park if you stay with your vehicle
- C. use these spaces, disabled or not
- D. not park there unless permitted

893 CAR

Your vehicle is parked on the road at night. When must you use sidelights?

Mark one answer
- A. Where there are continuous white lines in the middle of the road
- B. Where the speed limit exceeds 30mph
- C. Where you are facing oncoming traffic
- D. Where you are near a bus stop

894 CAR

On which THREE occasions MUST you stop your vehicle?

Mark three answers
- A. When in an accident where damage or injury is caused
- B. At a red traffic light
- C. When signalled to do so by a police officer
- D. At a junction with double broken white lines
- E. At a pelican crossing when the amber light is flashing and no pedestrians are crossing

895 CAR

You are on a road that is only wide enough for one vehicle. There is a car coming towards you. What should you do?

Mark one answer

- **A.** Pull into a passing place on your right
- **B.** Force the other driver to reverse
- **C.** Pull into a passing place if your vehicle is wider
- **D.** Pull into a passing place on your left

896 CAR

What MUST you have to park in a disabled space?

Mark one answer

- **A.** An orange or blue badge
- **B.** A wheelchair
- **C.** An advanced driver certificate
- **D.** A modified vehicle

897 CAR

You are driving at night with full beam headlights on. A vehicle is overtaking you. You should dip your lights

Mark one answer

- **A.** some time after the vehicle has passed you
- **B.** before the vehicle starts to pass you
- **C.** only if the other driver dips their headlights
- **D.** as soon as the vehicle passes you

898 CAR

When may you drive a motor car in this bus lane?

Mark one answer

- **A.** Outside its hours of operation
- **B.** To get to the front of a traffic queue
- **C.** You may not use it at any time
- **D.** To overtake slow-moving traffic

899 CAR

Signals are normally given by direction indicators and

Mark one answer

- **A.** brake lights
- **B.** sidelights
- **C.** fog lights
- **D.** interior lights

900 CAR & MOTORCYCLE

You are travelling on a motorway. You MUST stop when signalled to do so by which of these?

NI

Mark one answer

- **A.** Flashing amber lights above your lane
- **B.** A Highways Agency Traffic Officer
- **C.** Pedestrians on the hard shoulder
- **D.** A driver who has broken down

901 CAR & MOTORCYCLE

At a busy unmarked crossroads, which of the following has priority?

Mark one answer

- **A.** Vehicles going straight ahead
- **B.** Vehicles turning right
- **C.** None of the vehicles
- **D.** The vehicles that arrived first

902 MOTORCYCLE
How should you give an arm signal to turn left?

Mark one answer

A.

B.

C.

D.

903 MOTORCYCLE
You are giving an arm signal ready to turn left. Why should you NOT continue with the arm signal while you turn?

Mark one answer

A. Because you might hit a pedestrian on the corner

B. Because you will have less steering control

C. Because you will need to keep the clutch applied

D. Because other motorists will think that you are stopping on the corner

904 MOTORCYCLE
This sign is of particular importance to motorcyclists. It means

Mark one answer

A. side winds

B. airport

C. slippery road

D. service area

905 MOTORCYCLE
Which one of these signs are you allowed to ride past on a solo motorcycle?

Mark one answer

A.

B.

C.

D.

906 MOTORCYCLE
Which of these signals should you give when slowing or stopping your motorcycle?

Mark one answer

☐ A.

☐ B.

☐ C.

☐ D.

907 MOTORCYCLE
When drivers flash their headlights at you it means

Mark one answer

☐ A. that there is a radar speed trap ahead
☐ B. that they are giving way to you
☐ C. that they are warning you of their presence
☐ D. that there is something wrong with your motorcycle

908 MOTORCYCLE
You are riding on a motorway. There is a slow-moving vehicle ahead. On the back you see this sign. What should you do?

Mark one answer

☐ A. Pass on the right
☐ B. Pass on the left
☐ C. Leave at the next exit
☐ D. Drive no further

909 MOTORCYCLE
Why should you make sure that you cancel your indicators after turning?

Mark one answer

☐ A. To avoid flattening the battery
☐ B. To avoid misleading other road users
☐ C. To avoid dazzling other road users
☐ D. To avoid damage to the indicator relay

910 MOTORCYCLE
Your indicators are difficult to see due to bright sunshine. When using them you should

Mark one answer

☐ A. also give an arm signal
☐ B. sound your horn
☐ C. flash your headlight
☐ D. keep both hands on the handlebars

911 CAR & MOTORCYCLE
You MUST obey signs giving orders. These signs are mostly in

Mark one answer

☐ A. green rectangles
☐ B. red triangles
☐ C. blue rectangles
☐ D. red circles

912 CAR & MOTORCYCLE
Traffic signs giving orders are generally which shape?

Mark one answer

A.

B.

C.

D.

913 CAR & MOTORCYCLE
Which type of sign tells you NOT to do something?

Mark one answer

A.

B.

C.

D.

914 CAR & MOTORCYCLE
What does this sign mean?

Mark one answer

A. Maximum speed limit with traffic calming
B. Minimum speed limit with traffic calming
C. '20 cars only' parking zone
D. Only 20 cars allowed at any one time

915 CAR & MOTORCYCLE
Which sign means no motor vehicles are allowed?

Mark one answer

A.

B.

C.

D.

916 CAR & MOTORCYCLE
Which of these signs means no motor vehicles?

Mark one answer

A.

B.

C.

D.

917 CAR & MOTORCYCLE
What does this sign mean?

Mark one answer
- **A.** New speed limit 20mph
- **B.** No vehicles over 30 tonnes
- **C.** Minimum speed limit 30mph
- **D.** End of 20mph zone

918 CAR & MOTORCYCLE
What does this sign mean?

Mark one answer
- **A.** No overtaking
- **B.** No motor vehicles
- **C.** Clearway (no stopping)
- **D.** Cars and motorcycles only

919 CAR & MOTORCYCLE
What does this sign mean?

Mark one answer
- **A.** No parking
- **B.** No road markings
- **C.** No through road
- **D.** No entry

920 CAR & MOTORCYCLE
What does this sign mean?

Mark one answer
- **A.** Bend to the right
- **B.** Road on the right closed
- **C.** No traffic from the right
- **D.** No right turn

921 CAR & MOTORCYCLE
Which sign means 'no entry'?

Mark one answer

- **A.**
- **B.**
- **C.**
- **D.**

922 CAR & MOTORCYCLE
What does this sign mean?

Mark one answer

- [ ] **A.** Route for trams only
- [ ] **B.** Route for buses only
- [ ] **C.** Parking for buses only
- [ ] **D.** Parking for trams only

923 CAR & MOTORCYCLE
Which type of vehicle does this sign apply to?

Mark one answer

- [ ] **A.** Wide vehicles
- [ ] **B.** Long vehicles
- [ ] **C.** High vehicles
- [ ] **D.** Heavy vehicles

924 CAR & MOTORCYCLE
Which sign means NO motor vehicles allowed?

Mark one answer

- [ ] **A.**
- [ ] **B.**
- [ ] **C.**
- [ ] **D.**

925 CAR & MOTORCYCLE
What does this sign mean?

Mark one answer

- [ ] **A.** You have priority
- [ ] **B.** No motor vehicles
- [ ] **C.** Two-way traffic
- [ ] **D.** No overtaking

926 CAR & MOTORCYCLE
What does this sign mean?

Mark one answer

- [ ] **A.** Keep in one lane
- [ ] **B.** Give way to oncoming traffic
- [ ] **C.** Do not overtake
- [ ] **D.** Form two lanes

927 CAR & MOTORCYCLE
Which sign means no overtaking?

Mark one answer

A.

B.

C.

D.

928 CAR & MOTORCYCLE
What does this sign mean?

Mark one answer
- A. Waiting restrictions apply
- B. Waiting permitted
- C. National speed limit applies
- D. Clearway (no stopping)

929 CAR & MOTORCYCLE
What does this sign mean?

Mark one answer
- A. End of restricted speed area
- B. End of restricted parking area
- C. End of clearway
- D. End of cycle route

Zone ENDS

930 CAR & MOTORCYCLE
Which sign means 'no stopping'?

Mark one answer

A.

B.

C.

D.

931 CAR & MOTORCYCLE
What does this sign mean?

Mark one answer
- A. Roundabout
- B. Crossroads
- C. No stopping
- D. No entry

932 CAR & MOTORCYCLE
You see this sign ahead. It means

Mark one answer
- A. national speed limit applies
- B. waiting restrictions apply
- C. no stopping
- D. no entry

933 CAR & MOTORCYCLE
What does this sign mean?

Mark one answer
- A. Distance to parking place ahead
- B. Distance to public telephone ahead
- C. Distance to public house ahead
- D. Distance to passing place ahead

934 CAR & MOTORCYCLE
What does this sign mean?

Mark one answer
- A. Vehicles may not park on the verge or footway
- B. Vehicles may park on the left-hand side of the road only
- C. Vehicles may park fully on the verge or footway
- D. Vehicles may park on the right-hand side of the road only

935 CAR & MOTORCYCLE
What does this traffic sign mean?

Mark one answer
- A. No overtaking allowed
- B. Give priority to oncoming traffic
- C. Two-way traffic
- D. One-way traffic only

936 CAR & MOTORCYCLE
What is the meaning of this traffic sign?

Mark one answer
- A. End of two-way road
- B. Give priority to vehicles coming towards you
- C. You have priority over vehicles coming towards you
- D. Bus lane ahead

937 CAR & MOTORCYCLE
What MUST you do when you see this sign?

Mark one answer
- A. Stop, only if traffic is approaching
- B. Stop, even if the road is clear
- C. Stop, only if children are waiting to cross
- D. Stop, only if a red light is showing

938 CAR & MOTORCYCLE
What does this sign mean?

Mark one answer
- **A.** No overtaking
- **B.** You are entering a one-way street
- **C.** Two-way traffic ahead
- **D.** You have priority over vehicles from the opposite direction

939 CAR & MOTORCYCLE
What shape is a STOP sign at a junction?

Mark one answer
- **A.**
- **B.**
- **C.**
- **D.**

940 CAR & MOTORCYCLE
At a junction you see this sign partly covered by snow. What does it mean?

Mark one answer
- **A.** Crossroads
- **B.** Give way
- **C.** Stop
- **D.** Turn right

941 CAR & MOTORCYCLE
Which shape is used for a 'give way' sign?

Mark one answer
- **A.**
- **B.**
- **C.**
- **D.**

942 CAR & MOTORCYCLE
What does this sign mean?

Mark one answer
- **A.** Service area 30 miles ahead
- **B.** Maximum speed 30mph
- **C.** Minimum speed 30mph
- **D.** Lay-by 30 miles ahead

943 CAR & MOTORCYCLE
In some narrow residential streets you may find a speed limit of

Mark one answer
- **A.** 20mph
- **B.** 25mph
- **C.** 35mph
- **D.** 40mph

944 CAR & MOTORCYCLE
Which of these signs means turn left ahead?

Mark one answer

A.

B.

C.

D.

945 CAR & MOTORCYCLE
What does this sign mean?

Mark one answer

A. Buses turning

B. Ring road

C. Mini-roundabout

D. Keep right

946 CAR & MOTORCYCLE
What does this sign mean?

Mark one answer

A. Give way to oncoming vehicles

B. Approaching traffic passes you on both sides

C. Turn off at the next available junction

D. Pass either side to get to the same destination

947 CAR & MOTORCYCLE
What does this sign mean?

Mark one answer

A. Route for trams

B. Give way to trams

C. Route for buses

D. Give way to buses

948 CAR & MOTORCYCLE
What does a circular traffic sign with a blue background do?

Mark one answer

A. Give warning of a motorway ahead

B. Give directions to a car park

C. Give motorway information

D. Give an instruction

949 CAR & MOTORCYCLE
Which of these signs means that you are entering a one-way street?

Mark one answer

A.

B.

C.

D.

950 CAR & MOTORCYCLE
Where would you see a contraflow bus and cycle lane?

Mark one answer

A. On a dual carriageway
B. On a roundabout
C. On an urban motorway
D. On a one-way street

951 CAR & MOTORCYCLE
What does this sign mean?

Mark one answer

A. Bus station on the right
B. Contraflow bus lane
C. With-flow bus lane
D. Give way to buses

952 CAR & MOTORCYCLE
What does this sign mean?

Mark one answer

A. With-flow bus and cycle lane
B. Contraflow bus and cycle lane
C. No buses and cycles allowed
D. No waiting for buses and cycles

953 CAR & MOTORCYCLE
What does a sign with a brown background show?

Mark one answer

A. Tourist directions
B. Primary roads
C. Motorway routes
D. Minor routes

954 CAR & MOTORCYCLE
This sign means

Mark one answer

A. tourist attraction
B. beware of trains
C. level crossing
D. beware of trams

955 CAR & MOTORCYCLE
What are triangular signs for?

Mark one answer
- **A.** To give warnings
- **B.** To give information
- **C.** To give orders
- **D.** To give directions

956 CAR & MOTORCYCLE
What does this sign mean?

Mark one answer
- **A.** Turn left ahead
- **B.** T-junction
- **C.** No through road
- **D.** Give way

957 CAR & MOTORCYCLE
What does this sign mean?

Mark one answer
- **A.** Multi-exit roundabout
- **B.** Risk of ice
- **C.** Six roads converge
- **D.** Place of historical interest

958 CAR & MOTORCYCLE
What does this sign mean?

Mark one answer
- **A.** Crossroads
- **B.** Level crossing with gate
- **C.** Level crossing without gate
- **D.** Ahead only

959 CAR & MOTORCYCLE
What does this sign mean?

Mark one answer
- **A.** Ring road
- **B.** Mini-roundabout
- **C.** No vehicles
- **D.** Roundabout

960 CAR & MOTORCYCLE
Which FOUR of these would be indicated by a triangular road sign?

Mark four answers
- **A.** Road narrows
- **B.** Ahead only
- **C.** Low bridge
- **D.** Minimum speed
- **E.** Children crossing
- **F.** T-junction

961 CAR & MOTORCYCLE
What does this sign mean?

Mark one answer

- **A.** Cyclists must dismount
- **B.** Cycles are not allowed
- **C.** Cycle route ahead
- **D.** Cycle in single file

962 CAR & MOTORCYCLE
Which sign means that pedestrians may be walking along the road?

Mark one answer

A.   **B.**

C.   **D.**

963 CAR & MOTORCYCLE
Which of these signs warn you of a pedestrian crossing?

Mark one answer

A.   **B.**

C.   **D.**

964 CAR & MOTORCYCLE
What does this sign mean?

Mark one answer

- **A.** No footpath ahead
- **B.** Pedestrians only ahead
- **C.** Pedestrian crossing ahead
- **D.** School crossing ahead

965 CAR & MOTORCYCLE
What does this sign mean?

Mark one answer

- **A.** School crossing patrol
- **B.** No pedestrians allowed
- **C.** Pedestrian zone – no vehicles
- **D.** Pedestrian crossing ahead

966 CAR & MOTORCYCLE
Which of these signs means there is a double bend ahead?

Mark one answer

- [ ] A.
- [ ] B.
- [ ] C.
- [ ] D.

967 CAR & MOTORCYCLE
What does this sign mean?

Mark one answer

- [ ] A. Wait at the barriers
- [ ] B. Wait at the crossroads
- [ ] C. Give way to trams
- [ ] D. Give way to farm vehicles

968 CAR & MOTORCYCLE
What does this sign mean?

Mark one answer

- [ ] A. Humpback bridge
- [ ] B. Humps in the road
- [ ] C. Entrance to tunnel
- [ ] D. Soft verges

969 CAR & MOTORCYCLE
What does this sign mean?

Mark one answer

- [ ] A. Low bridge ahead
- [ ] B. Tunnel ahead
- [ ] C. Ancient monument ahead
- [ ] D. Accident black spot ahead

970 CAR & MOTORCYCLE
What does this sign mean?

Mark one answer

- [ ] A. Two-way traffic straight ahead
- [ ] B. Two-way traffic crosses a one-way road
- [ ] C. Two-way traffic over a bridge
- [ ] D. Two-way traffic crosses a two-way road

971 CAR & MOTORCYCLE
Which sign means 'two-way traffic crosses a one-way road'?

Mark one answer

A.

B.

C.

D.

972 CAR & MOTORCYCLE
Which of these signs means the end of a dual carriageway?

Mark one answer

A.

B.

C.

D.

973 CAR & MOTORCYCLE
What does this sign mean?

Mark one answer

A. End of dual carriageway

B. Tall bridge

C. Road narrows

D. End of narrow bridge

974 CAR & MOTORCYCLE
What does this sign mean?

Mark one answer

A. Two-way traffic ahead across a one-way road

B. Traffic approaching you has priority

C. Two-way traffic straight ahead

D. Motorway contraflow system ahead

975 CAR & MOTORCYCLE
What does this sign mean?

Mark one answer

A. Crosswinds

B. Road noise

C. Airport

D. Adverse camber

976 CAR & MOTORCYCLE
What does this traffic sign mean?

Mark one answer

A. Slippery road ahead

B. Tyres liable to punctures ahead

C. Danger ahead

D. Service area ahead

977 CAR & MOTORCYCLE
You are about to overtake when you see this sign. You should

Mark one answer
- A. overtake the other driver as quickly as possible
- B. move to the right to get a better view
- C. switch your headlights on before overtaking
- D. hold back until you can see clearly ahead

978 CAR & MOTORCYCLE
What does this sign mean?

Mark one answer
- A. Level crossing with gate or barrier
- B. Gated road ahead
- C. Level crossing without gate or barrier
- D. Cattle grid ahead

979 CAR & MOTORCYCLE
What does this sign mean?

Mark one answer
- A. No trams ahead
- B. Oncoming trams
- C. Trams crossing ahead
- D. Trams only

980 CAR & MOTORCYCLE
What does this sign mean?

Mark one answer
- A. Adverse camber
- B. Steep hill downwards
- C. Uneven road
- D. Steep hill upwards

981 CAR & MOTORCYCLE
What does this sign mean?

Mark one answer
- A. Uneven road surface
- B. Bridge over the road
- C. Road ahead ends
- D. Water across the road

982 CAR & MOTORCYCLE
What does this sign mean?

Mark one answer
- A. Humpback bridge
- B. Traffic calming hump
- C. Low bridge
- D. Uneven road

983
CAR & MOTORCYCLE
What does this sign mean?

Mark one answer
- A. Turn left for parking area
- B. No through road on the left
- C. No entry for traffic turning left
- D. Turn left for ferry terminal

984
CAR & MOTORCYCLE
What does this sign mean?

Mark one answer
- A. T-junction
- B. No through road
- C. Telephone box ahead
- D. Toilet ahead

985
CAR & MOTORCYCLE
Which sign means 'no through road'?

Mark one answer
- A.
- B.

- C.
- D.

986
CAR & MOTORCYCLE
Which of the following signs informs you that you are coming to a 'no through road'?

Mark one answer
- A.
- B.

- C.
- D.

987
CAR & MOTORCYCLE
What does this sign mean?

Mark one answer
- A. Direction to park-and-ride car park
- B. No parking for buses or coaches
- C. Directions to bus and coach park
- D. Parking area for cars and coaches

988
CAR & MOTORCYCLE
You are in a tunnel and you see this sign. What does it mean?

Mark one answer
- A. Direction to emergency pedestrian exit
- B. Beware of pedestrians, no footpath ahead
- C. No access for pedestrians
- D. Beware of pedestrians crossing ahead

989 CAR & MOTORCYCLE
Which is the sign for a ring road?

Mark one answer

☐ A.

☐ B.

☐ C.

☐ D.

990 CAR & MOTORCYCLE
What does this sign mean?

Mark one answer

☐ A. The right-hand lane ahead is narrow
☐ B. Right-hand lane for buses only
☐ C. Right-hand lane for turning right
☐ D. The right-hand lane is closed

991 CAR & MOTORCYCLE
What does this sign mean?

Mark one answer

☐ A. Change to the left lane
☐ B. Leave at the next exit
☐ C. Contraflow system
☐ D. One-way street

992 CAR & MOTORCYCLE
At a railway level crossing the red light signal continues to flash after a train has gone by. What should you do?

Mark one answer

☐ A. Phone the signal operator
☐ B. Alert drivers behind you
☐ C. Wait
☐ D. Proceed with caution

993
CAR & MOTORCYCLE
What does this sign mean?

Mark one answer
- [ ] **A.** Leave motorway at next exit
- [ ] **B.** Lane for heavy and slow vehicles
- [ ] **C.** All lorries use the hard shoulder
- [ ] **D.** Rest area for lorries

994
CAR & MOTORCYCLE
You are approaching a red traffic light. The signal will change from red to

Mark one answer
- [ ] **A.** red and amber, then green
- [ ] **B.** green, then amber
- [ ] **C.** amber, then green
- [ ] **D.** green and amber, then green

995
CAR & MOTORCYCLE
A red traffic light means

Mark one answer
- [ ] **A.** you should stop unless turning left
- [ ] **B.** stop, if you are able to brake safely
- [ ] **C.** you must stop and wait behind the stop line
- [ ] **D.** proceed with caution

996
CAR & MOTORCYCLE
At traffic lights, amber on its own means

Mark one answer
- [ ] **A.** prepare to go
- [ ] **B.** go if the way is clear
- [ ] **C.** go if no pedestrians are crossing
- [ ] **D.** stop at the stop line

997
CAR & MOTORCYCLE
You are approaching traffic lights. Red and amber are showing. This means

Mark one answer
- [ ] **A.** pass the lights if the road is clear
- [ ] **B.** there is a fault with the lights – take care
- [ ] **C.** wait for the green light before you cross the stop line
- [ ] **D.** the lights are about to change to red

998
CAR & MOTORCYCLE
You are at a junction controlled by traffic lights. When should you NOT proceed at green?

Mark one answer

- [ ] **A.** When pedestrians are waiting to cross
- [ ] **B.** When your exit from the junction is blocked
- [ ] **C.** When you think the lights may be about to change
- [ ] **D.** When you intend to turn right

999
CAR & MOTORCYCLE
You are in the left-hand lane at traffic lights. You are waiting to turn left. At which of these traffic lights must you NOT move on?

Mark one answer

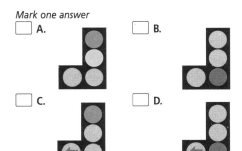

- [ ] **A.**
- [ ] **B.**
- [ ] **C.**
- [ ] **D.**

1000
CAR & MOTORCYCLE
What does this sign mean?

Mark one answer

- [ ] **A.** Traffic lights out of order
- [ ] **B.** Amber signal out of order
- [ ] **C.** Temporary traffic lights ahead
- [ ] **D.** New traffic lights ahead

1001
CAR & MOTORCYCLE
When traffic lights are out of order, who has priority?

Mark one answer

- [ ] **A.** Traffic going straight on
- [ ] **B.** Traffic turning right
- [ ] **C.** Nobody
- [ ] **D.** Traffic turning left

1002
CAR & MOTORCYCLE
These flashing red lights mean STOP. In which THREE of the following places could you find them?

Mark three answers

- [ ] **A.** Pelican crossings
- [ ] **B.** Lifting bridges
- [ ] **C.** Zebra crossings
- [ ] **D.** Level crossings
- [ ] **E.** Motorway exits
- [ ] **F.** Fire stations

1003 CAR & MOTORCYCLE
What do these zigzag lines at pedestrian crossings mean?

Mark one answer
- **A.** No parking at any time
- **B.** Parking allowed only for a short time
- **C.** Slow down to 20mph
- **D.** Sounding horns is not allowed

1004 CAR & MOTORCYCLE
When may you cross a double solid white line in the middle of the road?

Mark one answer
- **A.** To pass traffic that is queuing back at a junction
- **B.** To pass a car signalling to turn left ahead
- **C.** To pass a road maintenance vehicle travelling at 10mph or less
- **D.** To pass a vehicle that is towing a trailer

1005 CAR & MOTORCYCLE
What does this road marking mean?

Mark one answer
- **A.** Do not cross the line
- **B.** No stopping allowed
- **C.** You are approaching a hazard
- **D.** No overtaking allowed

1006 CAR & MOTORCYCLE
This marking appears on the road just before a

Mark one answer
- **A.** 'no entry' sign
- **B.** 'give way' sign
- **C.** 'stop' sign
- **D.** 'no through road' sign

1007 CAR & MOTORCYCLE
Where would you see this road marking?

Mark one answer
- **A.** At traffic lights
- **B.** On road humps
- **C.** Near a level crossing
- **D.** At a box junction

1008 CAR & MOTORCYCLE
Which is a hazard warning line?

Mark one answer

A.

B.

C.

D.

1009 CAR & MOTORCYCLE
At this junction there is a stop sign with a solid white line on the road surface. Why is there a stop sign here?

Mark one answer

A. Speed on the major road is de-restricted
B. It is a busy junction
C. Visibility along the major road is restricted
D. There are hazard warning lines in the centre of the road

1010 CAR & MOTORCYCLE
You see this line across the road at the entrance to a roundabout. What does it mean?

Mark one answer

A. Give way to traffic from the right
B. Traffic from the left has right of way
C. You have right of way
D. Stop at the line

1011 CAR & MOTORCYCLE
Where would you find these road markings?

Mark one answer

A. At a railway crossing
B. At a junction
C. On a motorway
D. On a pedestrian crossing

1012 CAR & MOTORCYCLE
How will a police officer in a patrol vehicle normally get you to stop?

Mark one answer

A. Flash the headlights, indicate left and point to the left
B. Wait until you stop, then approach you
C. Use the siren, overtake, cut in front and stop
D. Pull alongside you, use the siren and wave you to stop

1013 CAR & MOTORCYCLE
There is a police car following you. The police officer flashes the headlights and points to the left. What should you do?

Mark one answer
- **A.** Turn left at the next junction
- **B.** Pull up on the left
- **C.** Stop immediately
- **D.** Move over to the left

1014 CAR & MOTORCYCLE
You approach a junction. The traffic lights are not working. A police officer gives this signal. You should

Mark one answer
- **A.** turn left only
- **B.** turn right only
- **C.** stop level with the officer's arm
- **D.** stop at the stop line

1015 CAR & MOTORCYCLE
The driver of the car in front is giving this arm signal. What does it mean?

Mark one answer
- **A.** The driver is slowing down
- **B.** The driver intends to turn right
- **C.** The driver wishes to overtake
- **D.** The driver intends to turn left

1016 CAR & MOTORCYCLE
Where would you see these road markings?

Mark one answer
- **A.** At a level crossing
- **B.** On a motorway slip road
- **C.** At a pedestrian crossing
- **D.** On a single-track road

1017 CAR & MOTORCYCLE
When may you NOT overtake on the left?

Mark one answer
- **A.** On a free-flowing motorway or dual carriageway
- **B.** When the traffic is moving slowly in queues
- **C.** On a one-way street
- **D.** When the car in front is signalling to turn right

1018 CAR & MOTORCYCLE
What does this motorway sign mean?

Mark one answer
- **A.** Change to the lane on your left
- **B.** Leave the motorway at the next exit
- **C.** Change to the opposite carriageway
- **D.** Pull up on the hard shoulder

1019 CAR & MOTORCYCLE
What does this motorway sign mean?

Mark one answer

- [ ] **A.** Temporary minimum speed 50mph
- [ ] **B.** No services for 50 miles
- [ ] **C.** Obstruction 50 metres (164 feet) ahead
- [ ] **D.** Temporary maximum speed 50mph

1020 CAR & MOTORCYCLE
What does this sign mean?

Mark one answer

- [ ] **A.** Through traffic to use left lane
- [ ] **B.** Right-hand lane T-junction only
- [ ] **C.** Right-hand lane closed ahead
- [ ] **D.** 11 tonne weight limit

1021 CAR & MOTORCYCLE
On a motorway this sign means

Mark one answer

- [ ] **A.** move over on to the hard shoulder
- [ ] **B.** overtaking on the left only
- [ ] **C.** leave the motorway at the next exit
- [ ] **D.** move to the lane on your left

1022 CAR & MOTORCYCLE
What does '25' mean on this motorway sign?

Mark one answer

- [ ] **A.** The distance to the nearest town
- [ ] **B.** The route number of the road
- [ ] **C.** The number of the next junction
- [ ] **D.** The speed limit on the slip road

1023 CAR & MOTORCYCLE
The right-hand lane of a three-lane motorway is

Mark one answer

- [ ] **A.** for lorries only
- [ ] **B.** an overtaking lane
- [ ] **C.** the right-turn lane
- [ ] **D.** an acceleration lane

1024 CAR & MOTORCYCLE
Where can you find reflective amber studs on a motorway?

Mark one answer

- [ ] **A.** Separating the slip road from the motorway
- [ ] **B.** On the left-hand edge of the road
- [ ] **C.** On the right-hand edge of the road
- [ ] **D.** Separating the lanes

1025 CAR & MOTORCYCLE
Where on a motorway would you find green reflective studs?

Mark one answer
- [ ] **A.** Separating driving lanes
- [ ] **B.** Between the hard shoulder and the carriageway
- [ ] **C.** At slip road entrances and exits
- [ ] **D.** Between the carriageway and the central reservation

1026 CAR & MOTORCYCLE
You are travelling along a motorway. You see this sign. You should

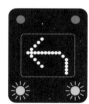

Mark one answer
- [ ] **A.** leave the motorway at the next exit
- [ ] **B.** turn left immediately
- [ ] **C.** change lane
- [ ] **D.** move onto the hard shoulder

1027 CAR & MOTORCYCLE
At a junction you see this signal. It means

Mark one answer
- [ ] **A.** cars must stop
- [ ] **B.** trams must stop
- [ ] **C.** both trams and cars must stop
- [ ] **D.** both trams and cars can continue

1028 CAR & MOTORCYCLE
What does this sign mean?

Mark one answer
- [ ] **A.** No motor vehicles
- [ ] **B.** End of motorway
- [ ] **C.** No through road
- [ ] **D.** End of bus lane

1029 CAR & MOTORCYCLE
Which of these signs means that the national speed limit applies?

Mark one answer
- [ ] **A.**
- [ ] **B.**

- [ ] **C.**
- [ ] **D.**

1030 CAR & MOTORCYCLE
What is the maximum speed on a single carriageway road?

Mark one answer
- [ ] **A.** 50mph
- [ ] **B.** 60mph
- [ ] **C.** 40mph
- [ ] **D.** 70mph

1031 CAR & MOTORCYCLE
What does this sign mean?

Mark one answer
- **A.** End of motorway
- **B.** End of restriction
- **C.** Lane ends ahead
- **D.** Free recovery ends

1032 CAR & MOTORCYCLE
This sign is advising you to

Mark one answer
- **A.** follow the route diversion
- **B.** follow the signs to the picnic area
- **C.** give way to pedestrians
- **D.** give way to cyclists

1033 CAR & MOTORCYCLE
Why would this temporary speed limit sign be shown?

Mark one answer
- **A.** To warn of the end of the motorway
- **B.** To warn you of a low bridge
- **C.** To warn you of a junction ahead
- **D.** To warn of road works ahead

1034 CAR & MOTORCYCLE
This traffic sign means there is

Mark one answer
- **A.** a compulsory maximum speed limit
- **B.** an advisory maximum speed limit
- **C.** a compulsory minimum speed limit
- **D.** an advised separation distance

1035 CAR & MOTORCYCLE
You see this sign at a crossroads. You should

Mark one answer
- **A.** maintain the same speed
- **B.** carry on with great care
- **C.** find another route
- **D.** telephone the police

1036 CAR & MOTORCYCLE
You are signalling to turn right in busy traffic. How would you confirm your intention safely?

Mark one answer
- **A.** Sound the horn
- **B.** Give an arm signal
- **C.** Flash your headlights
- **D.** Position over the centre line

1037
CAR & MOTORCYCLE
What does this sign mean?

Mark one answer
- A. Motorcycles only
- B. No cars
- C. Cars only
- D. No motorcycles

1038
CAR & MOTORCYCLE
You are on a motorway. You see this sign on a lorry that has stopped in the right-hand lane. You should

Mark one answer
- A. move into the right-hand lane
- B. stop behind the flashing lights
- C. pass the lorry on the left
- D. leave the motorway at the next exit

1039
CAR & MOTORCYCLE
You are on a motorway. Red flashing lights appear above your lane only. What should you do?

Mark one answer
- A. Continue in that lane and look for further information
- B. Move into another lane in good time
- C. Pull on to the hard shoulder
- D. Stop and wait for an instruction to proceed

1040
CAR & MOTORCYCLE
A red traffic light means

Mark one answer
- A. you must stop behind the white stop line
- B. you may go straight on if there is no other traffic
- C. you may turn left if it is safe to do so
- D. you must slow down and prepare to stop if traffic has started to cross

1041
CAR & MOTORCYCLE
The driver of this car is giving an arm signal. What are they about to do?

Mark one answer
- A. Turn to the right
- B. Turn to the left
- C. Go straight ahead
- D. Let pedestrians cross

1042 CAR & MOTORCYCLE
Which arm signal tells you that the car you are following is going to turn left?

Mark one answer

A. ☐

B. ☐

C. ☐

D. ☐

1043 CAR & MOTORCYCLE
When may you sound the horn?

Mark one answer

☐ A. To give you right of way
☐ B. To attract a friend's attention
☐ C. To warn others of your presence
☐ D. To make slower drivers move over

1044 CAR & MOTORCYCLE
You must not use your horn when you are stationary

Mark one answer

☐ A. unless a moving vehicle may cause you danger
☐ B. at any time whatsoever
☐ C. unless it is used only briefly
☐ D. except for signalling that you have just arrived

1045 CAR & MOTORCYCLE
What does this sign mean?

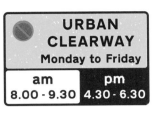

URBAN CLEARWAY
Monday to Friday

am	pm
8.00 - 9.30	4.30 - 6.30

Mark one answer

☐ A. You can park on the days and times shown
☐ B. No parking on the days and times shown
☐ C. No parking at all from Monday to Friday
☐ D. End of the urban clearway restrictions

1046 CAR & MOTORCYCLE
What does this sign mean?

Mark one answer

☐ A. Quayside or river bank
☐ B. Steep hill downwards
☐ C. Uneven road surface
☐ D. Road liable to flooding

1047 CAR & MOTORCYCLE
You see this amber traffic light ahead. Which light or lights will come on next?

Mark one answer

☐ A. Red alone
☐ B. Red and amber together
☐ C. Green and amber together
☐ D. Green alone

1048 CAR & MOTORCYCLE
This broken white line painted in the centre of the road means

Mark one answer
- A. oncoming vehicles have priority over you
- B. you should give priority to oncoming vehicles
- C. there is a hazard ahead of you
- D. the area is a national speed limit zone

1049 CAR & MOTORCYCLE
Which sign means you have priority over oncoming vehicles?

Mark one answer
- A.
- B.
- C.
- D.

1050 CAR & MOTORCYCLE
You see this signal overhead on the motorway. What does it mean?

Mark one answer
- A. Leave the motorway at the next exit
- B. All vehicles use the hard shoulder
- C. Sharp bend to the left ahead
- D. Stop, all lanes ahead closed

1051 CAR & MOTORCYCLE
A white line like this along the centre of the road is a

Mark one answer
- A. bus lane marking
- B. hazard warning
- C. give way marking
- D. lane marking

1052
CAR & MOTORCYCLE
What is the purpose of these yellow criss-cross lines on the road?

Mark one answer
- **A.** To make you more aware of the traffic lights
- **B.** To guide you into position as you turn
- **C.** To prevent the junction becoming blocked
- **D.** To show you where to stop when the lights change

1053
CAR & MOTORCYCLE
What is the reason for the yellow criss-cross lines painted on the road here?

Mark one answer
- **A.** To mark out an area for trams only
- **B.** To prevent queuing traffic from blocking the junction on the left
- **C.** To mark the entrance lane to a car park
- **D.** To warn you of the tram lines crossing the road

1054
CAR & MOTORCYCLE
What is the reason for the area marked in red and white along the centre of this road?

Mark one answer
- **A.** It is to separate traffic flowing in opposite directions
- **B.** It marks an area to be used by overtaking motorcyclists
- **C.** It is a temporary marking to warn of the road works
- **D.** It is separating the two sides of the dual carriageway

1055
CAR & MOTORCYCLE
Other drivers may sometimes flash their headlights at you. In which situation are they allowed to do this?

Mark one answer
- **A.** To warn of a radar speed trap ahead
- **B.** To show that they are giving way to you
- **C.** To warn you of their presence
- **D.** To let you know there is a fault with your vehicle

1056 CAR
You are approaching a zebra crossing where pedestrians are waiting. Which arm signal might you give?

Mark one answer

A.

B.

C.

D.

1057 CAR
The white line along the side of the road

Mark one answer

A. shows the edge of the carriageway
B. shows the approach to a hazard
C. means no parking
D. means no overtaking

1058 CAR
You see this white arrow on the road ahead. It means

Mark one answer

A. entrance on the left
B. all vehicles turn left
C. keep left of the hatched markings
D. road bending to the left

1059 CAR
How should you give an arm signal to turn left?

Mark one answer

A.

B.

C.

D.

1060 CAR
You are waiting at a T-junction. A vehicle is coming from the right with the left signal flashing. What should you do?

Mark one answer

A. Move out and accelerate hard
B. Wait until the vehicle starts to turn in
C. Pull out before the vehicle reaches the junction
D. Move out slowly

1061 CAR
When may you use hazard warning lights when driving?

Mark one answer
- [ ] **A.** Instead of sounding the horn in a built-up area between 11.30pm and 7am
- [ ] **B.** On a motorway or unrestricted dual carriageway, to warn of a hazard ahead
- [ ] **C.** On rural routes, after a warning sign of animals
- [ ] **D.** On the approach to toucan crossings where cyclists are waiting to cross

1062 CAR
You are driving on a motorway. There is a slow-moving vehicle ahead. On the back you see this sign. You should

Mark one answer
- [ ] **A.** pass on the right
- [ ] **B.** pass on the left
- [ ] **C.** leave at the next exit
- [ ] **D.** drive no further

1063 CAR
You should NOT normally stop on these markings near schools

SCHOOL KEEP CLEAR

Mark one answer
- [ ] **A.** except when picking up children
- [ ] **B.** under any circumstances
- [ ] **C.** unless there is nowhere else available
- [ ] **D.** except to set down children

1064 CAR
Why should you make sure that your indicators are cancelled after turning?

Mark one answer
- [ ] **A.** To avoid flattening the battery
- [ ] **B.** To avoid misleading other road users
- [ ] **C.** To avoid dazzling other road users
- [ ] **D.** To avoid damage to the indicator relay

1065 CAR
You are driving in busy traffic. You want to pull up on the left just after a junction on the left. When should you signal?

Mark one answer
- [ ] **A.** As you are passing or just after the junction
- [ ] **B.** Just before you reach the junction
- [ ] **C.** Well before you reach the junction
- [ ] **D.** It would be better not to signal at all

1066 MOTORCYCLE
After passing your motorcycle test you must exchange the pass certificate for a full motorcycle licence within

Mark one answer
- [ ] A. six months
- [ ] B. one year
- [ ] C. two years
- [ ] D. five years

1067 MOTORCYCLE
For which TWO of these must you show your motorcycle insurance certificate?

Mark two answers
- [ ] A. When you are taking your motorcycle test
- [ ] B. When buying or selling a machine
- [ ] C. When a police officer asks you for it
- [ ] D. When you are taxing your machine
- [ ] E. When having an MOT inspection

1068 MOTORCYCLE
You are a learner motorcyclist. The law states that you can carry a passenger when

Mark one answer
- [ ] A. your motorcycle is no larger than 125cc
- [ ] B. your pillion passenger is a full licence holder
- [ ] C. you have passed your test for a full licence
- [ ] D. you have had three years' experience of riding

1069 MOTORCYCLE
You hold a provisional motorcycle licence. This means you must NOT

Mark three answers
- [ ] A. exceed 30mph
- [ ] B. ride on a motorway
- [ ] C. ride after dark
- [ ] D. carry a pillion passenger
- [ ] E. ride without 'L' plates displayed

1070 MOTORCYCLE
Which of the following information is found on your motorcycle registration document?

Mark three answers
- [ ] A. Make and model
- [ ] B. Service history record
- [ ] C. Ignition key security number
- [ ] D. Engine size and number
- [ ] E. Purchase price
- [ ] F. Year of first registration

1071 MOTORCYCLE
A theory test pass certificate is valid for

Mark one answer
- [ ] A. two years
- [ ] B. three years
- [ ] C. four years
- [ ] D. five years

1072 MOTORCYCLE
A full category A1 licence will allow you to ride a motorcycle up to

Mark one answer
- [ ] A. 125cc
- [ ] B. 250cc
- [ ] C. 350cc
- [ ] D. 425cc

1073 MOTORCYCLE
Compulsory Basic Training (CBT) can only be carried out by

NI

Mark one answer
- [ ] A. any ADI (Approved Driving Instructor)
- [ ] B. any road safety officer
- [ ] C. any DSA (Driving Standards Agency) approved training body
- [ ] D. any motorcycle main dealer

1074 MOTORCYCLE
Before riding anyone else's motorcycle you should make sure that

Mark one answer
- A. the owner has third party insurance cover
- B. your own motorcycle has insurance cover
- C. the motorcycle is insured for your use
- D. the owner has the insurance documents with them

1075 MOTORCYCLE
Vehicle excise duty is often called 'Road Tax' or 'The Tax Disc'. You must

Mark one answer
- A. keep it with your registration document
- B. display it clearly on your motorcycle
- C. keep it concealed safely in your motorcycle
- D. carry it on you at all times

1076 MOTORCYCLE
Motorcycles must FIRST have an MOT test certificate when they are

NI

Mark one answer
- A. one year old
- B. three years old
- C. five years old
- D. seven years old

1077 MOTORCYCLE
Your motorcycle needs a current MOT certificate. You do not have one. Until you do have one you will not be able to renew your

Mark one answer
- A. driving licence
- B. motorcycle insurance
- C. road tax disc
- D. motorcycle registration document

1078 MOTORCYCLE
Which THREE of the following do you need before you can ride legally?

Mark three answers
- A. A valid driving licence with signature
- B. A valid tax disc displayed on your motorcycle
- C. Proof of your identity
- D. Proper insurance cover
- E. Breakdown cover
- F. A vehicle handbook

1079 MOTORCYCLE
Which THREE pieces of information are found on a registration document?

Mark three answers
- A. Registered keeper
- B. Make of the motorcycle
- C. Service history details
- D. Date of the MOT
- E. Type of insurance cover
- F. Engine size

1080 MOTORCYCLE
You have a duty to contact the licensing authority when

Mark three answers
- A. you go abroad on holiday
- B. you change your motorcycle
- C. you change your name
- D. your job status is changed
- E. your permanent address changes
- F. your job involves travelling abroad

1081 MOTORCYCLE
Your motorcycle is insured third party only. This covers

Mark two answers
- [ ] **A.** damage to your motorcycle
- [ ] **B.** damage to other vehicles
- [ ] **C.** injury to yourself
- [ ] **D.** injury to others
- [ ] **E.** all damage and injury

1082 MOTORCYCLE
Your motorcycle insurance policy has an excess of £100. What does this mean?

Mark one answer
- [ ] **A.** The insurance company will pay the first £100 of any claim
- [ ] **B.** You will be paid £100 if you do not have an accident
- [ ] **C.** Your motorcycle is insured for a value of £100 if it is stolen
- [ ] **D.** You will have to pay the first £100 of any claim

1083 MOTORCYCLE
When you apply to renew your motorcycle excise licence (tax disc) you must produce

Mark one answer
- [ ] **A.** a valid insurance certificate
- [ ] **B.** the old tax disc
- [ ] **C.** the motorcycle handbook
- [ ] **D.** a valid driving licence

1084 MOTORCYCLE
What is the legal minimum insurance cover you must have to ride on public roads?

Mark one answer
- [ ] **A.** Third party, fire and theft
- [ ] **B.** Fully comprehensive
- [ ] **C.** Third party only
- [ ] **D.** Personal injury cover

1085 MOTORCYCLE
You have a CBT (Compulsory Basic Training) certificate. How long is it valid?

Mark one answer
- [ ] **A.** 1 year
- [ ] **B.** 2 years   **NI**
- [ ] **C.** 3 years
- [ ] **D.** 4 years

1086 MOTORCYCLE
Your motorcycle road tax is due to expire. As well as the renewal form and fee you will also need to produce an MOT (if required). What else will you need?

Mark one answer
- [ ] **A.** Proof of purchase receipt
- [ ] **B.** Compulsory Basic Training certificate
- [ ] **C.** A valid certificate of insurance
- [ ] **D.** The vehicle registration document

1087 MOTORCYCLE
A vehicle registration document will show

Mark one answer
- [ ] **A.** the service history
- [ ] **B.** the year of first registration
- [ ] **C.** the purchase price
- [ ] **D.** the tyre sizes

1088 MOTORCYCLE
Which one of these details would you expect to see on an MOT?

Mark one answer
- [ ] **A.** Your name, address and telephone number
- [ ] **B.** The vehicle registration and chassis number
- [ ] **C.** The previous owners' details
- [ ] **D.** The next due date for servicing

1089 MOTORCYCLE
What is the purpose of having a vehicle test certificate (MOT)?

Mark one answer

- A. To make sure your motorcycle is roadworthy
- B. To certify how many miles per gallon it does
- C. To prove you own the motorcycle
- D. To allow you to park in restricted areas

1090 MOTORCYCLE
You want a licence to ride a large motorcycle via Direct Access. You will

Mark one answer **NI**

- A. not require 'L' plates if you have passed a car test
- B. require 'L' plates only when learning on your own machine
- C. require 'L' plates while learning with a qualified instructor
- D. not require 'L' plates if you have passed a moped test

1091 MOTORCYCLE
A theory test pass certificate will not be valid after

Mark one answer

- A. 6 months
- B. 1 year
- C. 18 months
- D. 2 years

1092 MOTORCYCLE
Before taking a practical motorcycle test you need

Mark one answer **NI**

- A. a full moped licence
- B. a full car licence
- C. a CBT (Compulsory Basic Training) certificate
- D. 12 months' riding experience

1093 MOTORCYCLE
You must notify the licensing authority when

Mark three answers

- A. your health affects your riding
- B. your eyesight does not meet a set standard
- C. you intend lending your motorcycle
- D. your motorcycle requires an MOT certificate
- E. you change your motorcycle

1094 MOTORCYCLE
You have just passed your practical motorcycle test. This is your first full licence. Within two years you get six penalty points. You will have to

Mark two answers

- A. retake only your theory test
- B. retake your theory and practical tests
- C. retake only your practical test
- D. reapply for your full licence immediately
- E. reapply for your provisional licence

1095 MOTORCYCLE
A motorcyclist may only carry a pillion passenger when

Mark three answers **NI**

- A. the rider has successfully completed CBT (Compulsory Basic Training)
- B. the rider holds a full licence for the category of motorcycle
- C. the motorcycle is fitted with rear footrests
- D. the rider has a full car licence and is over 21
- E. there is a proper passenger seat fitted
- F. there is no sidecar fitted to the machine

1096 CAR & MOTORCYCLE
An MOT certificate is normally valid for

Mark one answer

- A. three years after the date it was issued
- B. 10,000 miles
- C. one year after the date it was issued
- D. 30,000 miles

1097 CAR & MOTORCYCLE
A cover note is a document issued before you receive your

Mark one answer
- A. driving licence
- B. insurance certificate
- C. registration document
- D. MOT certificate

1098 CAR & MOTORCYCLE
A police officer asks to see your documents. You do not have them with you. You may produce them at a police station within

Mark one answer
- A. 5 days
- B. 7 days
- C. 14 days
- D. 21 days

1099 CAR & MOTORCYCLE
You have just passed your practical test. You do not hold a full licence in another category. Within two years you get six penalty points on your licence. What will you have to do?

Mark two answers
- A. Retake only your theory test
- B. Retake your theory and practical tests
- C. Retake only your practical test
- D. Reapply for your full licence immediately
- E. Reapply for your provisional licence

1100 CAR
To drive on the road learners MUST

Mark one answer
- A. have NO penalty points on their licence
- B. have taken professional instruction
- C. have a signed, valid provisional licence
- D. apply for a driving test within 12 months

1101 CAR
Before driving anyone else's motor vehicle you should make sure that

Mark one answer
- A. the vehicle owner has third party insurance cover
- B. your own vehicle has insurance cover
- C. the vehicle is insured for your use
- D. the owner has left the insurance documents in the vehicle

1102 CAR
Your car needs an MOT certificate. If you drive without one this could invalidate your

Mark one answer
- A. vehicle service record
- B. insurance
- C. road tax disc
- D. vehicle registration document

1103 CAR
When is it legal to drive a car over three years old without an MOT certificate?

Mark one answer **NI**
- A. Up to seven days after the old certificate has run out
- B. When driving to an MOT centre to arrange an appointment
- C. Just after buying a second-hand car with no MOT
- D. When driving to an appointment at an MOT centre

1104 CAR
To supervise a learner driver you must

Mark two answers

- A. have held a full licence for at least 3 years
- B. be at least 21 years old
- C. be an approved driving instructor
- D. hold an advanced driving certificate

1105 CAR
How old must you be to supervise a learner driver?

Mark one answer

- A. 18 years old
- B. 19 years old
- C. 20 years old
- D. 21 years old

1106 CAR
A newly qualified driver must

Mark one answer

- A. display green 'L' plates
- B. not exceed 40mph for 12 months
- C. be accompanied on a motorway
- D. have valid motor insurance

1107 CAR
You have third party insurance. What does this cover?

Mark three answers

- A. Damage to your own vehicle
- B. Damage to your vehicle by fire
- C. Injury to another person
- D. Damage to someone's property
- E. Damage to other vehicles
- F. Injury to yourself

1108 CAR
For which TWO of these must you show your motor insurance certificate?

Mark two answers

- A. When you are taking your driving test
- B. When buying or selling a vehicle
- C. When a police officer asks you for it
- D. When you are taxing your vehicle
- E. When having an MOT inspection

1109 CAR
Vehicle excise duty is often called 'Road Tax' or 'The Tax Disc'. You must

Mark one answer

- A. keep it with your registration document
- B. display it clearly on your vehicle
- C. keep it concealed safely in your vehicle
- D. carry it on you at all times

1110 CAR
Motor cars must first have an MOT test certificate when they are

NI

Mark one answer

- A. one year old
- B. three years old
- C. five years old
- D. seven years old

1111 CAR
Your vehicle needs a current MOT certificate. You do not have one. Until you do have one you will not be able to renew your

Mark one answer

- A. driving licence
- B. vehicle insurance
- C. road tax disc
- D. vehicle registration document

1112 CAR
Which THREE pieces of information are found on a vehicle registration document?

Mark three answers

- [ ] A. Registered keeper
- [ ] B. Make of the vehicle
- [ ] C. Service history details
- [ ] D. Date of the MOT
- [ ] E. Type of insurance cover
- [ ] F. Engine size

1113 CAR
You have a duty to contact the licensing authority when

Mark three answers

- [ ] A. you go abroad on holiday
- [ ] B. you change your vehicle
- [ ] C. you change your name
- [ ] D. your job status is changed
- [ ] E. your permanent address changes
- [ ] F. your job involves travelling abroad

1114 CAR
You must notify the licensing authority when

Mark three answers

- [ ] A. your health affects your driving
- [ ] B. your eyesight does not meet a set standard
- [ ] C. you intend lending your vehicle
- [ ] D. your vehicle requires an MOT certificate
- [ ] E. you change your vehicle

1115 CAR
Your vehicle is insured third party only. This covers

Mark two answers

- [ ] A. damage to your vehicle
- [ ] B. damage to other vehicles
- [ ] C. injury to yourself
- [ ] D. injury to others
- [ ] E. all damage and injury

1116 CAR
Your motor insurance policy has an excess of £100. What does this mean?

Mark one answer

- [ ] A. The insurance company will pay the first £100 of any claim
- [ ] B. You will be paid £100 if you do not have an accident
- [ ] C. Your vehicle is insured for a value of £100 if it is stolen
- [ ] D. You will have to pay the first £100 of any claim

1117 CAR
When you apply to renew your vehicle excise licence (tax disc) you must produce

Mark one answer

- [ ] A. a valid insurance certificate
- [ ] B. the old tax disc
- [ ] C. the vehicle handbook
- [ ] D. a valid driving licence

1118 CAR
What is the legal minimum insurance cover you must have to drive on public roads?

Mark one answer

- [ ] A. Third party, fire and theft
- [ ] B. Comprehensive
- [ ] C. Third party only
- [ ] D. Personal injury cover

1119 CAR
Which THREE of the following do you need before you can drive legally?

Mark three answers
- [ ] **A.** A valid driving licence with signature
- [ ] **B.** A valid tax disc displayed on your vehicle
- [ ] **C.** A vehicle service record
- [ ] **D.** Proper insurance cover
- [ ] **E.** Breakdown cover
- [ ] **F.** A vehicle handbook

1120 CAR
The cost of your insurance may reduce if you

Mark one answer **NI**
- [ ] **A.** are under 25 years old
- [ ] **B.** do not wear glasses
- [ ] **C.** pass the driving test first time
- [ ] **D.** take the Pass Plus scheme

1121 CAR
Which of the following may reduce the cost of your insurance?

Mark one answer **NI**
- [ ] **A.** Having a valid MOT certificate
- [ ] **B.** Taking a Pass Plus course
- [ ] **C.** Driving a powerful car
- [ ] **D.** Having penalty points on your licence

1122 CAR
The Pass Plus scheme has been created for new drivers. What is its main purpose?

Mark one answer **NI**
- [ ] **A.** To allow you to drive faster
- [ ] **B.** To allow you to carry passengers
- [ ] **C.** To improve your basic skills
- [ ] **D.** To let you drive on motorways

1123 CAR & MOTORCYCLE
How long will a Statutory Off Road Notification (SORN) last for?

Mark one answer
- [ ] **A.** 12 months
- [ ] **B.** 24 months
- [ ] **C.** 3 years
- [ ] **D.** 10 years

1124 CAR & MOTORCYCLE
What is a Statutory Off Road Notification (SORN) declaration?

Mark one answer **NI**
- [ ] **A.** A notification to tell VOSA that a vehicle does not have a current MOT
- [ ] **B.** Information kept by the police about the owner of the vehicle
- [ ] **C.** A notification to tell DVLA that a vehicle is not being used on the road
- [ ] **D.** Information held by insurance companies to check the vehicle is insured

1125 CAR & MOTORCYCLE
A Statutory Off Road Notification (SORN) declaration is

Mark one answer **NI**
- [ ] **A.** to tell DVLA that your vehicle is being used on the road but the MOT has expired
- [ ] **B.** to tell DVLA that you no longer own the vehicle
- [ ] **C.** to tell DVLA that your vehicle is not being used on the road
- [ ] **D.** to tell DVLA that you are buying a personal number plate

1126 CAR & MOTORCYCLE
A Statutory Off Road Notification (SORN) is valid

Mark one answer
- [ ] **A.** for as long as the vehicle has an MOT
- [ ] **B.** for 12 months only
- [ ] **C.** only if the vehicle is more than 3 years old
- [ ] **D.** provided the vehicle is insured

1127 CAR & MOTORCYCLE
A Statutory Off Road Notification (SORN) will last

Mark one answer

- A. for the life of the vehicle
- B. for as long as you own the vehicle
- C. for 12 months only
- D. until the vehicle warranty expires

1128 CAR & MOTORCYCLE
What is the maximum specified fine for driving without insurance?

Mark one answer **NI**

- A. £50
- B. £500
- C. £1,000
- D. £5,000

1129 CAR
You claim on your insurance to have your car repaired. Your policy has an excess of £100. What does this mean?

Mark one answer

- A. The insurance company will pay the first £100 of any claim
- B. You will be paid £100 if you do not claim within one year
- C. Your vehicle is insured for a value of £100 if it is stolen
- D. You will have to pay the first £100 of the cost of repair to your car

1130 CAR & MOTORCYCLE
When should you update your Vehicle Registration Certificate (V5C)?

Mark one answer

- A. When you pass your driving test
- B. When you move house
- C. When your vehicle needs an MOT
- D. When you have an accident

1131 CAR & MOTORCYCLE
Who is legally responsible for ensuring that a Vehicle Registration Certificate (V5C) is updated?

Mark one answer

- A. The registered vehicle keeper
- B. The vehicle manufacturer
- C. Your insurance company
- D. The licensing authority

1132 CAR
The Pass Plus scheme is designed to

Mark one answer **NI**

- A. give you a discount on your MOT
- B. improve your basic driving skills
- C. increase your mechanical knowledge
- D. allow you to drive anyone else's vehicle

1133 CAR
By taking part in the Pass Plus scheme you will

Mark one answer **NI**

- A. never get any points on your licence
- B. be able to service your own car
- C. allow you to drive anyone else's vehicle
- D. improve your basic driving skills

1134 CAR
The Pass Plus scheme is aimed at all newly qualified drivers. It enables them to

Mark one answer **NI**

- A. widen their driving experience
- B. supervise a learner driver
- C. increase their insurance premiums
- D. avoid mechanical breakdowns

1135 CAR

New drivers can take further training after passing the practical test. A Pass Plus course will help to

Mark two answers NI

- [ ] **A.** improve your basic skills
- [ ] **B.** widen your experience
- [ ] **C.** increase your insurance premiums
- [ ] **D.** get cheaper road tax

1136 CAR

The Pass Plus Scheme is operated by DSA for newly qualified drivers. It is intended to

Mark one answer NI

- [ ] **A.** improve your basic skills
- [ ] **B.** reduce the cost of your driving licence
- [ ] **C.** prevent you from paying congestion charges
- [ ] **D.** allow you to supervise a learner driver

1137 MOTORCYCLE
Your motorcycle has broken down on a motorway. How will you know the direction of the nearest emergency telephone?

Mark one answer
- [ ] **A.** By walking with the flow of traffic
- [ ] **B.** By following an arrow on a marker post
- [ ] **C.** By walking against the flow of traffic
- [ ] **D.** By remembering where the last phone was

1138 MOTORCYCLE
You are travelling on a motorway. A bag falls from your motorcycle. There are valuables in the bag. What should you do?

Mark one answer
- [ ] **A.** Go back carefully and collect the bag as quickly as possible
- [ ] **B.** Stop wherever you are and pick up the bag, but only when there is a safe gap
- [ ] **C.** Stop on the hard shoulder and use the emergency telephone to inform the police
- [ ] **D.** Stop on the hard shoulder and then retrieve the bag yourself

1139 MOTORCYCLE
You should use the engine cut-out switch to

Mark one answer
- [ ] **A.** stop the engine in an emergency
- [ ] **B.** stop the engine on short journeys
- [ ] **C.** save wear on the ignition switch
- [ ] **D.** start the engine if you lose the key

1140 MOTORCYCLE
You are involved in an accident. How can you reduce the risk of fire to your motorcycle?

Mark one answer
- [ ] **A.** Keep the engine running
- [ ] **B.** Open the choke
- [ ] **C.** Turn the fuel tap to reserve
- [ ] **D.** Use the engine cut-out switch

1141 MOTORCYCLE
You are riding on a motorway. The car in front switches on its hazard warning lights whilst moving. This means

Mark one answer
- [ ] **A.** they are going to take the next exit
- [ ] **B.** there is a danger ahead
- [ ] **C.** there is a police car in the left lane
- [ ] **D.** they are trying to change lanes

1142 MOTORCYCLE
You are on the motorway. Luggage falls from your motorcycle. What should you do?

Mark one answer
- [ ] **A.** Stop at the next emergency telephone and contact the police
- [ ] **B.** Stop on the motorway and put on hazard lights whilst you pick it up
- [ ] **C.** Walk back up the motorway to pick it up
- [ ] **D.** Pull up on the hard shoulder and wave traffic down

1143 MOTORCYCLE
You are involved in an accident with another vehicle. Someone is injured. Your motorcycle is damaged. Which FOUR of the following should you find out?

Mark four answers

- A. Whether the driver owns the other vehicle involved
- B. The other driver's name, address and telephone number
- C. The make and registration number of the other vehicle
- D. The occupation of the other driver
- E. The details of the other driver's vehicle insurance
- F. Whether the other driver is licensed to drive

1144 MOTORCYCLE
You have broken down on a motorway. When you use the emergency telephone you will be asked

Mark three answers

- A. for the number on the telephone that you are using
- B. for your driving licence details
- C. for the name of your vehicle insurance company
- D. for details of yourself and your motorcycle
- E. whether you belong to a motoring organisation

1145 MOTORCYCLE
You are on a motorway. When can you use hazard warning lights?

Mark one answer

- A. When a vehicle is following too closely
- B. When you slow down quickly because of danger ahead
- C. When you are being towed by another vehicle
- D. When riding on the hard shoulder

1146 MOTORCYCLE
Your motorcycle breaks down in a tunnel. What should you do?

Mark one answer

- A. Stay with your motorcycle and wait for the police
- B. Stand in the lane behind your motorcycle to warn others
- C. Stand in front of your motorcycle to warn oncoming drivers
- D. Switch on hazard lights then go and call for help immediately

1147 MOTORCYCLE
You are riding through a tunnel. Your motorcycle breaks down. What should you do?

Mark one answer

- A. Switch on hazard warning lights
- B. Remain on your motorcycle
- C. Wait for the police to find you
- D. Rely on CCTV cameras seeing you

1148 CAR & MOTORCYCLE
At the scene of an accident you should

Mark one answer

- A. not put yourself at risk
- B. go to those casualties who are screaming
- C. pull everybody out of their vehicles
- D. leave vehicle engines switched on

1149 CAR & MOTORCYCLE
You are the first to arrive at the scene of an accident. Which FOUR of these should you do?

Mark four answers
- A. Leave as soon as another motorist arrives
- B. Switch off the vehicle engine(s)
- C. Move uninjured people away from the vehicle(s)
- D. Call the emergency services
- E. Warn other traffic

1150 CAR & MOTORCYCLE
An accident has just happened. An injured person is lying in a busy road. What is the FIRST thing you should do to help?

Mark one answer
- A. Treat the person for shock
- B. Warn other traffic
- C. Place them in the recovery position
- D. Make sure the injured person is kept warm

1151 CAR & MOTORCYCLE
You are the first person to arrive at an accident where people are badly injured. Which THREE should you do?

Mark three answers
- A. Switch on your own hazard warning lights
- B. Make sure that someone telephones for an ambulance
- C. Try and get people who are injured to drink something
- D. Move the people who are injured clear of their vehicles
- E. Get people who are not injured clear of the scene

1152 CAR & MOTORCYCLE
You arrive at the scene of a motorcycle accident. The rider is injured. When should the helmet be removed?

Mark one answer
- A. Only when it is essential
- B. Always straight away
- C. Only when the motorcyclist asks
- D. Always, unless they are in shock

1153 CAR & MOTORCYCLE
You arrive at a serious motorcycle accident. The motorcyclist is unconscious and bleeding. Your main priorities should be to

Mark three answers
- A. try to stop the bleeding
- B. make a list of witnesses
- C. check the casualty's breathing
- D. take the numbers of the vehicles involved
- E. sweep up any loose debris
- F. check the casualty's airways

1154 CAR & MOTORCYCLE
You arrive at an accident. A motorcyclist is unconscious. Your FIRST priority is the casualty's

Mark one answer
- A. breathing
- B. bleeding
- C. broken bones
- D. bruising

1155 CAR & MOTORCYCLE
At an accident a casualty is unconscious. Which THREE of the following should you check urgently?

Mark three answers
- A. Circulation
- B. Airway
- C. Shock
- D. Breathing
- E. Broken bones

1156 CAR & MOTORCYCLE
You arrive at the scene of an accident. It has just happened and someone is unconscious. Which of the following should be given urgent priority to help them?

Mark three answers
- A. Clear the airway and keep it open
- B. Try to get them to drink water
- C. Check that they are breathing
- D. Look for any witnesses
- E. Stop any heavy bleeding
- F. Take the numbers of vehicles involved

1157 CAR & MOTORCYCLE
At an accident someone is unconscious. Your main priorities should be to

Mark three answers
- A. sweep up the broken glass
- B. take the names of witnesses
- C. count the number of vehicles involved
- D. check the airway is clear
- E. make sure they are breathing
- F. stop any heavy bleeding

1158 CAR & MOTORCYCLE
You have stopped at the scene of an accident to give help. Which THREE things should you do?

Mark three answers
- A. Keep injured people warm and comfortable
- B. Keep injured people calm by talking to them reassuringly
- C. Keep injured people on the move by walking them around
- D. Give injured people a warm drink
- E. Make sure that injured people are not left alone

1159 CAR & MOTORCYCLE
You arrive at the scene of an accident. It has just happened and someone is injured. Which THREE of the following should be given urgent priority?

Mark three answers
- A. Stop any severe bleeding
- B. Get them a warm drink
- C. Check that their breathing is OK
- D. Take numbers of vehicles involved
- E. Look for witnesses
- F. Clear their airway and keep it open

1160 CAR & MOTORCYCLE
At an accident a casualty has stopped breathing. You should

Mark two answers
- A. remove anything that is blocking the mouth
- B. keep the head tilted forwards as far as possible
- C. raise the legs to help with circulation
- D. try to give the casualty something to drink
- E. tilt the head back gently to clear the airway

1161 CAR & MOTORCYCLE
You are at the scene of an accident. Someone is suffering from shock. You should

Mark four answers
- A. reassure them constantly
- B. offer them a cigarette
- C. keep them warm
- D. avoid moving them if possible
- E. avoid leaving them alone
- F. give them a warm drink

1162 CAR & MOTORCYCLE
Which of the following should you NOT do at the scene of an accident?

Mark one answer

- A. Warn other traffic by switching on your hazard warning lights
- B. Call the emergency services immediately
- C. Offer someone a cigarette to calm them down
- D. Ask drivers to switch off their engines

1163 CAR & MOTORCYCLE
There has been an accident. The driver is suffering from shock. You should

Mark two answers

- A. give them a drink
- B. reassure them
- C. not leave them alone
- D. offer them a cigarette
- E. ask who caused the accident

1164 CAR & MOTORCYCLE
You have to treat someone for shock at the scene of an accident. You should

Mark one answer

- A. reassure them constantly
- B. walk them around to calm them down
- C. give them something cold to drink
- D. cool them down as soon as possible

1165 CAR & MOTORCYCLE
You arrive at the scene of a motorcycle accident. No other vehicle is involved. The rider is unconscious, lying in the middle of the road. The first thing you should do is

Mark one answer

- A. move the rider out of the road
- B. warn other traffic
- C. clear the road of debris
- D. give the rider reassurance

1166 CAR & MOTORCYCLE
At an accident a small child is not breathing. When giving mouth to mouth you should breathe

Mark one answer

- A. sharply
- B. gently
- C. heavily
- D. rapidly

1167 CAR & MOTORCYCLE
To start mouth to mouth on a casualty you should

Mark three answers

- A. tilt their head forward
- B. clear the airway
- C. turn them on their side
- D. tilt their head back gently
- E. pinch the nostrils together
- F. put their arms across their chest

1168 CAR & MOTORCYCLE
When you are giving mouth to mouth you should only stop when

Mark one answer

- A. you think the casualty is dead
- B. the casualty can breathe without help
- C. the casualty has turned blue
- D. you think the ambulance is coming

1169 CAR & MOTORCYCLE
You arrive at the scene of an accident. There has been an engine fire and someone's hands and arms have been burnt. You should NOT

Mark one answer
- A. douse the burn thoroughly with cool liquid
- B. lay the casualty down
- C. remove anything sticking to the burn
- D. reassure them constantly

1170 CAR & MOTORCYCLE
You arrive at an accident where someone is suffering from severe burns. You should

Mark one answer
- A. apply lotions to the injury
- B. burst any blisters
- C. remove anything stuck to the burns
- D. douse the burns with cool liquid

1171 CAR & MOTORCYCLE
You arrive at the scene of an accident. A pedestrian has a severe bleeding wound on their leg, although it is not broken. What should you do?

Mark two answers
- A. Dab the wound to stop bleeding
- B. Keep both legs flat on the ground
- C. Apply firm pressure to the wound
- D. Raise the leg to lessen bleeding
- E. Fetch them a warm drink

1172 CAR & MOTORCYCLE
You arrive at the scene of a crash. Someone is bleeding badly from an arm wound. There is nothing embedded in it. What should you do?

Mark one answer
- A. Apply pressure over the wound and keep the arm down
- B. Dab the wound
- C. Get them a drink
- D. Apply pressure over the wound and raise the arm

1173 CAR & MOTORCYCLE
At an accident a casualty is unconscious but still breathing. You should only move them if

Mark one answer
- A. an ambulance is on its way
- B. bystanders advise you to
- C. there is further danger
- D. bystanders will help you to

1174 CAR & MOTORCYCLE
At an accident you suspect a casualty has back injuries. The area is safe. You should

Mark one answer
- A. offer them a drink
- B. not move them
- C. raise their legs
- D. offer them a cigarette

1175 CAR & MOTORCYCLE
At an accident it is important to look after the casualty. When the area is safe, you should

Mark one answer
- A. get them out of the vehicle
- B. give them a drink
- C. give them something to eat
- D. keep them in the vehicle

1176 CAR & MOTORCYCLE
A tanker is involved in an accident. Which sign would show that the tanker is carrying dangerous goods?

Mark one answer

A.

B.
LONG VEHICLE

2YE
1089

C.

D.

1177 CAR & MOTORCYCLE
The police may ask you to produce which three of these documents following an accident?

Mark three answers
- A. Vehicle registration document
- B. Driving licence
- C. Theory test certificate
- D. Insurance certificate
- E. MOT test certificate
- F. Road tax disc

1178 CAR & MOTORCYCLE
You see a car on the hard shoulder of a motorway with a HELP pennant displayed. This means the driver is most likely to be

Mark one answer
- A. a disabled person
- B. first aid trained
- C. a foreign visitor
- D. a rescue patrol person

1179 CAR & MOTORCYCLE
On the motorway the hard shoulder should be used

Mark one answer
- A. to answer a mobile phone
- B. when an emergency arises
- C. for a short rest when tired
- D. to check a road atlas

1180 CAR & MOTORCYCLE
For which TWO should you use hazard warning lights?

Mark two answers
- A. When you slow down quickly on a motorway because of a hazard ahead
- B. When you have broken down
- C. When you wish to stop on double yellow lines
- D. When you need to park on the pavement

1181 CAR & MOTORCYCLE
When are you allowed to use hazard warning lights?

Mark one answer

- A. When stopped and temporarily obstructing traffic
- B. When travelling during darkness without headlights
- C. When parked for shopping on double yellow lines
- D. When travelling slowly because you are lost

1182 CAR & MOTORCYCLE
You are on a motorway. A large box falls on to the road from a lorry. The lorry does not stop. You should

Mark one answer

- A. go to the next emergency telephone and inform the police
- B. catch up with the lorry and try to get the driver's attention
- C. stop close to the box until the police arrive
- D. pull over to the hard shoulder, then remove the box

1183 CAR & MOTORCYCLE
There has been an accident. A motorcyclist is lying injured and unconscious. Unless it's essential, why should you usually not attempt to remove their helmet?

Mark one answer

- A. Because they may not want you to
- B. This could result in more serious injury
- C. They will get too cold if you do this
- D. Because you could scratch the helmet

1184 CAR & MOTORCYCLE
After an accident, someone is unconscious in their vehicle. When should you call the emergency services?

Mark one answer

- A. Only as a last resort
- B. As soon as possible
- C. After you have woken them up
- D. After checking for broken bones

1185 CAR & MOTORCYCLE
An accident casualty has an injured arm. They can move it freely, but it is bleeding. Why should you get them to keep it in a raised position?

Mark one answer

- A. Because it will ease the pain
- B. It will help them to be seen more easily
- C. To stop them touching other people
- D. It will help to reduce the bleeding

1186 CAR & MOTORCYCLE
You are going through a congested tunnel and have to stop. What should you do?

Mark one answer

- A. Pull up very close to the vehicle in front to save space
- B. Ignore any message signs as they are never up to date
- C. Keep a safe distance from the vehicle in front
- D. Make a U-turn and find another route

1187 CAR & MOTORCYCLE
You are going through a tunnel. What should you look out for that warns of accidents or congestion?

Mark one answer

- A. Hazard warning lines
- B. Other drivers flashing their lights
- C. Variable message signs
- D. Areas marked with hatch markings

1188 CAR & MOTORCYCLE
You are going through a tunnel. What systems are provided to warn of any accidents or congestion?

Mark one answer

- A. Double white centre lines
- B. Variable message signs
- C. Chevron 'distance markers'
- D. Rumble strips

1189 CAR
While driving, a warning light on your vehicle's instrument panel comes on. You should

Mark one answer

- A. continue if the engine sounds all right
- B. hope that it is just a temporary electrical fault
- C. deal with the problem when there is more time
- D. check out the problem quickly and safely

1190 CAR
You have broken down on a two-way road. You have a warning triangle. You should place the warning triangle at least how far from your vehicle?

Mark one answer

- A. 5 metres (16 feet)
- B. 25 metres (82 feet)
- C. 45 metres (147 feet)
- D. 100 metres (328 feet)

1191 CAR
You break down on a level crossing. The lights have not yet begun to flash. Which THREE things should you do?

Mark three answers

- A. Telephone the signal operator
- B. Leave your vehicle and get everyone clear
- C. Walk down the track and signal the next train
- D. Move the vehicle if a signal operator tells you to
- E. Tell drivers behind what has happened

1192 CAR
Your vehicle has broken down on an automatic railway level crossing. What should you do FIRST?

Mark one answer

- A. Get everyone out of the vehicle and clear of the crossing
- B. Phone the signal operator so that trains can be stopped
- C. Walk along the track to give warning to any approaching trains
- D. Try to push the vehicle clear of the crossing as soon as possible

1193 CAR
Your tyre bursts while you are driving. Which TWO things should you do?

Mark two answers
- [ ] **A.** Pull on the handbrake
- [ ] **B.** Brake as quickly as possible
- [ ] **C.** Pull up slowly at the side of the road
- [ ] **D.** Hold the steering wheel firmly to keep control
- [ ] **E.** Continue on at a normal speed

1194 CAR
Which TWO things should you do when a front tyre bursts?

Mark two answers
- [ ] **A.** Apply the handbrake to stop the vehicle
- [ ] **B.** Brake firmly and quickly
- [ ] **C.** Let the vehicle roll to a stop
- [ ] **D.** Hold the steering wheel lightly
- [ ] **E.** Grip the steering wheel firmly

1195 CAR
Your vehicle has a puncture on a motorway. What should you do?

Mark one answer
- [ ] **A.** Drive slowly to the next service area to get assistance
- [ ] **B.** Pull up on the hard shoulder. Change the wheel as quickly as possible
- [ ] **C.** Pull up on the hard shoulder. Use the emergency phone to get assistance
- [ ] **D.** Switch on your hazard lights. Stop in your lane

1196 CAR
Which of these items should you carry in your vehicle for use in the event of an accident?

Mark three answers
- [ ] **A.** Road map
- [ ] **B.** Can of petrol
- [ ] **C.** Jump leads
- [ ] **D.** Fire extinguisher
- [ ] **E.** First aid kit
- [ ] **F.** Warning triangle

1197 CAR
You are in an accident on a two-way road. You have a warning triangle with you. At what distance before the obstruction should you place the warning triangle?

Mark one answer
- [ ] **A.** 25 metres (82 feet)
- [ ] **B.** 45 metres (147 feet)
- [ ] **C.** 100 metres (328 feet)
- [ ] **D.** 150 metres (492 feet)

1198 CAR
You have broken down on a two-way road. You have a warning triangle. It should be displayed

Mark one answer
- [ ] **A.** on the roof of your vehicle
- [ ] **B.** at least 150 metres (492 feet) behind your vehicle
- [ ] **C.** at least 45 metres (147 feet) behind your vehicle
- [ ] **D.** just behind your vehicle

1199 CAR
You have stalled in the middle of a level crossing and cannot restart the engine. The warning bell starts to ring. You should

Mark one answer

- **A.** get out and clear of the crossing
- **B.** run down the track to warn the signal operator
- **C.** carry on trying to restart the engine
- **D.** push the vehicle clear of the crossing

1200 CAR
You are on the motorway. Luggage falls from your vehicle. What should you do?

Mark one answer

- **A.** Stop at the next emergency telephone and contact the police
- **B.** Stop on the motorway and put on hazard lights while you pick it up
- **C.** Walk back up the motorway to pick it up
- **D.** Pull up on the hard shoulder and wave traffic down

1201 CAR
You are on a motorway. When can you use hazard warning lights?

Mark two answers

- **A.** When a vehicle is following too closely
- **B.** When you slow down quickly because of danger ahead
- **C.** When you are towing another vehicle
- **D.** When driving on the hard shoulder
- **E.** When you have broken down on the hard shoulder

1202 CAR
You are involved in an accident with another vehicle. Someone is injured. Your vehicle is damaged. Which FOUR of the following should you find out?

Mark four answers

- **A.** Whether the driver owns the other vehicle involved
- **B.** The other driver's name, address and telephone number
- **C.** The make and registration number of the other vehicle
- **D.** The occupation of the other driver
- **E.** The details of the other driver's vehicle insurance
- **F.** Whether the other driver is licensed to drive

1203 CAR
You have broken down on a motorway. When you use the emergency telephone you will be asked

Mark three answers

- **A.** for the number on the telephone that you are using
- **B.** for your driving licence details
- **C.** for the name of your vehicle insurance company
- **D.** for details of yourself and your vehicle
- **E.** whether you belong to a motoring organisation

1204 CAR
You lose control of your car and damage a garden wall. No one is around. What must you do?

Mark one answer **NI**

- [ ] **A.** Report the accident to the police within 24 hours
- [ ] **B.** Go back to tell the house owner the next day
- [ ] **C.** Report the accident to your insurance company when you get home
- [ ] **D.** Find someone in the area to tell them about it immediately

1205 CAR
Your engine catches fire. What should you do first?

Mark one answer

- [ ] **A.** Lift the bonnet and disconnect the battery
- [ ] **B.** Lift the bonnet and warn other traffic
- [ ] **C.** Call a breakdown service
- [ ] **D.** Call the fire brigade

1206 CAR
Before driving through a tunnel what should you do?

Mark one answer

- [ ] **A.** Switch your radio off
- [ ] **B.** Remove any sunglasses
- [ ] **C.** Close your sunroof
- [ ] **D.** Switch on windscreen wipers

1207 CAR
You are driving through a tunnel and the traffic is flowing normally. What should you do?

Mark one answer

- [ ] **A.** Use parking lights
- [ ] **B.** Use front spot lights
- [ ] **C.** Use dipped headlights
- [ ] **D.** Use rear fog lights

1208 CAR
When approaching a tunnel it is good advice to

Mark one answer

- [ ] **A.** put on your sunglasses
- [ ] **B.** check tyre pressures
- [ ] **C.** change to a lower gear
- [ ] **D.** tune your radio to a local channel

1209 CAR
You are driving through a tunnel. Your vehicle breaks down. What should you do?

Mark one answer

- [ ] **A.** Switch on hazard warning lights
- [ ] **B.** Remain in your vehicle
- [ ] **C.** Wait for the police to find you
- [ ] **D.** Rely on CCTV cameras seeing you

1210 CAR
Your vehicle breaks down in a tunnel. What should you do?

Mark one answer

- [ ] **A.** Stay in your vehicle and wait for the police
- [ ] **B.** Stand in the lane behind your vehicle to warn others
- [ ] **C.** Stand in front of your vehicle to warn oncoming drivers
- [ ] **D.** Switch on hazard lights then go and call for help immediately

1211 CAR
You have an accident while driving through a tunnel. You are not injured but your vehicle CANNOT be driven. What should you do first?

Mark one answer

- [ ] **A.** Rely on other drivers phoning for the police
- [ ] **B.** Switch off the engine and switch on hazard lights
- [ ] **C.** Take the names of witnesses and other drivers
- [ ] **D.** Sweep up any debris that is in the road

1212
CAR
When driving through a tunnel you should

Mark one answer

- **A.** Look out for variable message signs
- **B.** Use your air conditioning system
- **C.** Switch on your rear fog lights
- **D.** Always use your windscreen wipers

1213
CAR
What TWO safeguards could you take against fire risk to your vehicle?

Mark two answers

- **A.** Keep water levels above maximum
- **B.** Carry a fire extinguisher
- **C.** Avoid driving with a full tank of petrol
- **D.** Use unleaded petrol
- **E.** Check out any strong smell of petrol
- **F.** Use low octane fuel

1214
CAR
Your vehicle catches fire while driving through a tunnel. It is still driveable. What should you do?

Mark one answer

- **A.** Leave it where it is with the engine running
- **B.** Pull up, then walk to an emergency telephone point
- **C.** Park it away from the carriageway
- **D.** Drive it out of the tunnel if you can do so

1215
CAR
You are driving through a tunnel. Your vehicle catches fire. What should you do?

Mark one answer

- **A.** Continue through the tunnel if you can
- **B.** Turn your vehicle around immediately
- **C.** Reverse out of the tunnel
- **D.** Carry out an emergency stop

1216
CAR
You are in a tunnel. Your vehicle is on fire and you CANNOT drive it. What should you do?

Mark two answers

- **A.** Stay in the vehicle and close the windows
- **B.** Switch on hazard warning lights
- **C.** Leave the engine running
- **D.** Try and put out the fire
- **E.** Switch off all of your lights
- **F.** Wait for other people to phone for help

1217
CAR
You are driving through a tunnel. There has been an accident and the car in front is on fire and blocking the road. What should you do?

Mark one answer

- **A.** Overtake and continue as quickly as you can
- **B.** Lock all the doors and windows
- **C.** Switch on hazard warning lights
- **D.** Stop, then reverse out of the tunnel

1218 CAR & MOTORCYCLE
You are at an incident where a casualty is unconscious. Their breathing should be checked. This should be done for at least

Mark one answer
- A. 2 seconds
- B. 10 seconds
- C. 1 minute
- D. 2 minutes

1219 CAR & MOTORCYCLE
Following a collision someone has suffered a burn. The burn needs to be cooled. What is the shortest time it should be cooled for?

Mark one answer
- A. 5 minutes
- B. 10 minutes
- C. 15 minutes
- D. 20 minutes

1220 CAR & MOTORCYCLE
After a collision someone has suffered a burn. The burn needs to be cooled. What is the shortest time it should be cooled for?

Mark one answer
- A. 30 seconds
- B. 60 seconds
- C. 5 minutes
- D. 10 minutes

1221 CAR & MOTORCYCLE
A casualty is not breathing normally. Chest compressions should be given. At what rate?

Mark one answer
- A. 50 per minute
- B. 100 per minute
- C. 200 per minute
- D. 250 per minute

1222 CAR & MOTORCYCLE
A casualty is not breathing. To maintain circulation compressions should be given. What is the correct depth to press?

Mark one answer
- A. 1 to 2 centimetres
- B. 4 to 5 centimetres
- C. 10 to 15 centimetres
- D. 15 to 20 centimetres

1223 CAR & MOTORCYCLE
A person has been injured. They may be suffering from shock. What are the warning signs to look for?

Mark one answer
- A. Flushed complexion
- B. Warm dry skin
- C. Slow pulse
- D. Pale grey skin

1224 CAR & MOTORCYCLE

You suspect that an injured person may be suffering from shock. What are the warning signs to look for?

Mark one answer

- A. Warm dry skin
- B. Sweating
- C. Slow pulse
- D. Skin rash

1225 CAR & MOTORCYCLE

A person is injured and lying on their back. They are unconscious but breathing normally. What treatment should be given?

Mark one answer

- A. Try to get them to drink water
- B. Raise their legs above head height
- C. Place them in the recovery position
- D. Leave them in the position found

1226 CAR & MOTORCYCLE

An injured person has been placed in the recovery position. They are unconscious but breathing normally. What else should be done?

Mark one answer

- A. Press firmly between the shoulders
- B. Place their arms by their side
- C. Give them a hot sweet drink
- D. Check the airway is clear

1227 MOTORCYCLE
If a trailer swerves or snakes when you are towing it you should

Mark one answer

- A. ease off the throttle and reduce your speed
- B. let go of the handlebars and let it correct itself
- C. brake hard and hold the brake on
- D. increase your speed as quickly as possible

1228 MOTORCYCLE
When riding with a sidecar attached for the first time you should

Mark two answers

- A. keep your speed down
- B. be able to stop more quickly
- C. accelerate quickly round bends
- D. approach corners more carefully

1229 MOTORCYCLE
You hold a provisional motorcycle licence. Are you allowed to carry a pillion passenger?

Mark one answer

- A. Only if the passenger holds a full licence
- B. Not at any time
- C. Not unless you are undergoing training
- D. Only if the passenger is under 21

1230 MOTORCYCLE
Which THREE must a learner motorcyclist under 21 NOT do?

Mark three answers

- A. Ride a motorcycle with an engine capacity greater than 125cc
- B. Pull a trailer
- C. Carry a pillion passenger
- D. Ride faster than 30mph
- E. Use the right-hand lane on dual carriageways

1231 MOTORCYCLE
When carrying extra weight on a motorcycle, you may need to make adjustments to the

Mark three answers

- A. headlight
- B. gears
- C. suspension
- D. tyres
- E. footrests

1232 MOTORCYCLE
To obtain the full category 'A' licence through the accelerated or direct access scheme, your motorcycle must be

Mark one answer NI

- A. solo with maximum power 25kw (33bhp)
- B. solo with maximum power of 11kw (14.6bhp)
- C. fitted with a sidecar and have minimum power of 35kw (46.6bhp)
- D. solo with minimum power of 35kw (46.6bhp)

1233 MOTORCYCLE
Any load that is carried on a luggage rack MUST be

Mark one answer

- A. securely fastened when riding
- B. carried only when strictly necessary
- C. visible when you are riding
- D. covered with plastic sheeting

1234 MOTORCYCLE
Pillion passengers should

Mark one answer
- [ ] A. have a provisional motorcycle licence
- [ ] B. be lighter than the rider
- [ ] C. always wear a helmet
- [ ] D. signal for the rider

1235 MOTORCYCLE
Pillion passengers should

Mark one answer
- [ ] A. give the rider directions
- [ ] B. lean with the rider when going round bends
- [ ] C. check the road behind for the rider
- [ ] D. give arm signals for the rider

1236 MOTORCYCLE
When you are going around a corner your pillion passenger should

Mark one answer
- [ ] A. give arm signals for you
- [ ] B. check behind for other vehicles
- [ ] C. lean with you on bends
- [ ] D. lean to one side to see ahead

1237 MOTORCYCLE
Which of these may need to be adjusted when carrying a pillion passenger?

Mark one answer
- [ ] A. Indicators
- [ ] B. Exhaust
- [ ] C. Fairing
- [ ] D. Headlight

1238 MOTORCYCLE
You are towing a trailer with your motorcycle. You should remember that your

Mark one answer
- [ ] A. stopping distance may increase
- [ ] B. fuel consumption will improve
- [ ] C. tyre grip will increase
- [ ] D. stability will improve

1239 MOTORCYCLE
Carrying a heavy load in your top box may

Mark one answer
- [ ] A. cause high-speed weave
- [ ] B. cause a puncture
- [ ] C. use less fuel
- [ ] D. improve stability

1240 MOTORCYCLE
Heavy loads in a motorcycle top box may

Mark one answer
- ☐ **A.** improve stability
- ☐ **B.** cause low-speed wobble
- ☐ **C.** cause a puncture
- ☐ **D.** improve braking

1241 MOTORCYCLE
You want to tow a trailer behind your motorcycle. You should

Mark two answers
- ☐ **A.** display a 'long vehicle' sign
- ☐ **B.** fit a larger battery
- ☐ **C.** have a full motorcycle licence
- ☐ **D.** ensure that your engine is more than 125cc
- ☐ **E.** ensure that your motorcycle has shaft drive

1242 MOTORCYCLE
Overloading your motorcycle can seriously affect the

Mark two answers
- ☐ **A.** gearbox
- ☐ **B.** steering
- ☐ **C.** handling
- ☐ **D.** battery life
- ☐ **E.** journey time

1243 MOTORCYCLE
Who is responsible for making sure that a motorcycle is not overloaded?

Mark one answer
- ☐ **A.** The rider of the motorcycle
- ☐ **B.** The owner of the items being carried
- ☐ **C.** The licensing authority
- ☐ **D.** The owner of the motorcycle

1244 MOTORCYCLE
Before fitting a sidecar to a motorcycle you should

Mark one answer
- ☐ **A.** have the wheels balanced
- ☐ **B.** have the engine tuned
- ☐ **C.** pass the extended bike test
- ☐ **D.** check that the motorcycle is suitable

1245 MOTORCYCLE
You are using throwover saddlebags. Why is it important to make sure they are evenly loaded?

Mark one answer
- ☐ **A.** They will be uncomfortable for you to sit on
- ☐ **B.** They will slow your motorcycle down
- ☐ **C.** They could make your motorcycle unstable
- ☐ **D.** They will be uncomfortable for a pillion passenger to sit on

1246 MOTORCYCLE
You are carrying a bulky tank bag. What could this affect?

Mark one answer
- ☐ **A.** Your ability to steer
- ☐ **B.** Your ability to accelerate
- ☐ **C.** Your view ahead
- ☐ **D.** Your insurance premium

1247 MOTORCYCLE
To carry a pillion passenger you must

Mark one answer
- A. hold a full car licence
- B. hold a full motorcycle licence
- C. be over the age of 21
- D. be over the age of 25

1248 MOTORCYCLE
When carrying a heavy load on your luggage rack, you may need to adjust your

Mark one answer
- A. carburettor
- B. fuel tap
- C. seating position
- D. tyre pressures

1249 MOTORCYCLE
You are carrying a pillion passenger. When following other traffic, which of the following should you do?

Mark one answer
- A. Keep to your normal following distance
- B. Get your passenger to keep checking behind
- C. Keep further back than you normally would
- D. Get your passenger to signal for you

1250 MOTORCYCLE
You should only carry a child as a pillion passenger when

Mark one answer
- A. they are over 14 years old
- B. they are over 16 years old
- C. they can reach the floor from the seat
- D. they can reach the handholds and footrests

1251 MOTORCYCLE
You have fitted a sidecar to your motorcycle. You should make sure that the sidecar

Mark one answer
- A. has a registration plate
- B. is correctly aligned
- C. has a waterproof cover
- D. has a solid cover

1252 MOTORCYCLE
You are riding a motorcycle and sidecar. The extra weight

Mark one answer
- A. will allow you to corner more quickly
- B. will allow you to brake later for hazards
- C. may increase your stopping distance
- D. will improve your fuel consumption

1253 MOTORCYCLE
You are carrying a pillion passenger. To allow for the extra weight which of the following is most likely to need adjustment?

Mark one answer
- A. Preload on the front forks
- B. Preload on the rear shock absorber(s)
- C. The balance of the rear wheel
- D. The front and rear wheel alignment

1254 MOTORCYCLE
A trailer on a motorcycle must be no wider than

Mark one answer
- A. 0.5 metres (1 foot 8 inches)
- B. 1 metre (3 feet 3 inches)
- C. 1.5 metres (4 feet 11 inches)
- D. 2 metres (6 feet 6 inches)

1255 MOTORCYCLE
To carry a pillion passenger your motorcycle should be fitted with

Mark two answers
- A. rear footrests
- B. an engine of 250cc or over
- C. a top box
- D. a grab handle
- E. a proper pillion seat

1256 MOTORCYCLE
You want to tow a trailer with your motorcycle. Which one applies?

Mark one answer
- A. The motorcycle should be attached to a sidecar
- B. The trailer should weigh more than the motorcycle
- C. The trailer should be fitted with brakes
- D. The trailer should NOT be more than 1 metre (3 feet 3 inches) wide

1257 MOTORCYCLE
Your motorcycle is fitted with a top box. It is unwise to carry a heavy load in the top box because it may

Mark three answers
- A. reduce stability
- B. improve stability
- C. make turning easier
- D. cause high-speed weave
- E. cause low-speed wobble
- F. increase fuel economy

1258 MOTORCYCLE
You have a sidecar fitted to your motorcycle. What effect will it have?

Mark one answer
- A. Reduce stability
- B. Make steering lighter
- C. Increase stopping distance
- D. Increase fuel economy

1259 CAR & MOTORCYCLE
You are towing a small trailer on a busy three-lane motorway. All the lanes are open. You must

Mark two answers
- A. not exceed 60mph
- B. not overtake
- C. have a stabiliser fitted
- D. use only the left and centre lanes

1260 CAR
Any load that is carried on a roof rack should be

Mark one answer
- A. securely fastened when driving
- B. loaded towards the rear of the vehicle
- C. visible in your exterior mirror
- D. covered with plastic sheeting

1261 CAR
You are planning to tow a caravan. Which of these will mostly help to aid the vehicle handling?

Mark one answer
- A. A jockey wheel fitted to the tow bar
- B. Power steering fitted to the towing vehicle
- C. Anti-lock brakes fitted to the towing vehicle
- D. A stabiliser fitted to the tow bar

1262 CAR
If a trailer swerves or snakes when you are towing it you should

Mark one answer

- A. ease off the accelerator and reduce your speed
- B. let go of the steering wheel and let it correct itself
- C. brake hard and hold the pedal down
- D. increase your speed as quickly as possible

1263 CAR
How can you stop a caravan snaking from side to side?

Mark one answer

- A. Turn the steering wheel slowly to each side
- B. Accelerate to increase your speed
- C. Stop as quickly as you can
- D. Slow down very gradually

1264 CAR
On which TWO occasions might you inflate your tyres to more than the recommended normal pressure?

Mark two answers

- A. When the roads are slippery
- B. When driving fast for a long distance
- C. When the tyre tread is worn below 2mm
- D. When carrying a heavy load
- E. When the weather is cold
- F. When the vehicle is fitted with anti-lock brakes

1265 CAR
A heavy load on your roof rack will

Mark one answer

- A. improve the road holding
- B. reduce the stopping distance
- C. make the steering lighter
- D. reduce stability

1266 CAR
Are passengers allowed to ride in a caravan that is being towed?

Mark one answer

- A. Yes, if they are over 14
- B. No, not at any time
- C. Only if all the seats in the towing vehicle are full
- D. Only if a stabiliser is fitted

1267 CAR
You are towing a caravan along a motorway. The caravan begins to swerve from side to side. What should you do?

Mark one answer

- A. Ease off the accelerator slowly
- B. Steer sharply from side to side
- C. Do an emergency stop
- D. Speed up very quickly

1268 CAR
A trailer must stay securely hitched up to the towing vehicle. What additional safety device can be fitted to the trailer braking system?

Mark one answer

- A. Stabiliser
- B. Jockey wheel
- C. Corner steadies
- D. Breakaway cable

1269 CAR
Overloading your vehicle can seriously affect the

Mark two answers
- [ ] A. gearbox
- [ ] B. steering
- [ ] C. handling
- [ ] D. battery life
- [ ] E. journey time

1270 CAR
Who is responsible for making sure that a vehicle is not overloaded?

Mark one answer
- [ ] A. The driver of the vehicle
- [ ] B. The owner of the items being carried
- [ ] C. The person who loaded the vehicle
- [ ] D. The licensing authority

1271 CAR
You are carrying a child in your car. They are under three years of age. Which of these is a suitable restraint?

Mark one answer
- [ ] A. A child seat
- [ ] B. An adult holding a child
- [ ] C. An adult seat belt
- [ ] D. An adult lap belt

1272 CAR
Why would you fit a stabiliser before towing a caravan?

Mark one answer
- [ ] A. It will help with stability when driving in crosswinds
- [ ] B. It will allow heavy items to be loaded behind the axle
- [ ] C. It will help you to raise and lower the jockey wheel
- [ ] D. It will allow you to tow without the breakaway cable

1273 CAR
You wish to tow a trailer. Where would you find the maximum noseweight of your vehicle's tow ball?

Mark one answer
- [ ] A. In the vehicle handbook
- [ ] B. In The Highway Code
- [ ] C. In your vehicle registration certificate
- [ ] D. In your licence documents

Glossary

Accelerate

To make the vehicle move faster by pressing the right-hand pedal.

Advanced stop lines

A marked area on the road at traffic lights, which permits cyclists or buses to wait in front of other traffic.

Adverse weather

Bad weather that makes driving difficult or dangerous.

Alert

Quick to notice possible hazards.

Anticipation

Looking out for hazards and taking action before a problem starts.

Anti-lock brakes

Brakes that stop the wheels locking so that you are less likely to skid on a slippery road.

Aquaplane

To slide out of control on a wet road surface.

Articulated vehicle

A long vehicle that is divided into two or more sections joined by cables.

Attitude

The way you think or feel, which affects the way you drive. Especially, whether you are patient and polite, or impatient and aggressive.

Automatic

A vehicle with gears that change by themselves as you speed up or slow down.

Awareness

Taking notice of the road and traffic conditions around you at all times.

Black ice

An invisible film of ice that forms over the road surface, creating very dangerous driving conditions.

Blind spot

The section of road behind you which you cannot see in your mirrors. You 'cover' your blind spot by looking over your shoulder before moving off or overtaking.

Brake fade

Loss of power to the brakes when you have been using them for a long time without taking your foot off the brake pedal. For example, when driving down a steep hill. The brakes will overheat and not work properly.

Braking distance

The distance you must allow to slow the vehicle in order to come to a stop.

Brow

The highest point of a hill.

Built-up area

A town, or place with lots of buildings.

Carriageway

One side of a road or motorway. A 'dual carriageway' has two lanes on each side of a central reservation.

Catalytic converter

A piece of equipment fitted in the exhaust system that changes harmful gases into less harmful ones.

Chicane

A sharp double bend that has been put into a road to make traffic slow down.

Child restraint

A child seat or special seat belt for children. It keeps them safe and stops them moving around in the car.

Clearway

A road where no stopping is allowed at any time. The sign for a clearway is a red cross in a red circle on a blue background.

Coasting

Driving a vehicle without using any of the gears. That is, with your foot on the clutch pedal and the car in neutral.

Commentary driving

Talking to yourself about what you see on the road ahead and what action you are going to take – an aid to concentration.

Comprehensive insurance

A motor insurance policy that pays for repairs even if you cause an accident.

Concentration

Keeping all your attention on your driving.

Conditions

How good or bad the road surface is, volume of traffic on the road, and what the weather is like.

Congestion

Heavy traffic that makes it difficult to get to where you want to go.

Consideration

Thinking about other road users and not just yourself. For example, letting another driver go first at a junction, or stopping at a zebra crossing to let pedestrians cross over.

Contraflow

When traffic on a motorway follows signs to move to the opposite carriageway for a short distance because of roadworks. (During a contraflow, there is traffic driving in both directions on the same side of the motorway.)

Coolant

Liquid in the radiator that removes heat from the engine.

Defensive driving

Driving safely without taking risks, looking out for hazards and thinking for others.

Disqualified

Stopped from doing something (eg driving) by law, because you have broken the law.

Distraction

Anything that stops you concentrating on your driving, such as chatting to passengers or on your mobile phone.

Document

An official paper or card, eg your driving licence.

Dual carriageway

One side of a road or motorway, with two lanes on each side of a central reservation.

Engine braking – see also gears

Using the low gears to keep your speed down. For example, when you are driving down a steep hill and you want to stop the vehicle running away. Using the gears instead of braking will help to prevent brake fade.

Environment

The world around us and the air we breathe.

Exceed

Go higher than an upper limit.

Exhaust emissions

Gases that come out of the exhaust pipe to form part of the outside air.

Field of vision

How far you can see in front and around you when you are driving.

Filler cap

Provides access to the vehicle's fuel tank, for filling up with petrol or diesel.

Fog lights

Extra bright rear (and sometimes front) lights which may be switched on in conditions of very poor visibility. You must remember to switch them off when visibility improves, as they can dazzle and distract other drivers.

Ford

A place in a stream or river which is shallow enough to drive across with care.

Four-wheel drive (4WD)

On a conventional vehicle, steering and engine speed affect just two 'drive' wheels. On 4WD, they affect all four wheels, ensuring optimum grip on loose ground.

Frustration

Feeling annoyed because you cannot drive as fast as you want to because of other drivers or heavy traffic.

Fuel consumption

The amount of fuel (petrol or diesel) that your vehicle uses. Different vehicles have different rates of consumption. Increased fuel consumption means using more fuel. Decreased fuel consumption means using less fuel.

Fuel gauge

A display or dial on the instrument panel that tells you how much fuel (petrol or diesel) you have left.

Gantry

An overhead platform like a high narrow bridge that displays electric signs on a motorway.

Gears

Control the speed of the engine in relation to the vehicle's speed. May be hand operated (manual) or automatically controlled. In a low gear (such as first or second) the engine runs more slowly. In a high gear (such as fourth or fifth), it runs more quickly. Putting the car into a lower gear as you drive can create the effect of engine braking – forcing the engine to run more slowly.

Handling

How well your vehicle moves or responds when you steer or brake.

Harass

To drive in away that makes other road users afraid.

Hard shoulder

The single lane to the left of the inside lane on a motorway, which is for emergency use only. You should not drive on the hard shoulder except in an emergency, or when there are signs telling you to use the hard shoulder because of roadworks.

Harsh braking (or harsh acceleration)

Using the brake or accelerator too hard so as to cause wear on the engine.

Hazard warning lights

Flashing amber lights which you should use only when you have broken down. On a motorway you can use them to warn other drivers behind of a hazard ahead.

High-sided vehicle

A van or truck with tall sides, or a tall trailer such as a caravan or horse-box, that is at risk of being blown off-course in strong winds.

Impatient

Not wanting to wait for pedestrians and other road users.

Inflate

To blow up – to put air in your tyres until they are at the right pressures.

Instrument panel

The car's electrical controls and gauges, set behind the steering wheel. Also called the dashboard.

Intimidate

To make someone feel afraid.

Involved

Being part of something. For example, being one of the drivers in an accident.

Jump leads

A pair of thick electric cables with clips at either end. You use it to charge a flat battery by connecting it to the live battery in another vehicle.

Junction

A place where two or more roads join.

Liability

Being legally responsible.

Manoeuvre

Using the controls to make your car move in a particular direction. For example turning, reversing or parking.

Manual

By hand. In a car that is a 'manual' or has manual gears, you have to change the gears yourself.

Maximum

The largest possible; 'maximum speed' is the highest speed allowed.

Minimum

The smallest possible.

Mirrors

Modern cars have a minimum of three rear view mirrors: one in the centre of the windscreen, and one on each front door. Additional mirrors may be required on longer vehicles, or when towing a high trailer such as a caravan. Some mirrors may be curved (convex or concave) to increase the field of vision. The mirror on the windscreen can be turned to anti-dazzle position, if glare from headlights behind creates a distraction.

Mobility

The ability to move around easily.

Monotonous

Boring. For example, a long stretch of motorway with no variety and nothing interesting to see.

MOT

The test that proves your car is safe to drive. Your MOT certificate is one of the important documents for your vehicle.

Motorway

A fast road that has two or more lanes on each side and a hard shoulder. Drivers must join or leave it on the left, via a motorway junction. Many kinds of slower vehicles – such as bicycles – are not allowed on motorways.

Multiple-choice questions

Questions with several possible answers where you have to try to choose the right one.

Observation

The ability to notice important information, such as hazards developing ahead.

Obstruct

To get in the way of another road user.

Octagonal

Having eight sides.

Oil level

The amount of oil needed for the engine to run effectively. The oil level should be checked as part of your regular maintenance routine, and the oil replaced as necessary.

Pedestrian

A person walking.

Pegasus crossing

An unusual kind of crossing. It has a button high up for horse riders to push (Pegasus was a flying horse in Greek legend).

Pelican crossing

A crossing with traffic lights that pedestrians can use by pushing a button. Cars must give way to pedestrians on the crossing while the amber light is flashing. You must give pedestrians enough time to get to the other side of the road.

Perception

Seeing or noticing (as in Hazard Perception).

Peripheral vision

The area around the edges of your field of vision.

Positive attitude

Being sensible and obeying the law when you drive.

Priority

The vehicle or other road user that is allowed by law to go first is the one that has priority.

Provisional licence

A first driving licence. all learner drivers must get one before they start having lessons.

Puffin crossing

A type of pedestrian crossing that does not have a flashing amber light phase.

Reaction time

The amount of time it takes you to see a hazard and decide what to do about it.

Red route

You see these in London and some other cities. Double red lines at the edge of the road tell you that you must not stop or park there at any time. Single red lines have notices with times when you must not stop or park. Some red routes have marked bays for either parking or loading at certain times.

Red warning triangle

An item of safety equipment to carry in your car in case you break down. You can place the triangle 45m behind your car on the same side of the road. It warns traffic that your vehicle is causing an obstruction. (Do not use these on motorways.)

Residential areas

Areas of housing where people live. The speed limit is 30mph or sometimes 20mph.

Road hump

A low bump built across the road to slow vehicles down. Also called 'sleeping policemen'.

Rumble strips

Raised strips across the road near a roundabout or junction that change the sound the tyres make on the road surface, warning drivers to slow down. They are also used on motorways to separate the main carriageway from the hard shoulder.

Safety margin

The amount of space you need to leave between your vehicle and the one in front so that you are not in danger of crashing into it if the driver slows down suddenly or stops. Safety margins have to be longer in wet or icy conditions.

Separation distance

The amount of space you need to leave between your vehicle and the one in front so that you are not in danger of crashing into it if the driver slows down suddenly or stops. The separation distance must be longer in wet or icy conditions.

Security coded radio

To deter thieves, a radio or CD unit which requires a security code (or pin number) to operate it.

Single carriageway

Generally, a road with one lane in each direction.

Skid

When the tyres fail to grip the surface of the road, the subsequent loss of control of the vehicle's movement is called a skid. Usually caused by harsh or fierce braking, steering or acceleration.

Snaking

Moving from side to side. This sometimes happens with caravans or trailers when you drive too fast, or they are not properly loaded.

Staggered junction

Where you drive cross another road. Instead of going straight across, you have to go a bit to the right or left.

Steering

Control of the direction of the vehicle. May be affected by road surface conditions: when the steering wheel turns very easily, steering is 'light', and when you have to pull hard on the wheel it is described as 'heavy'.

Sterile

Clean and free from bacteria.

Stopping distance

The time it takes for you to stop your vehicle – made up of 'thinking distance' and 'braking distance'.

Supervisor

Someone who sits in the passenger seat with a learner driver. They must be over 21 and have held a full driving licence for at least three years.

Tailgating

Driving too closely behind another vehicle – either to harass the driver in front or to help you in thick fog.

Tax disc

The disc you display on your windscreen to show that you have taxed your car (see Vehicle Excise Duty, below).

Thinking distance

The time it takes you to notice something and take the right action. You need to add thinking distance to your braking distance to make up your total stopping distance.

Third party insurance

An insurance policy that insures you against any claim by passengers or other persons for damage or injury to their person or property.

Toucan crossing

A type of pedestrian crossing that does not have a flashing amber light phase, and cyclists are allowed to ride across.

Tow

To pull something behind your vehicle. It could be a caravan or trailer.

Traffic calming measures

Speed humps, chicanes and other devices placed in roads to slow traffic down.

Tram

A public transport vehicle which moves along the streets on fixed rails, usually electrically powered by overhead lines.

Tread depth

The depth of the grooves in a car's tyres that help them grip the road surface. The grooves must all be at least 1.6mm deep.

Turbulence

Strong movement of air. For example, when a large vehicle passes a much smaller one.

Two-second rule

In normal driving, the ideal minimum distance between you and the vehicle in front can be timed using the 'two-second' rule. As the vehicle in front passes a fixed object (such as a signpost), say to yourself 'Only a fool breaks the two second rule'. It takes two seconds to say it. If you have passed the same object before you finish, you are too close – pull back.

Tyre pressures

The amount of air which must be pumped into a tyre in order for it to be correctly blown up.

Vehicle Excise Duty

The tax you pay for your vehicle so that you may drive it on public roads.

Vehicle Registration Document

A record of details about a vehicle and its owner.

Vehicle watch scheme

A system for identifying vehicles that may have been stolen.

Vulnerable

At risk of harm or injury.

Waiting restrictions

Times when you may not park or load your vehicle in a particular area.

Wheel balancing

To ensure smooth rotation at all speeds, wheels need to be 'balanced' correctly. This is a procedure done at a garage or tyre centre, when each wheel is removed for testing. Balancing may involve minor adjustment with the addition of small weights, to avoid wheel wobble.

Wheel spin

When the vehicle's wheels spin round out of control with no grip on the road surface.

Zebra crossing

A pedestrian crossing without traffic lights. It has an orange light, and is marked by black and white stripes on the road. Drivers must stop for pedestrians to cross.

Answers to Questions

Answers to Questions – Section 16

ALERTNESS – SECTION 1

1 AE	2 B	3 B	4 D	5 A	6 C	7 B	8 C	9 C
10 D	11 A	12 D	13 C	14 A	15 C	16 D	17 A	18 B
19 C	20 C	21 C	22 D	23 D	24 C	25 BDF	26 C	27 D
28 C	29 C	30 C	31 C	32 B	33 D	34 AC	35 ABCD	36 AD
37 AB	38 AB	39 ABCD	40 B	41 D	42 B	43 C	44 B	45 B
46 ABE	47 C	48 B	49 B	50 D	51 C	52 C	53 C	54 A
55 D	56 D	57 B	58 A	59 D	60 B	61 B	62 B	

ATTITUDE – SECTION 2

63 B	64 D	65 C	66 B	67 C	68 BD	69 D	70 A	71 C
72 B	73 C	74 D	75 D	76 B	77 B	78 BCD	79 ABE	80 A
81 D	82 B	83 A	84 A	85 B	86 A	87 A	88 C	89 A
90 B	91 D	92 D	93 D	94 A	95 A	96 B	97 C	98 A
99 C	100 A	101 C	102 B	103 C	104 DE	105 B	106 D	107 B
108 C	109 AB	110 D	111 C	112 A	113 A	114 D	115 B	116 A
117 C								

SAFETY AND YOUR VEHICLE – SECTION 3

118 D	119 C	120 D	121 A	122 A	123 B	124 B	125 C	126 D
127 C	128 A	129 B	130 A	131 ABC	132 B	133 D	134 ACD	135 AE
136 BE	137 C	138 D	139 A	140 D	141 A	142 B	143 D	144 B
145 D	146 A	147 B	148 B	149 BC	150 BCDE	151 AD	152 CD	153 C
154 D	155 C	156 A	157 A	158 C	159 D	160 B	161 A	162 C
163 D	164 A	165 C	166 D	167 C	168 D	169 B	170 C	171 C
172 B	173 C	174 D	175 A	176 A	177 A	178 D	179 B	180 B
181 AB	182 ABF	183 BEF	184 C	185 ACF	186 C	187 B	188 D	189 C
190 D	191 D	192 D	193 A	194 AE	195 D	196 B	197 D	198 D
199 A	200 B	201 BCDF	202 D	203 D	204 BC	205 BC	206 A	207 D
208 A	209 B	210 B	211 D	212 C	213 D	214 D	215 D	216 B
217 B	218 B	219 D	220 ABF	221 ABC	222 ABC	223 BDF	224 ADE	225 BD
226 B	227 CDE	228 B	229 B	230 C	231 B	232 DE	233 A	234 C
235 B	236 D	237 D	238 D	239 B	240 C	241 A	242 B	243 D
244 C	245 A	246 B	247 AB	248 A	249 D	250 B	251 BCD	252 C
253 CD	254 A	255 A	256 D	257 C	258 B	259 B	260 B	261 D
262 ABE	263 ADE	264 D	265 A	266 B	267 C	268 D	269 A	270 B
271 C	272 D	273 A	274 C	275 D	276 B	277 B	278 A	279 A
280 B	281 B	282 D	283 B	284 A	285 C	286 D	287 B	288 B
289 D	290 B	291 B	292 C	293 A	294 A	295 A	296 D	

SAFETY MARGINS – SECTION 4

297 C	298 B	299 D	300 B	301 A	302 A	303 C	304 AB	305 BDE
306 D	307 BC	308 D	309 D	310 D	311 D	312 BD	313 BE	314 B
315 D	316 A	317 B	318 AB	319 A	320 ABDF	321 AB	322 C	323 D
324 D	325 D	326 D	327 A	328 C	329 B	330 A	331 CD	332 D
333 D	334 BC	335 B	336 D	337 D	338 C	339 C	340 A	341 B
342 A	343 B	344 A	345 B	346 AE	347 C	348 B	349 C	350 BDEF
351 B	352 D	353 A	354 C	355 A	356 AD	357 C	358 B	359 B
360 B	361 C	362 C	363 B	364 B	365 BC	366 C	367 C	368 B
369 C	370 D	371 BC	372 B	373 ACE	374 D	375 D	376 D	377 A
378 D	379 BD	380 D	381 B	382 A	383 D	384 A	385 B	386 B

HAZARD AWARENESS – SECTION 5

387 AD	388 D	389 D	390 ABC	391 B	392 ACE	393 D	394 AB	395 A
396 D	397 C	398 B	399 B	400 D	401 B	402 A	403 D	404 A
405 D	406 ACD	407 CD	408 B	409 C	410 A	411 D	412 ACE	413 D
414 C	415 A	416 C	417 C	418 D	419 B	420 B	421 A	422 A
423 A	424 C	425 C	426 CD	427 A	428 B	429 A	430 A	431 C
432 BF	433 B	434 AE	435 A	436 D	437 D	438 C	439 B	440 B
441 C	442 A	443 B	444 B	445 CD	446 B	447 D	448 B	449 A
450 A	451 D	452 A	453 B	454 AE	455 C	456 B	457 BC	458 D
459 B	460 B	461 C	462 D	463 C	464 CD	465 AC	466 AB	467 A
468 A	469 B	470 A	471 ABC	472 C	473 C	474 C	475 ABE	476 C
477 D	478 D	479 C	480 C	481 D	482 ABD	483 ABC	484 D	485 C
486 AB	487 B	488 B	489 CD	490 D	491 ACE	492 ABE	493 A	494 A
495 D	496 D	497 A	498 D	499 A	500 B	501 B	502 ACE	503 C

VULNERABLE ROAD USERS – SECTION 6

504 D	505 B	506 ABC	507 A	508 A	509 A	510 A	511 D	512 B
513 AE	514 B	515 B	516 C	517 C	518 AD	519 C	520 D	521 D
522 C	523 C	524 B	525 D	526 D	527 A	528 B	529 C	530 D
531 A	532 D	533 D	534 B	535 D	536 B	537 D	538 D	539 C
540 AC	541 C	542 C	543 A	544 D	545 C	546 D	547 ABC	548 C
549 B	550 B	551 AC	552 ABD	553 B	554 D	555 A	556 A	557 D
558 D	559 A	560 A	561 C	562 C	563 C	564 D	565 ACE	566 D
567 B	568 A	569 C	570 D	571 C	572 C	573 A	574 D	575 D
576 A	577 A	578 B	579 B	580 D	581 C	582 C	583 B	584 C
585 AE	586 D	587 C	588 C	589 B	590 B	591 D	592 D	593 A
594 C	595 C	596 D	597 D	598 B	599 A	600 D	601 B	602 B
603 C	604 D	605 A						

OTHER TYPES OF VEHICLE – SECTION 7

606 C	607 AB	608 A	609 A	610 B	611 B	612 D	613 B	614 A
615 BC	616 B	617 D	618 A	619 A	620 C	621 B	622 D	623 D
624 D	625 B	626 B	627 B	628 AC	629 BD	630 B	631 D	632 D
633 A	634 A							

VEHICLE HANDLING – SECTION 8

635 B	636 AD	637 C	638 D	639 AB	640 A	641 BDE	642 BE	643 A
644 CE	645 D	646 C	647 B	648 C	649 A	650 C	651 C	652 A
653 ABC	654 C	655 D	656 C	657 D	658 A	659 D	660 D	661 ABD
662 D	663 A	664 A	665 C	666 D	667 A	668 A	669 A	670 D
671 ACDE	672 B	673 B	674 ACE	675 A	676 CD	677 D	678 A	679 BDF
680 C	681 D	682 C	683 DE	684 D	685 B	686 C	687 C	688 D
689 D	690 D	691 C	692 C	693 BD	694 BD	695 D	696 B	697 C
698 CE	699 C	700 D	701 A	702 A	703 C	704 B	705 ABDF	706 A
707 D	708 B	709 B	710 AB	711 BD	712 A	713 ACD	714 B	715 A
716 C	717 B	718 A	719 A	720 C	721 C	722 A	723 B	724 C
725 D	726 B	727 D	728 ABD	729 D	730 C	731 C	732 C	733 D
734 D	735 A	736 B						

MOTORWAY RULES – SECTION 9

737 A	738 C	739 A	740 C	741 D	742 D	743 A	744 B	745 A
746 ADEF	747 ADEF	748 D	749 D	750 D	751 D	752 A	753 B	754 C
755 BE	756 C	757 A	758 C	759 A	760 D	761 A	762 C	763 C
764 C	765 C	766 C	767 C	768 B	769 C	770 B	771 B	772 A
773 B	774 B	775 D	776 CDF	777 C	778 D	779 C	780 D	781 A
782 B	783 B	784 D	785 C	786 A	787 B	788 D	789 A	790 D
791 D	792 A	793 C	794 B	795 B	796 C	797 A	798 A	799 B
800 D	801 D	802 B	803 D	804 D	805 B	806 C	807 D	808 D
809 C	810 A	811 D						

RULES OF THE ROAD – SECTION 10

812 A	813 DE	814 A	815 ACF	816 B	817 C	818 B	819 D	820 D
821 D	822 ABC	823 D	824 B	825 A	826 C	827 C	828 D	829 B
830 A	831 C	832 D	833 ADF	834 AD	835 A	836 B	837 A	838 B
839 A	840 D	841 A	842 D	843 D	844 C	845 A	846 ACE	847 B
848 C	849 D	850 BD	851 B	852 A	853 D	854 C	855 A	856 B
857 CDE	858 B	859 AE	860 B	861 A	862 ABD	863 A	864 B	865 B
866 A	867 D	868 A	869 D	870 C	871 D	872 D	873 BEF	874 D
875 D	876 D	877 C	878 C	879 D	880 A	881 A	882 A	883 C
884 B	885 A	886 D	887 AB	888 A	889 D	890 D	891 A	892 D
893 B	894 ABC	895 D	896 A	897 D	898 A	899 A	900 B	901 C

ROAD AND TRAFFIC SIGNS – SECTION 11

902 C	903 B	904 A	905 D	906 A	907 C	908 B	909 B	
910 A	911 D	912 D	913 A	914 A	915 B	916 A	917 D	
918 B	919 D	920 D	921 D	922 A	923 C	924 B	925 D	
926 C	927 B	928 A	929 B	930 B	931 C	932 C	933 A	
934 C	935 B	936 C	937 B	938 D	939 D	940 C	941 D	
942 C	943 A	944 B	945 C	946 D	947 A	948 D	949 B	
950 D	951 B	952 A	953 A	954 A	955 A	956 B	957 B	
958 A	959 D	960 ACEF	961 C	962 A	963 A	964 C	965 D	
966 B	967 C	968 B	969 B	970 B	971 B	972 C	973 A	
974 C	975 A	976 C	977 D	978 A	979 C	980 B	981 D	
982 A	983 B	984 B	985 C	986 C	987 A	988 A	989 C	
990 D	991 C	992 C	993 B	994 A	995 C	996 D	997 C	
998 B	999 A	1000 A	1001 C	1002 BDF	1003 A	1004 C	1005 C	
1006 B	1007 B	1008 A	1009 C	1010 A	1011 B	1012 A	1013 B	
1014 D	1015 D	1016 B	1017 A	1018 A	1019 D	1020 C	1021 D	
1022 C	1023 B	1024 C	1025 C	1026 A	1027 B	1028 B	1029 D	
1030 B	1031 B	1032 A	1033 D	1034 A	1035 B	1036 B	1037 D	
1038 C	1039 B	1040 A	1041 B	1042 A	1043 C	1044 A	1045 B	
1046 A	1047 A	1048 C	1049 C	1050 A	1051 B	1052 C	1053 B	
1054 A	1055 C	1056 A	1057 A	1058 C	1059 C	1060 B	1061 B	
1062 B	1063 B	1064 B	1065 A					

DOCUMENTS – SECTION 12

1066 C	1067 CD	1068 C	1069 BDE	1070 ADF	1071 A	1072 A	1073 C
1074 C	1075 B	1076 B	1077 C	1078 ABD	1079 ABF	1080 BCE	1081 BD
1082 D	1083 A	1084 C	1085 B	1086 C	1087 B	1088 B	1089 A
1090 C	1091 D	1092 C	1093 ABE	1094 BE	1095 BCE	1096 C	1097 B
1098 B	1099 BE	1100 C	1101 C	1102 B	1103 D	1104 AB	1105 D
1106 D	1107 CDE	1108 CD	1109 B	1110 B	1111 C	1112 ABF	1113 BCE
1114 ABE	1115 BD	1116 D	1117 A	1118 C	1119 ABD	1120 D	1121 B
1122 C	1123 A	1124 C	1125 C	1126 B	1127 C	1128 D	1129 D
1130 B	1131 A	1132 B	1133 D	1134 A	1135 AB	1136 A	

ACCIDENTS – SECTION 13

1137 B	1138 C	1139 A	1140 D	1141 B	1142 A	1143 ABCE	1144 ADE
1145 B	1146 D	1147 A	1148 A	1149 BCDE	1150 B	1151 ABE	1152 A
1153 ACF	1154 A	1155 ABD	1156 ACE	1157 DEF	1158 ABE	1159 ACF	1160 AE
1161 ACDE	1162 C	1163 BC	1164 A	1165 B	1166 B	1167 BDE	1168 B
1169 C	1170 D	1171 CD	1172 D	1173 C	1174 B	1175 D	1176 B
1177 BDE	1178 A	1179 B	1180 AB	1181 A	1182 A	1183 B	1184 B
1185 D	1186 C	1187 C	1188 B	1189 D	1190 C	1191 ABD	1192 A
1193 CD	1194 CE	1195 C	1196 DEF	1197 B	1198 C	1199 A	1200 A
1201 BE	1202 ABCE	1203 ADE	1204 A	1205 D	1206 B	1207 C	1208 D
1209 A	1210 D	1211 B	1212 A	1213 BE	1214 D	1215 A	1216 BD
1217 C	1218 B	1219 B	1220 D	1221 B	1222 B	1223 D	1224 B
1225 C	1226 D						

VEHICLE LOADING – SECTION 14

1227 A	1228 AD	1229 B	1230 ABC	1231 ACD	1232 D	1233 A	1234 C
1235 B	1236 C	1237 D	1238 A	1239 A	1240 B	1241 CD	1242 BC
1243 A	1244 D	1245 C	1246 A	1247 B	1248 D	1249 C	1250 D
1251 B	1252 C	1253 B	1254 B	1255 AE	1256 D	1257 ADE	1258 C
1259 AD	1260 A	1261 D	1262 A	1263 D	1264 BD	1265 D	1266 B
1267 A	1268 D	1269 BC	1270 A	1271 A	1272 A	1273 A	

AA driving school
0800 107 2045
www.AAdrivingschool.co.uk

Driving Standards Agency (DSA)
You can book your Theory or Practical Test

Online: www.direct.gov.uk

By phone: 0870 0101 372

By fax: 0870 0102 372

Welsh speakers: 0870 0100 372

Minicom: 0870 0107 372

To book your Theory Test you will need:

- The driver number on your licence

- Your debit/credit card details

To book your Practical Test you will need:

- The driver number on your licence

- Theory Test pass date and certificate number

- Driving school code (if known)

- Your preferred date

- Unacceptable days or periods

- If you can accept a test at short notice

- Details of any disability or any special circumstances

- Your credit/debit card details

Saturday and weekday evening tests are available at some driving test centres. The fee is higher than for a driving test during normal working hours on weekdays. Evening tests are available during the summer months only.

Pass Plus scheme
For information on the Pass Plus scheme ask your Advanced Driving Instructor, see www.passplus.org.uk or call the DSA on 0115 901 2633

Driver and Vehicle Licensing Agency (DVLA)
www.dvla.gov.uk

For enquiries about your driving licence
Phone: 0870 240 0009

Or write to:
Drivers Customer Services (DCS)
Correspondence Team
DVLA
Swansea
SA6 7JL

The Highway Code
www.highwaycode.gov.uk

St John Ambulance
www.sja.org.uk
08700 10 49 50

St Andrew's First Aid
www.firstaid.org.uk
0141 332 4031

Personal Information

My driver number

Driving instructor's name and phone number

Driving instructor's number

Theory Test date and time

Theory Test pass date

Theory Test certificate number

Driving school code

Practical Test date and time

Acknowledgements

Illustrations: Chris Orr & Associates

Notes